Just Being Difficult?

Cultural Memory
in
the
Present

Mieke Bal and Hent de Vries, Editors

Just Being Difficult?

Academic Writing in the Public Arena

Edited by JONATHAN CULLER
and KEVIN LAMB

Stanford University Press
Stanford, California
2003

Stanford University Press
Stanford, California
www.sup.org

Portions of Margaret Ferguson's essay appear in slightly different form in
Dido's Daughters: Literacy, Gender, and Empire in Early Modern England and France
by Margaret W. Ferguson. © 2003 by The University of Chicago. All rights reserved.

A longer version of Michael Warner's essay appears in his book, *Publics and
Counterpublics.* © 2002 by Zone Books. Reprinted by permission.

Library of Congress Cataloging-in-Publication Data

Just being difficult? : academic writing in the public arena / edited by
Jonathan Culler and Kevin Lamb.
        p.   cm. (Cultural memory in the present)
    Includes bibliographical references and index.
    ISBN 0-8047-4709-1 (alk. paper).—ISBN 0-8047-4710-5 (pbk. : alk paper)
    1. Academic writing   2. Scholarly publishing.   3. Learning and scholar-
ship.   4. English language—Style.   5. English language—Rhetoric.   6.
College teachers—Language.   I. Culler, Jonathan D.   II. Lamb, Kevin,
1975–   III. Series.
PN146.J87   2003
808'.02—dc21   2002014744

808·066 CUL
Original printing 2003

Last figure below indicates year of this printing:
12   11   10   09   08   07   06   05   04   03

Printed in the United States of America on acid-free, archival-quality
paper.

Designed and typeset at Stanford University Press in 10.5/12 Bembo

Contents

Introduction: Dressing Up, Dressing Down   *1*

JONATHAN CULLER AND KEVIN LAMB

Part 1. In Search of a Common Language; or, Language Debates and the History of Philosophy

1. Difficult Style and "Illustrious" Vernaculars: A Historical Perspective   *15*

MARGARET FERGUSON

2. Hume's Learned and Conversable Worlds   *29*

ROBIN VALENZA AND JOHN BENDER

3. Bad Writing and Good Philosophy   *43*

JONATHAN CULLER

4. The Metaphysics of Clarity and the Freedom of Meaning   *58*

JOHN MCCUMBER

Part 2. Institutions, Publics, Intellectual Labor

5. Feminism's Broken English   *75*

ROBYN WIEGMAN

6. The Resistance of Theory; or, The Worth of Agony   *95*

REY CHOW

7. Styles of Intellectual Publics   *106*

MICHAEL WARNER

Part 3. Modernist Poetics and Critical Badness

8. On Difficulty, the Avant-Garde, and Critical Moribundity   *129*

   PETER BROOKS

9. Difficulty in Modern Poetry and Aesthetics   *139*

   ROBERT KAUFMAN

10. Bad Writing   *157*

   BARBARA JOHNSON

Part 4. Address to the Other: Ethics and Acknowledgment

11. The Morality of Form; or, What's "Bad" about "Bad Writing"?   *171*

   DAVID PALUMBO-LIU

12. The Politics of the Production of Knowledge: An Interview with Gayatri Chakravorty Spivak   *181*

   STUART J. MURRAY

13. Values of Difficulty   *199*

   JUDITH BUTLER

   Contributors   *217*

   Index   *221*

Just Being Difficult?

JONATHAN CULLER AND KEVIN LAMB

Introduction: Dressing Up, Dressing Down

THIS COLLECTION emerges from recent debates about bad or obscure writing in the humanities, although many of the essays show that the issue is scarcely new. What is at stake when the work of prominent thinkers is attacked as "just bad writing" or as needlessly obscure? And why should what might seem a local academic matter have graced the pages of the *New York Times*, the *New Republic*, the *Wall Street Journal*, and the *London Review of Books*, as well as university publications such as *Lingua Franca* and *South Atlantic Quarterly*? The current controversy was stimulated in particular by the journal *Philosophy and Literature*, which for several years garnered publicity by announcing recipients of a bad writing award, recipients who—doubtless no surprise—turned out to be highly influential scholars and, more specifically, ones engaged in what has come to be known as "theory," with its odd cachet of both political radicalism and intellectual abstraction. In something like an academic version of *Entertainment Weekly*'s "worst dresses" of the Oscars, the editors of *Philosophy and Literature* sought out instances of the "ugliest, most stylistically awful"[1] prose, and, as with such awards at the Oscars, the targets' acknowledged star status certainly appears to be a prerequisite for disparagement. But if this concern with writing were all *merely* a matter of style, what could be the cause for such commotion? And if it were not only a matter of style, what else could the charge of bad writing possibly signify?

This volume sets out to inquire into the underlying stakes of these debates. The essays gathered here are less about proving innocence than contesting the terms of the allegations, exposing to interrogation the history, conventions, and assumptions underlying the designation "bad writing" and its almost inarguable efficacy. For the most striking feature of the accusation of bad writing is that it seems not to require explanation or demonstration, as if all one has to do is quote a sentence and people will instantly recognize how awful it is. Although obscurity is a charge one can contest by trying to show that, taken in context, for an appropriately informed reader the sentence is actually quite intelligible, badness seems to brook no argument. The editor of *Philosophy and Literature*, indeed, felt no need to explain what made a particular winning specimen the worst writing he had found, and when he did speak about criteria of badness, he cited ugliness and opacity. The allegation of *bad writing* works, then, through an appeal to transparency that assigns badness to opacity. But if the most credible gloss for *bad* in *bad writing* is simply "unclear," doesn't the word itself—as an unclear substitution for the word *unclear*—enact the same failure of clarity it decries? And insofar as, in this model of transparency, clarity is what provokes immediate recognition, bad writing might be above all merely unfamiliar.

As one might expect, the allegations of bad writing under scrutiny center on the twin demons of difficulty and obscurity, but like the bad writing itself, these constitute a special class of difficulty and obscurity. Literary and philosophical texts have often been characterized by elevated language, abstruseness, unconventional syntax, idiosyncratic style, even (horrors!) ungrammatical usage. But when the object under consideration inhabits the literary canon, difficulty is treated as richness and intricacy, the very qualities that make literature an object of exegetical energy and classroom study. Even in philosophy, grappling with Kant or Hegel is considered fruitful because they are important objects of knowledge whose stylistic complexity correlates with the task of precision demanded in the elucidation of complicated ideas. The obscure way of writing endemic to much philosophy is presumably one of the reasons the academy undertakes to teach philosophy at all and often in the format of explicatory lectures. But why, then, should certain other types of difficulty be scorned? Since scientists and even social scientists are not vilified in the public press for bad writing, the answer must lie in the status of the humanities, which is conceived not as a realm where specialized or recondite reflection is needed but as a set of disciplines devoted to transmitting a cultural heritage. To be more precise, specialized research may be needed to work out problems in the history of culture, but insofar as it is significant, this research should be "written up," as we say, in terms that are broadly accessible.

We will return to the questions this assumption raises about the tasks of the humanities. But what of difficulty? Critics of bad writing claim that the problem is not difficulty per se; rather, the writing of current literary and cultural theory is *needlessly* obscure. Doubtless the reason for charging writing with badness rather than opacity comes from the conviction that obscurity is unnecessary. Its badness, even wickedness—for moral indignation quickly bubbles to the surface here—comes from its refusal to communicate, from its adoption of jargon, abstraction, and complicated syntax that make it inaccessible.

The claim not to understand might seem an innocent posture that people would seldom adopt willingly, but in fact it is one of considerable power, in which authorities often entrench themselves. Eve Sedgwick has described the "epistemological privilege of unknowing," whereby "obtuseness arms the powerful against their enemies," as when a bilingual diplomat must negotiate in the language of his monolingual counterpart from another country.[2] Something of that structure underlies charges of excess difficulty. The claim not to understand carries a presumption that the writer ought to communicate in terms familiar to the reader, who thus comes to have an interest in not understanding, since that is what strengthens his or her position. The person who does not understand or declines to understand, the interlocutor who has or pretends to have the less broadly knowledgeable understanding, gets to determine the terms of the encounter. This is particularly salient in laws on rape, where, Sedgwick writes—with some overstatement, one hopes—"it matters not at all what the raped woman perceives or wants, so long as the man raping her can claim not to have noticed" or understood—a matter in which our culture provides masculine sexuality with a certain amount of training.[3]

Does something comparable happen in other cultural spheres? When difficulty is seen as elitist, inimical to the ideal of democracy, a disinclination to try to understand anything complicated can readily cloak itself in self-righteousness. When American students are treated as customers who should be satisfied, their resistance to difficulty can become a source of power. Above all, our educational system, treating difficulty as something to be postponed until it doesn't seem difficult, declines to value the struggle with complexity except when that struggle succeeds in dissipating it.[4] In this context it is striking but scarcely surprising how securely the power of the enemies of theory is anchored not in their command of knowledge, their superior understanding of the texts they would impugn, but precisely in their ignorance, their claim not to understand.

But the critics of theoretical writing swiftly proffer a different, and to some extent contradictory, charge: it is not that theorists incompetently conceal a simple meaning in obscure formulations. On the contrary, they know exactly what they are doing and deliberately write obscurely in order to sound profound when in fact they have nothing to say. According to such reasoning obscurantism is purely suggestive display. It produces the expectation that deciphering is in order, only to elude the reader's effort with hollow mystification.

This charge has the merit of recognizing the performative dimension of writing, that it does not simply transmit a thought or a content but performs an action, takes up a stance. Of course, this fact about writing is itself part of the problem: instead of self-effacingly conveying information, difficult writing puts itself forward, seeks to act on the reader, providing an experience as it structures experience. And one of the performative effects of writing is indeed the establishment of authority, although it is scarcely clear that writing obscurely succeeds in conferring authority, as critics of academic writing seem to believe. There is a great deal of obscure writing out there, and few of those who write obscurely become invested with authority. Far more often readers are put off, and the writing languishes. Obscure writing may connote profundity of thought, but it rarely achieves the end of promoting its author as a profound thinker.

However, critics are not concerned with the mass of obscure writers, who produce difficult prose to no end, but with the famous ones, those thought, precisely, to have something important to say. The problem with these prominent writers, critics charge, is that their prose not only obfuscates any meaning but, more insidiously, produces an aura of authority. Theoretical jargon, pervasive allusions, syntactic complexity, in short, difficult style, commands the respect of the unwitting reader, they claim, because the rhetorical flourish that bars the transmission of meaning also stands in for meaning's presence. Obscurity in style, therefore, becomes a pretext for ferreting out the impersonators and exposing bad writers' complexity as the masquerade it is.

Accused of donning the vestments of authority without purveying the substance worthy of difficulty, these writers find themselves in a telling dilemma. If they assert, "Yes, I have content, and here it is in plain language," they grant that the difficulty was needless and can hope, at best, that their critics will acknowledge that there is credible content. But explaining to the critics of bad writing what a difficult sentence means invariably seems somewhat beside the point. They are not curious about the concealed or possibly missing meaning but angry at the obscurantism, which seems both to thwart comprehension and to signal the authors' more serious intellectual, moral, and political failings.

As many of the essays in this compilation make clear, the accusation of obscurantism (and even of intellectual vacuity) goes hand in hand with charges of professional irresponsibility, neglect of political realities, even collaboration with evil. Given the still vague definition of what qualifies as bad writing in this context, it may be unremarkable that these attacks can and do come from vastly different quarters of the political map, from the left and the right. The lack of immediate communicability—and therefore the lack of immediate content or politics of the sort to which lucid prose would supposedly guarantee access—is taken to reflect writers' willful resistance to commitments in the world, their refusal of, in Robyn Wiegman's terms, "the political real" or, in David Palumbo-Liu's terms, "sociability." But since critics can scarcely claim that transparency and simplicity correlate with political responsibility or that one should read only what is immediately clear and familiar, that one should never read anything the least bit difficult, they have, instead, recourse to a distinction between good and bad difficulty by differentiating interior from exterior, what is inherently difficult from what is only superficially so—a position that allows that truly substantive complexity may make unusual linguistic demands of the reader but still inveighs against purely stylistic obscurity.

Critics' attempts, however, to separate real difficulty from merely apparent difficulty—the latter being equated with bad writing—is perhaps unwittingly and transferentially a displacement of the problem of which the bad writers in question are often so acutely aware: the problem of a criticism that aspires to find language about language yet is always already working through and with the tools about which it seeks to perform its explanatory magic. For Paul de Man this problem was the site both of theory and of its resistance. He writes, "Nothing can overcome the resistance to theory since theory *is* itself this resistance."[5] Nowhere are these paradoxes more in evidence than in the debate that has emerged around the badness of particular academic writing.

Inasmuch as theory takes language as an object of critical inquiry, it is forever working both within and against linguistic constraints, seeking the distance implied by interrogation yet snared in the intimacy of language as the ultimate dwelling place of descriptive possibility. This effort has placed determining importance not only on language but on its subset of metalanguage, on language about language. *Bad writing* is precisely a metalinguistic designation, a form of writing about writing. Yet, as we've suggested already, the manifest sense of what one means by *bad writing* is only assured by familiarity with its absence; the meaning that the label "bad writing" makes present consists in isolating writing's failure to produce meaning. Of course, the enabling ground on which all metalanguage functions is its reference to something *else* called language. The referent is, thus, always eluding its description, perpetually absent at the moment it is, in fact, speaking on its behalf. According to de Man it is even in appealing to our most intuitive notions of language that we are perhaps most adrift in the problem of theory, for "we seem to assume all too readily that, when we refer to something called 'language,' we know what it is we are talking about, although there is probably no word to be found in language that is as overdetermined, self-evasive, disfigured and disfiguring as 'language.'"[6]

That theory aims to account for language necessarily implies that theory must examine the metalinguistic tools at its disposal. And if theory has seemed to be self-critical, even self-parodying, it must be, in part, because theory resists *itself*. To the extent that theory is enmeshed in language's refusal of literal self-description, charges against academic writing may highlight the central task of theory: to engage, expose, describe, and even resist this defining resistance of and to language. The very difficulty toward which the designation "bad writing" gestures—that writing is *bad* when it is opaque or extrusive, when it is seen as primarily or merely writing, without the precious nucleus we designate content—appears mistakenly as theory's outside; but it is, on the contrary, internal to the objects it describes, characteristic rather than independent of the theory it purports merely to characterize. For if language were to be transparent in relation to itself, it would be inescapably opaque, presenting itself as the object by simultaneously claiming only to refer to language and only to be language. The label "bad writing" is, hence, a fine specimen not only of de Man's resistance to theory but also of the quandary of theory as resistance, caught up in its impossibility as its condition of possibility. Indeed, at bottom, the failure of critical metalanguage is what drives all theory.

The recent example of Judith Butler's selection as *Philosophy and Literature*'s bad writer of the year is especially revealing with respect to the task of theory and its relation to the prevailing distinction in these debates between real or essential complexity and purely accessory or stylistic difficulty. Strangely enough, parody has seemed at issue in the recent controversy. One of the contest's rules states, "Entries must be non-ironic, from serious, published academic journals or books. Deliberate parody cannot be allowed in a field where unintended self-parody is so widespread."[7] In explaining the journal's goal to readers of the *Wall Street Journal*, editor Denis Dutton goes on to define "theory" (his quotes) as "mostly inept philosophy applied to literature and culture." To show how "jargon has become the emperor's clothing of choice" for literary theory, Dutton cites a passage from a recent article by Paul Fry, which he characterizes as follows: "The writing is intended to look *as though* Mr. Fry is a physicist struggling to make clear the Copenhagen interpretation of Quantum Mechanics. Of course, he's *just* an English professor showing off."[8] Turning his attention to the year's prizewinner, Dutton contrasts Judith Butler and previous prizewinners—so-called kitsch theorists—with Kant, Aristotle, and Wittgenstein, where the former, it is claimed, only "mimic the effects of rigor and profundity without actually doing serious intellectual work."[9] In a separate and very different attack on Butler, Martha Nussbaum accuses "The Professor of Parody" (her title for Butler) of encouraging dangerous flirtation with gender travesty as a substitute for the real politics of advocating legal equality for women and gays and lesbians. Like Dutton, who describes theory as "intellectual kitsch" and as "analogous to bad art," Nussbaum seems interested in ripping off the frock of gender subversion and exposing it as a bad charade of real political engagement.

This charge of impersonation is particularly interesting for the way in which it takes on the questions of earnest performance, mimesis, and parody thematized by Butler's work, questions at the heart of her claims about the constitution of identity and of the social realm. Butler's point—that reality itself has been delimited by the concretizing effects of language and that drag performance is perhaps one way of seeing anew the materiality of everyday self-presentation as already imitative, linguistic, repetitive—ironically becomes the very ground of attack, as though Butler were merely a carbon copy, flitting around decked out in all the trappings of intellectual abstraction and political radicalism but with neither the substance of theoretical complexity nor the bite of genuine activism. One of Butler's enduring insights, however, is that the example of drag performance, of acting "as though a woman," uncovers in all gender identity a form of impersonation or performance predicated on the certitude of belief guaranteed over again by language and by its invisibility. If Butler herself was merely *impersonating* the real labor of intellectuals, acting *as though* an intellectual, she was, by the logic of her own account, simultaneously exposing the natural performance of such labor as already imitative, as relying on the transparency of meaning that could only be guaranteed by powerfully obscure linguistic conventions, conventions requiring language's invisibility and designating as parodic—and bad—thought that appears garishly overdressed in language.

Pretending "as though" or "as if"—a function treated at greater length and in more detail in Barbara Johnson's contribution to this volume—traditionally sustains our encounters with fiction, not criticism. But as Dutton's analogy to kitsch suggests, bad critical writing has seemed to be *like* bad art, in part, because it has ceased to be properly *critical*, because the difference from the object of criticism has diminished to the point where theoretical writing, maintaining vaunted pretensions to be "real philosophy," appears at times to mimic the allusive, metaphorical, convoluted structure of its literary objects, becoming itself literary. Many of the essays in this collection also point to this perceptible overlap between the literary and the critical, emphasizing the continuity between modernist writers' attempts in the early twentieth century to enable the representation of new realities and contemporary theorists' efforts in the latter half of that century to make newly strange familiar ones. Even what alerts critics of bad writing to its presence is ostensibly a structure of fictional self-presentation, a structure in which authority is claimed under false pretenses; for resemblance to abstraction is taken as the real thing in its absence, as though fooling readers into buying the novelistic surrogate by way of a persuasive likeness to reality. But what if the task of criticism is the unmasking of various fictional self-presentations as the stuff of reality? What would it mean to present the substance of reality as certain types of linguistic masquerade yet to avoid masquerade? The seeming literariness of theory may then be its own self-difference as an undertaking of theory at all, which is to say that its moment of writing—and hence of coming into being—is also its moment of fictionality. As Barbara Johnson has argued elsewhere, "The difference between literature and criticism consists perhaps only in the fact that criticism is more likely to be blind to the way in which its own critical difference from itself makes it, in the final analysis, literary."[10]

When deconstruction discovered in the writing of philosophy the disavowal of writing—writing as the supplement to conversation in its absence, of an address to the other in the other's absence—it made explicit that for philosophy badness and writing have perhaps always belonged together and that the potential failure of acknowledgment seemed peculiarly the condition of writing at all. It should seem unsurprising, thus, that deconstruction and the work of many continental philosophers who influenced a linguistic turn in modern thought found their most hospitable home in the United States not in departments of philosophy but of literature, where writing constitutes the object of study and where the reliability of language and its relation to reality may be brought into question. In the philosophical tradition beginning with Plato, in which writing is an encumbrance to be rarefied to a vitreous surface, Derrida and others encountered an unmistakable figurality that turned against the description of language even at the moment of its supposed clarity. In specifying its office, language was supposed to guarantee the idea's presence yet was instead relying on rhetorical tropes—the metaphor, for example, of glass—even in its act of discrediting rhetoric. The ineluctability of the rhetorical, the figural, in other words, the literary, became central to much of the task of investigating language and meaning making that characterized semiotics, deconstruction, and, later, simply theory. That critical writing should seem not only the explication but also the uncanny double of its literary object reflects perhaps theory's central dilemma in finding literality shot through with its own figural otherness as always other than the literal, as itself a figure of the literal. If theory's task were to challenge commonsense notions about language and make apparent the role of language in relaying, producing, and structuring everyday phenomena understood as reality, how would it stretch, even deform, language to render discernible the contours of language itself?

This question brings us back to the role of writing in the humanities. Insofar as charges of bad writing take clarity and transparency as the norm, they appear to treat the humanistic disciplines as means of transmission of a cultural heritage. If they are, rather, the testing of the elements of that heritage in a critical writing of it, or even the unwriting of what culture has taught us to take for granted, then critical prose must call attention to itself as an act that cannot be seen through. Roland Barthes suggests that the writer's task is not "to express the inexpressible" but "to unexpress the expressible," to unwrite what is already inscribed in the discourses that subtend our world.[11]

Perhaps, then, the more serious criticism levied against certain theoretical writing is that it reflects merely a consolidation of local vernaculars, that in the process of challenging common sense it has failed to question its own intellectual "common sense" and that of fellow left-leaning scholars in the humanities. The weak version of this claim rehearses the common assumption in this debate about disciplinary distinctions, the assumption that comes through loud and clear, for instance, when Denis Dutton accuses Paul Fry of acting "*as though*" he were a physicist when he is "*just* an English professor showing off." However, a more interesting argument—and certainly the strong version of this claim—would be that, far from being too difficult or merely difficult for difficulty's sake, so-called bad writers aren't difficult enough; their idiom is too settled, not sufficiently creative, perhaps not even adequately neologistic. Rather than discouraging difficulty, this latter claim seems a call to difficulty not unlike the call to theory, desperately seeking a metalanguage able to allow the most deftly self-critical operations necessary to explain language within language itself. If we are to move beyond the current debate around bad writing in the humanities, it seems fitting to start at exactly this point of conjunction, where badness in writing means only, in the end, not treating writing with the difficulty it deserves.

The essays in Part 1, "In Search of a Common Language," start from precisely this question of common ground by taking issue with assumptions about transparency, persuasion, and intuition in the writing of philosophical ideas. Collectively, they represent insightful attempts to unearth and to think beyond the historical primacy of clarity as the arbiter for intersubjective contact. The first two essays of the section trace the status of language from the early Greek philosophers' repudiation of the Sophists through the advent of the modern academic disciplines in eighteenth-century England. Margaret Ferguson's essay on "illustrious vernaculars" in Dante's *De Vulgari Eloquentia* examines, in particular, the troubling position that foreigners and inscrutability occupy in the coemergence of ideologies of national unity and common language, ideologies that, often deployed in the service of imperialist expansion, tend to connect moral virtue with one form of argumentation, a form of argumentation that has at its heart the hierarchical exclusion of various others. With similar historical rigor and detail Robin Valenza and John Bender look closely at two texts from Hume taken as the translation between "learned" and "conversable" worlds, arguing that the term *translation* is itself inadequate to describe the movement between specialized, disciplinary knowledge and its more broadly accessible representation. By placing language debates in the context of the nascent disciplinary division between "natural philosophy" and "moral philosophy," they demonstrate that the movement in Hume's worlds betrays not only a difference in the representation of knowledge but a transformation in the very ways of knowing.

Jonathan Culler's and John McCumber's essays move the question of common language and communication into the modern philosophical context, where the authors propose the potential of difficulty to enable new ways of engaging subjectivity and meaning. Closely reading the hard prose of Stanley Cavell, Culler shows the promise of a style that convincingly describes the knots, dilemmas, desires, and identities of the writer. By breaking up the process of reading and interfering with the accustomed modes of understanding a text, "stylish" philosophical writing, Culler argues, may go past mere assessment and give persuasion a chance to happen. Locating the origin of philosophy's insistence on clarity in Aristotle and in the law of preservation of form, McCumber highlights the historical domination of matter by form. He concludes that when "matter"—that is, the body repressed and denied—speaks, its speech may ultimately need to reject both the Aristotelian mode of clarity (occupying the extant vocabularies of experience) and the Hegelian mode (treating obscurity as a necessary prelude to clarity) and rather to undertake a more experimental relation to obscurity, one that neither relegates obscurity to failed communication nor ties it to the ultimate goal of its own transcending.

Part 2, "Institutions, Publics, Intellectual Labor," centers on the politics embedded in theoretical discourses in the academy and elsewhere. Robyn Wiegman opens the discussion by showing how disciplinary divisions have, in themselves, abetted and reproduced the conventional estrangement between a "political real" and a "theoretical imaginary," cementing the opposition of activism versus abstraction. Her essay argues that feminism needs to reclaim a "theoretical humanities" as a vital site for considering afresh some of the many articulations between poststructuralism and left politics. Echoing many of the concerns raised by Wiegman, Rey Chow moves the discussion from the domestic politics of debates over bad writing to the flow of intellectual capital abroad, investigating, with surprising results, how globalization has affected the value attached to difficulty and the potential of obscurity to circulate in new, unanticipated ways. In the final essay of the section Michael Warner provides a nuanced account of the pressures, paradoxes, dilemmas, and unpredictability of writing that aspires to transform the world. Scrutinizing the different functions complexity in writing style plays in intellectual affiliation and change, Warner teases out the implications of

publishing circuits, political participation, and the anteriority of "world making" theory to its audience proper.

That the contemporary theory in question is itself a continuation of certain types of literary experimentation forms the organizing center of the essays in the next part. As the title "Modernist Poetics and Critical Badness"
suggests, the authors of these essays find in modernism the roots of a simultaneously literary and critical enterprise in which stylistic complexity and
the renegotiation of the subjective go together and in which the transgress-
ing of linguistic conventions—in the lyric, the novel, the essay, even the
boundary between the poetic and the prosaic, on the one hand, or art and
interpretation, on the other—diverts from general circulation works deeply
interested in the masses and in everyday experience and common sense.
Whereas Peter Brooks, by taking a historical view onto the emergence of
criticism and its alignment with the literary avant-garde, affirms hope for a
renewal of exegesis and its role in an aesthetic education, Robert Kaufman
provides a detailed example of such an inquiry into the complexity of
modernism in the example of contemporary poetry and Theodor Adorno's
aesthetic theory. Barbara Johnson's piece closes the section with the impossibility of closure, acting appropriately instead "as if" concluded. Her far-
reaching use of notions of "badness" from Baudelaire and Mallarmé shows
the existing currents of contemporary debates to be still deeply embedded
in prevailing notions of language that have the denial of self-obscurity as
their precondition and, therefore, project difficulties in comprehension to
moral failings of authors.

The final part of the collection, "Address to the Other," deals at greater
length with precisely this question of ethics raised by obscure academic
prose. The authors in this section engage with readers' refusal of acknowledgment to the seemingly opaque and inscrutable, or the less than immediately intuitive and transparent. David Palumbo-Liu's essay shows this refusal
to be rooted in conditions of sociability whereby notions of bad writing, bad
people, and nonnormativity work together to constrain what qualifies as legitimate intercourse, even as they function within the circuit of politics as
usual, in which different groups vie for predominance. The interview with
Gayatri Spivak places the question of difficulty in the terrain of left academic
politics and knowledge production and dissemination. By looking at the
"law of curvature," the different temporality now attached to books, and the
role of teaching, Spivak argues for wedging apart the question of the validity of knowledge from the relative level of difficulty attached to its expression. In the final essay Judith Butler revisits the frequently cited example of
Adorno by way of a significant detour through Henry James's *Washington
Square*. Through Adorno's correspondence with friend and colleague Walter
Benjamin, Butler argues that Adorno signifies not only difficulty but also

difficulty's limits, the terrifying points at which difficulty is reconstituted into orthodoxy and withdraws recognition to those who transgress its entrenched parameters. Proposing that the world may be understood anew in unfamiliar and unconventional writing, Butler also advocates reexamining the ethics of reading difficulty and of judgment in the face of incomprehension. By attaching ethical value to encounters with the "inadequacy of explanation," Butler challenges us to honor that which cannot be fully understood or mastered in the other.

Notes

1. The contest was conducted through the list serve, PHIL-LIT, for the journal *Philosophy and Literature*. The rules were posted on the Internet and have since been quoted in a number of places, in virtually identical form. The quotation here appears on the following Web page: Denis Dutton, "Bad Writing Contest: Results for Round Three," posted at www.miami.edu/phi/misc/badwrit3.htm.

2. Eve Sedgwick, *The Epistemology of the Closet* (Berkeley: University of California Press, 1990), 4–7.

3. Ibid., 5.

4. For discussion see Helen Regueiro Elam, "The Difficulty of Reading," in *The Idea of Difficulty in Literature*, ed. Alan Purves (Albany: SUNY Press, 1991), 73–79.

5. Paul de Man, "The Resistance to Theory," in *The Resistance to Theory* (Minneapolis: University of Minnesota Press, 1986), 19 (de Man's emphasis).

6. Ibid., 13.

7. Denis Dutton, "Bookmarks: The Somewhat Exaggerated Death of Primitive Art," *Philosophy and Literature* 23 (1999): 252.

8. Denis Dutton, "Language Crimes," *Wall Street Journal*, Feb. 5, 1999, W11 (our emphasis).

9. Ibid.

10. Barbara Johnson, "The Critical Difference: BartheS/BalZac," in *The Critical Difference: Essays in the Contemporary Rhetoric of Reading* (Baltimore, Md.: Johns Hopkins University Press, 1980), 12.

11. Roland Barthes, *Critical Essays* (Evanston, Ill.: Northwestern University Press, 1972), x.

PART I

In Search of a Common Language; or, Language Debates and the History of Philosophy

Difficult Style and "Illustrious" Vernaculars

A Historical Perspective

Ever since Socrates distinguished philosophy from what the sophists and the
rhetoricians were doing, it has been a discourse of equals who trade arguments
and counter-arguments without any obscurantist sleight of hand. In that way,
he claimed, philosophy showed respect for the soul, while the others' manipulative methods showed only disrespect.

—Martha Nussbaum, "The Professor of Parody"

The Sophists were disliked for different reasons both by philosophers like
Socrates and Plato and by leading citizens. The odium which they incurred in
the eyes of the establishment was not only due to the subjects they professed;
their own status [as "foreigners" to Athens] was against them.

—W. K. C. Guthrie, *The Sophists*

PHILOSOPHERS, Martha Nussbaum suggests, demonstrate their moral
goodness by using good language. Good language is clear language; it avoids
any "obscurantist sleight of hand" and conducts its arguments without any
trace of those "manipulative methods" that Plato's Socrates associated with
the Sophists. That group of language users and teachers, whose name allies
them with *sophia*, wisdom, have nonetheless come, in Western history, to be
vilified as false claimants to philosophy's goods. Those who possess some cultural literacy of the kind defined by E. D. Hirsch know that a sophistical argument is a specious one; and those who read and allowed themselves to be
persuaded by Nussbaum's denunciation of Judith Butler's writing style (and
ideas) in a 1999 issue of the *New Republic* know that those associated with
Sophists, even at the turn of the millennium in a country far from Greece,
are rhetoricians who seek to manipulate their readers' minds rather than re-
specting their souls. When they assessed Nussbaum's highly manipulative
rhetorical gesture of associating Judith Butler with the Sophists, however, did
the readers of the *New Republic* know that the Sophists were foreigners,
"provincials" (in the eyes of Athenians) who lacked legal standing in Athens

and whose habit, as Plato describes it, was to wander "from city to city . . . having no settled home of their own" (*Timaeus*, 19e)?[1]

The Sophists' status as foreigners is less likely to figure in a Hirschean conception of modern American cultural literacy, I suspect, than is their reputation as amoral, or even immoral, rhetoricians. In truth (but beware such a phrase: it may be attempting to manipulate you), the question of what constitutes foreignness in language use and among language users is intricately bound up with debates (past and present) about what constitutes "good" writing (or speaking) in English. By *English* I mean, in the context of this essay and this volume, that standardized form of the language that some sociolinguists call a "high prestige dialect" and see emerging, as a concept and a set of prescribed practices, over the course of many centuries starting in the early Renaissance era.[2] What counts as "bad" English has often been defined as a function of what the Athenians called barbarism or, more precisely, *solecism*. This term, which I vividly remember first seeing in the margin of one of my graduate school essays, where it accompanied a circled phrase the professorial reader regarded as extremely infelicitous and as a mark of my gross ignorance, denotes, according to the *Oxford English Dictionary*, "speaking incorrectly," a "violation of the rules of grammar or syntax." Ancient writers used the word to refer to "the corruption of the Attic dialect among the Athenian colonists at *Soloi* in Cilicia." Solecisms are thus usages judged to be improper or (later) "nonstandard" by those who know the rules of the prestige dialect, which is often, historically, the dialect spoken at the court and/or in the dominant city of a region or (later) of a nation-state.

By looking at a few moments in the history of the concept of a standard language or, as Dante called it, an "illustrious" vernacular, I hope in this essay to question a tendency I see not only in Martha Nussbaum's approach to the problem of Butler's "difficult" style but also in that of many well-educated persons who have written more generally, and in various fora, against the "obscure" language, often called "jargon," of recent literary and cultural theory. The tendency against which I'm writing here—and which I've certainly exhibited myself, at moments of irritation when I've felt that life is just too short to wade through one more convoluted sentence by (for instance) Luce Irigaray, or Jacques Derrida, or Theodor Adorno, or Cicero, or Milton—is to project one's irritation with stylistic difficulty as a negative *moral* judgment on the author of the text in question. It may of course be the case that the author is or was a liar or a criminal; but the difficulty of his or her style is, I contend, much less likely to reflect a given author's moral qualities than to refract a complex set of interactions between the features of a text (its grammar, its lexicon, its habits of allusion, but also, perhaps, the size of its print and the quality of its paper), on the one hand, and, on the other, variously educated and socially positioned readers whose tolerance for certain kinds of unfamiliarity may vary not only according to their education and social class but also according to their health and mood on a given day. My general aim, then, is to disaggregate the problem of stylistic difficulty, to separate some of its components so that it becomes less easy to recognize and judge than it seems to be in Nussbaum's construction of the phenomenon. I'm particularly interested here in opening a historical perspective onto the reasons why different readers may have different degrees of tolerance for aspects of a text's language that seem alien, foreign, unknown, or, at the least, hard to know without some considerable expenditure of time and energy.

Consider Nussbaum's statement that during a long plane trip she found Butler's prose "fatiguing" (40). Turning from Butler's writing to a student dissertation about "Hume's views of personal identity," however, Nussbaum found her spirits "reviving." "Doesn't she write clearly, I thought with pleasure, and a tiny bit of pride." It's not the expression of a preference in reading matter to which I object, nor is it Nussbaum's rhetorical gesture of recounting a personal experience to illustrate her argument: the Sophists, as well as Aristotle, recommended that rhetoricians enhance their authority by demonstrating aspects of their "ethos" or "good character." I do object, however, to Nussbaum's implied judgment that both Hume and the student writing "clear" prose about Hume's theories of personal identity are morally superior to Butler because their writing styles (presumably quite different) are less fatiguing (to Nussbaum) than Butler's is: "what a fine, what a gracious spirit" is Hume's; "how kindly he respects the reader's intelligence, even at the cost of exposing his own uncertainty," Nussbaum exclaims (40). Butler, however, is not "kindly" toward the reader; her style is "ponderous and obscure . . . dense with allusions to other theorists, drawn from a wide range of different theoretical traditions," half of them (in the list Nussbaum gives) from non-Anglophone countries. Hume is praised for exposing his "uncertainties" to us, but Butler is chided for using too many questions and for failing to tell us "whether she approves of the view described." Hume's way of expressing uncertainty seems to be good because it is somehow in a Platonic tradition of "equals trading arguments," whereas Butler's way of (perhaps) expressing uncertainty seems to be bad because it is alleged to be in a sophistical tradition of manipulating the reader. I suspect that matters are more complex than this, and Hume might well have agreed, on the evidence of an essay Nussbaum doesn't mention, an essay first published in 1742 and entitled "Of Simplicity and Refinement in Writing."

This essay is, to my mind, by no means easy to follow. In it Hume discusses the difficulty of finding a mean or balance between the two shifty concepts denoted by his title terms and yoked there, rather debatably, it turns out, by *and*. "Simplicity," as Hume explains this abstraction, is allied with "nature" and is a stylistic ideal that few readers will appreciate if it is not accompanied by "refinement," which includes "elegant" language and "un-common" observations.[3] The title terms, as the essay gradually unfolds their multiple meanings, seem to exist in more of an antithetical relation ("simplicity or refinement"?) than a complementary one. Hume's aim, however, is to discover what constitutes a "just mixture of simplicity and refinement in writing" (193). The answer to this question leads Hume to a discussion of a "proper medium" of style that "lies not in a point, but admits of a considerable latitude"—a latitude explained by a wide variety of examples signaled simply by capitalized proper names of figures from different eras and writing in different languages and traditions. Occupying Hume's "proper medium" of style are Pope, Parnell, Lucretius, Corneille, Congreve, Sophocles, Terence, Virgil, and Racine; the latter two are singled out as being "nearest the center," that is, "the farthest removed from both the extremities" of "refinement and simplicity" (193–94). Only a reader of considerable education and with considerable power to infer stylistic qualities from Hume's very elliptical illustrations will grasp what this concept of a "proper medium" of style entails; indeed, Hume's argument comes to be more about the nature and education of readers than about "simplicity and refinement," understood as qualities intrinsic to a style of writing. Simplicity, allied with a concept of "the natural" and—obliquely, I suggest, with Puritan theories about the virtue of "plain speaking"—is a more relative notion than most readers, even the "persons of taste" to whom Hume's essay seems to be addressed (191), may have thought; for, as Hume begins to explain in his second paragraph, sentiments that are "merely natural" "affect not the mind with any pleasure." Hume illustrates this point by referring to the mental and verbal productions of four lower-class groups or types: "The pleasantries of a waterman, the observations of a peasant, the ribaldry of a porter or hackney coachmen, all of these are natural, and disagreeable" (191). Whether as producers of "hackneyed" discourse or as objects to be imitated in the discourse of "persons of taste," such lower-class persons will not properly illustrate the ideal of natural simplicity that Hume is complexly defining. "Nothing can please persons of taste, but nature drawn with all her graces and ornaments, *la belle nature*" (192). Hume's statement here, with its untranslated French phrase ("the beautiful nature"), implicitly defines "persons of taste" as those who know more than one language—and also as those who reject Puritan injunctions against verbal "ornament." The proper mixture of "simplicity and refinement," the essay seems to say, is as much a function of the reader as of the writer.

I am by no means offering a full interpretation of Hume's short but highly dialectical essay; I am, however, hoping that my citations of and reflections on Hume will show that his prose style displays some of the very qualities Nussbaum so dislikes in Butler's prose ("casual allusion," for instance, where the disagreements among the figures invoked are not fully ex-

plained). In the significant although shifting weight Hume gives to the notion of "uncommon opinions," moreover, he joins Butler, Theodor Adorno,
Walter Benjamin, and Fredric Jameson (among others) in pointing to the intellectual value of not being too kind to your real or imagined readers.
"Only what they do not need first to understand, they consider understandable; only the word coined by commerce, and really alienated, touches them
as familiar," Adorno wrote in the *Minima Moralia*, in a sentence that has been
quoted more than once in recent debates about "badness" in academic writing.[4] Brecht's stress on the value of the "alienation effect" in drama (*Verfremd-
ungseffekt*); the Russian formalists' interest in strategies of "defamiliarization"
(ostranenie), including techniques of "barbarizing" or "deforming" stylistic
norms; Adorno's scorn for the "ideologies" of "lucidity, objectivity, and con-
cise precision," as he called them in his 1956 essay "Punctuation Marks";[5]
Benjamin's concept of "writing against the grain"—these are well-known
modernist versions, I suggest, of Hume's search for a style capable of expressing "uncommon opinions." The modernist versions, however, have
seemingly relinquished Hume's hope (hedged by irony) that "uncommon"
opinions and "refinement" of language could somehow be "mixed" with
something that a "person of taste" would recognize as stylistic "simplicity."

The quest for a style that would convey "uncommon opinions," whether
through Humean "simplicity" or through modernist gestures of aggressive
violation of "common" notions of decorum in prose or poetry, is also a quest
for a certain kind of reader, one educated, as I now want to suggest, in what
has been, for many centuries in the West, an altogether "uncommon" language. That language cannot be simply described as "one" language, nor can
it accurately be described as one's own vernacular tongue. Although ideas of
moral goodness (and social superiority) have historically accompanied this
language (these languages), such ideas are perhaps, at this historical juncture,
more in need of analysis than of endorsement. To illustrate this point, let me
turn to the tradition of writing about language that separates one "good" or
"noble" language from many languages considered "bad" or "vulgar"; moral
judgments are intricately tied to social ones in this tradition, which helped
to shape many later formulations about the relation between good writing
and moral (or social) superiority of a few over the many or, in the modern
American inversion of this idea, of the many over the few. Historically, the
literate elite happened to be mostly men; and the kind of language use they
defined as good was allied to an ideal of Latin as a universal, imperial, and
written, as well as spoken, language superior to local dialects. These latter
were, for most of the medieval period, spoken but not written languages.
One name for them, in some territories claimed by the French monarchy,
was *patois*. Before the fifteenth century this word denoted "incomprehensible speech"; between the fifteenth and the seventeenth centuries, however,

it came, according to Pierre Bourdieu, to signify "a corrupted and coarse speech, such as that of the common or 'vulgar' people."[6] Predating and helping us to understand that symptomatic change in the way in which the sociological fact of linguistic diversity was perceived by members of a literate elite is Roger Bacon's treatise on *Greek Grammar*. Written in the late thirteenth century, Bacon's text reflects on the distinction between the "one" (Latin derived from Greek) and the "many" (vernacular dialects). He defines the former as a "substance" to be discerned in the usage of those who know Latin; the vernaculars, in contrast to the philosophically and theologically charged notion of *substancia*, are implicitly defined as like the Aristotelian "attributes" of Absolute Being. Bacon thus neatly occludes the fact that *some* vernaculars (languages he classifies as "Teutonic," for instance) were *not* descended from Latin and hence are not properly described by the *substancia* metaphor, which makes subordinate languages ontologically dependent on Latin. Linguistic "substance" thus, with elegant circularity, becomes a quasi-divine and all-encompassing phenomenon revealed only in the usage of the "literate," defined as clerks and others who know Latin; variability is ejected, by definition, from the *idea* of Latin:

In lingua enim latina que vna est, sunt multa idiomata. Substancia enim ipsius lingue consistit in hijs in quibus communicant clerici et literati omnes. Idiomata vero sunt multa secundum multitudinem nacionum vtencium hac lingua. Quia aliter in multis pronunciant et scribunt ytalici, et aliter hyspani, et aliter gallici, et aliter teutonici et aliter anglici et ceteri.

[For in that Latin language which is one, there are many idioms. But their substance consists in that language in which clerks and literate persons communicate. Idioms are many according to the number of nations using that language. Therefore it is pronounced and written differently by Italians, and differently by Hispanics, and differently by Gauls, and by us, and by English people etcetera.][7]

Late medieval clerkly arguments like Bacon's for Latin as "one" versus the vernacular tongues as "many" frequently define Latin as the lineal heir to the two other ancient languages most closely associated with divine being and learning, Greek and Hebrew. This view of Latin implicitly privileges a foreign language learned in school by a small and mostly male portion of the population over native or "mother" tongues of various kinds. Building on this line of speculation, some medieval theorists of language insisted that the "conventional" mode of signification that Aristotle had regarded as characteristic of language in general is truly typical only of vernacular languages; Latin words, in contrast, signify in an "almost ontological" way, as the modern critic Serge Lusignan puts it in his book *Parler Vulgairement* (42–43). The notion of a divine ground (and origin) of Latin signification contributes not a little, Lusignan speculates, to the exalted idea of grammar we find in many late-medieval treatises; and the synonymy of grammar and Latin contributes in turn to an idea we find in works from Giles de Rome's *De regimine principum* (c. 1285) through Dante's *De Vulgari Eloquentia* (c. 1306) to Joachim Du Bellay's *Deffense et illustration de la langue françoyse* (1549) and Richard Mulcaster's *Positions* (1581). This is the idea that the "paternal" language of Latin is more "complete and perfect" than any vulgar tongue, a better instrument for expressing "the nature of things, the customs of men, the course of the stars and all of that which [men] wish to discuss."[8]

Theories of the vernacular influenced by this idea (ideology) of Latin had many results for educational practices in the West; one of the most significant of these results, for my argument here, was that standard or "national" languages came to be "difficult" languages for most people, languages that require schooling to learn and that are full of words derived from the "foreign" tongue revered by those who shaped our ideologies of the vernacular. Latin, and Latin-trained clerks, literally helped to create almost all the vernaculars of Western Europe; English, however, was critically shaped—"invaded," one might say—not only by Latin but also by Norman French. Indeed, as George Puttenham observed in an early statement prescribing a "courtly" standard for proper English, the "language" of England is a hybrid produced by history and still a locus of contention in 1589, when Puttenham wrote his *Arte of English Poetrie*:

When I say language, I meane the speach wherein the poet or maker writeth be it Greek or Latine, or as our case is the vulgar English, and when it is peculiar unto a contrey it is called the mother speach of that people: the Greekes terme it *Idioma*: so is ours at this day the Norman English. Before the Conquest of the Normans, it [the mother tongue] was the Anglesaxon, and before that the British, which as some will, is at this day, the Walsh, or as others affirme, the Cornish: I for my part thinke neither of them both, as they be now spoken and p[r]onounced . . . [Y]e shall therefore take the usuall speach of the Court, and that of London and the shires lying about London within lx. myles, and not much above.[9]

To illustrate my argument that what counts as our English vernacular standard has not only been infiltrated, for a very long time, by elements of the foreign, but has also presented significant lexical and grammatical difficulties for "native" speakers of the language or languages of a given political territory, I want to look briefly at Dante's famous treatise about an "illustrious" vernacular tongue. As we debate the question of what constitutes a good style in modern academic writing—specifically, that by humanists, who are expected to conform to standards of clarity and "jargon-free" usage by which scientific writing is seldom judged—Dante merits a place at the table. For he was the first European (to my knowledge) who thought to put an "illustrious" vernacular in the place previously occupied by Latin in discussions of "superordinate" languages versus the many or vulgar tongues.

Ironically, Dante makes his argument for a Latinate and grammaticized vernacular—a "superior" vulgar tongue, as it were—in Latin rather than in Italian; this dramatizes the fact that the Italian language for which Dante is arguing does not yet, in his view, exist. It is thus "standard" only in a highly
utopian sense.

The *De Vulgari Eloquentia*, unfinished in Dante's lifetime, circulated in
manuscript and was debated by theorists of the Italian language such as
Bembo and Trissino. The treatise was first printed in Paris, in its Latin original, in 1577. Its central notion of an "eloquent" vernacular contributed to the
construction of that set of theories about language, with corresponding
practices, that we associate with the Renaissance humanists and with print
capitalism. I want to view these theories as indebted to a masculinized
scribal culture that worked across Europe for many centuries and that produced ideas of linguistic unity profoundly important for modern ideologies
of national unity and national languages. Dante's treatise was written by a
political visionary actively attempting to promote a "unified" Italy that
would not in truth arrive, even as an official fiction, until the nineteenth
century, when, perhaps not coincidentally, the idea of an Italian Renaissance
would also take on many of the features it continues to have in modern
Western societies and school curricula. In 1861, just a year after Burckhardt's
Civilization of the Renaissance in Italy was published, one historian estimates
that "not more than 2 to 3% of the Italian population would have understood Italian."[10] Dante explicitly promotes his vision of an "eloquent vernacular" as the appropriate linguistic vehicle for an Italian nation modeled
(in Dante's vision) on the ancient Roman Empire. His "eloquent vernacular" belongs to no single region of Italy, not even Tuscany; rather, it unites
what is best from each "native" dialect and thus produces a higher, more
powerful, entity. As he explains, "[B]y the vulgar tongue I mean that which
we learn without any rule, in imitating our nurse. From this we have another, secondary language, which the Romans called grammar (vulgarem lo-
cutionem asserimus, quam sine omni regula nutricem imitantes accipimus.
Est et inde alia locutio secundaria nobis, quam Romani grammaticam vo-
caverunt)."[11]

Dante describes this regionally hybrid language as "cardinal, courtly, and
curial" and explains the middle adjective (*aulicus*) in clearly political terms:

The reason we call it courtly is as follows: if we Italians had a court it would be an
imperial one; and if a court is a common home of all the realm, and an august ruler
of all parts of the realm, it would be fitting that whatever is of such a character as to
be common to all parts without being peculiar to any should frequent this court and
dwell there: nor is there any other abode worthy of so great an inmate (Quia vero
aulicum nominamus, illud causa est, quod, si aulam nos Ytali haberemus, palatinum
foret. Nam si aula totius regni comunis est domus et omnium regni partium guber-

natrix augusta, quicquid tale est ut omnibus sit comune nec proprium ulli, conveniens est ut in ea conversetur et habitet; nec aliquod aliud habitaculum tanto dignum est habitante). (1.18.2, Marigo ed., 150–52)

Dante's theory of the illustrious vernacular anticipates a tendency to conflate the ideas of *nation* and *empire* in many later discussions of a national language in countries with expansionist aspirations. Such discussions often highlight the violence done to the "provinces"—eventually including colonial territories—and to languages and language speakers defined as provincial or colonial—in the process of nation building that has traditionally been seen as heralding the end of feudalism in many Western European countries.[12] It therefore behooves us to look closely, if briefly, at the way in which Dante articulates a theory of the "illustrious vernacular" through a highly elaborate set of *discriminations* between "good" and "bad" types of language. These discriminations are expressed, not accidentally, in terms that imply distinctions between language users of different genders and social statuses. The illustrious language, a "paternal" language made for "noble" men, involves an explicit devaluation, region by region, of the various mother tongues of Italy, the "native" languages that Dante examines and finds inadequate to his purposes. His illustrated prescriptions for an illustrious language, the product of his fantastic clerkly learning and imagination, are flagrantly, even deliriously, ideological. Dante's treatise offers, indeed, a useful perspective on a field in which grammar and biology are, as it were, at the extremes of a social spectrum, each exerting pressures on what the other is thought to be "by nature."

Dante articulates his vision of the "illustrious," "eloquent," "cardinal," "curial," and "courtly" vernacular, after showing that it belongs to no single region of Italy, through the central metaphor of the sieve (*cribrum*);[13] the "sifting" Dante prescribes and performs entails distinguishing not only among genres, forms, and words but also among persons. The illustrious language, as he explains, "just like our behavior in other matters and our dress, demands men of like quality to its own," men "who excel in genius and knowledge" ("Exigit ergo istud sibi consimiles viros, quaemadmodum alii nostri mores et habitus. . . . excellentes ingenio et scientia querit") (2.1.5–6, Marigo ed., 164–65). The illustrious language is not only "suited" for a certain kind of man but has a fatherly authority given it by its preponderance of "manly words" (*virilia*). These are contrasted to "childish" words (like the names children use, in their native dialects, for their mothers and fathers)[14] and to "feminine" words (2.7.4). It is important to note that by "feminine" words Dante does not simply mean words grammatically feminine in gender. In the category of "muliebra" he places words he considers excessively "soft"—in terms of both semantics and sound, it seems: *dolciada* et *placevole* are his examples (2.7.4, Marigo ed., 228). Within the preferred category of *virilia* he also makes discriminations that have strong social resonances, with reference not only to hierarchies of gender but also to those of class. Dividing "manly" words into the categories of "silvestria" and "urbana," he fantastically subdivides each of these categories into "good" and "bad" kinds of diction. Good "urban" words are "combed out" (*pexa*) and "shaggy" (*irsuta*), whereas bad "urban" words are "glossy" (*lubrica*) and "rumpled" (*reburra*). Examples of these last two (bad) categories are, respectively, the words *femina* and *corpo* (2.7.4, Marigo ed., 228). The illustrations are not innocent, and they have at least two resonant ironies for our inquiry. One is that the feminine was often equated with the corporeal in hierarchies of value such as Neoplatonism, which placed the masculine and the spiritual above the feminine and the corporeal. The second irony is that manuals for *vernacular* language instruction, in contrast to Latin and Greek grammars, were frequently addressed to women, and even ventriloquized women's voices, as they performed their pedagogical function of teaching "elementary" things, including names for the parts of the body.[15] In a multilingual treatise written during the reign of England's Henry V, for instance, which uncannily anticipates the French-language-teaching scenes in Shakespeare's play about that king, the author explains that he has entitled his work *Femina* because "as women teach infants the maternal speech, so this book will seek to teach young peoples in the speech and rhetoric of Gaul" (Liber iste vocatur femina quia sicut femina docet infantem loqui maternam, sic docet iste liber iuvenes rethorice loqui Gallicum prout infra patebit).[16]

Through its descriptions of types of diction "unsuitable" for the illustrious vernacular, Dante's treatise offers an exemplary formulation of a theory that appropriates for the "illustrated" and masculinized vernacular the qualities that clerks like Roger Bacon attributed to Latin. The notion of *grammar* would seem to be the mediating concept in this process; once one's vernacular has a grammar, it is more like Latin than it is like the spoken *idioma* used by those who are *illiterati* in a historically new sense: ignorant of their "own" language (as a phenomenon with a grammar) rather than simply ignorant of Latin, which is the dominant medieval meaning of *illiteratus*. In imbuing not only his prescriptions but his examples with hierarchical social meanings, Dante may be seen, then, as an illustrious father of a key intellectual enterprise of the Renaissance, the enterprise undertaken by humanist writers of constructing their vernaculars as tongues suitable for ambitious men and capable of competing against other "national/imperial" languages, as well as against the great ancient tongues of Latin and Greek. Such vernaculars—along with Latin and occasionally Greek—were taught in the "grammar schools" of Renaissance England and in the humanist "collèges" of France, the secondary schools that prepared some boys for the all-male institution of the university. Although many of us think of early modern grammar schools as teaching chiefly the Latin language, in truth, as Spenser's teacher Richard Mulcaster knew, such schools also taught English to many boys from the middling and upper classes whose writings would later fill pages and pages of the *Norton Anthology of English Literature*. The English they learned at grammar school through the method of "dual translation" was not, however, as I've been attempting to suggest, much like the languages that most people living in English territories learned at their mothers' or nurses' knees. This is a point often forgotten today, when (an idea of) "the vernacular" is commonly counterposed to and seen as somehow more democratic than Latin.

An ideal of muscular clarity—in French or English or Latin writing—was also upheld in and through the Renaissance grammar school curriculum. This ideal coexisted with a great variety of highly convoluted and difficult vernacular language practices in the early modern period—practices often defined, as Patricia Parker has shown, as "effeminate" or "Asiatic."[17] "Clarity" associated with masculinity remains a central educational value in the tradition I have attempted, rather sweepingly, to sketch here. This is the tradition of an "illustrious vernacular" that is at once a set of valued and prescribed stylistic practices and a set of theories about language and its social value. Historically linked to an ideal of Latinity and, I've been suggesting, to a vision of the Latin language as a supraregional phenomenon that must be learned through the social institution of the school, the illustrious vernacular, in theory and in practice, is also historically linked to ideas of empire.

If you entertain this hypothesis, you will see why the stylistic ideal of clarity is misunderstood, or at the least very partially understood, if it's associated chiefly with moral qualities such as "kindness" to the reader. Which reader? Born where? How educated? Considering the matter historically, we can discern some links between the generally educated reader Martha Nussbaum and others hypostatize—the presumably nongendered citizen of the modern democracy whose interests are allegedly not served by writing that is too difficult, too laden with terms from foreign languages and specialized discourses, not to mention with names of thinkers whose theoretical "differences" from each other aren't fully explained—on the one hand, and, on the other, the imperial subject adduced by Antonio Elio de Nebrija in a treatise written in 1492, the year of Columbus's fateful landfall on the island of San Salvador, which the natives called (something like) "Guanahani." In the preface to his *Gramática de la lengua castellana* Nebrija recounts what has become a well-known anecdote in the history of Spanish culture, an anecdote in which a writer describes, to a royal patron, the usefulness or political end of a vernacular grammar book:

Now, Your Majesty, let me come to the last advantage that you shall gain from my grammar. For the purpose, recall the time when I presented you with a draft of this book earlier this year in Salamanca. At this time, you asked me what end such a grammar could possibly serve. Upon this, the Bishop of Avila interrupted to answer in my stead. What he said was this: "Soon Your Majesty will have placed her yoke upon many barbarians who speak outlandish tongues. By this, your victory, these people shall stand in a new need: the need for the laws the victor owes to the vanquished, and the need for the language we shall bring with us." My grammar shall serve to impart them the Castilian tongue, as we have used grammar to teach Latin to our young.[18]

It may seem far-fetched to compare the outlaws and barbarians envisioned by Nebrija as persons capable of being brought into the pale of the Spanish empire by means of the newly grammaticized language of Castilian with the generally educated reader of the *New Republic* addressed, in an apparently kindly way, by Martha Nussbaum. There is, however, a political and historical tie that binds these groups, as pedagogical subjects, just as there is a political and historical tie that binds the Platonic philosopher, the late-medieval and early modern fashioner of illustrious vernaculars, and the Sophists—the foreigners or outlaws in Athens who compete with Socrates and Plato for pedagogical authority and cultural capital. The ties are many-stranded; I've done no more here than argue for their existence and begin to outline some of their features. I hope, however, to have driven a bit of a wedge between the notion of a "clear" style, on the one hand, and, on the other, any Platonic corner on the market for moral virtue.

Notes

1. Quoted in W. K. C. Guthrie, *The Sophists* (Cambridge, U.K.: Cambridge University Press, 1971), 40.

2. For valuable discussions of the notion of prestige dialects and the problems inherent in the concept of "standard" languages, see Tony Crowley, *Standard English and the Politics of Language* (Urbana: University of Illinois Press, 1989), chap. 3; and Juliet Fleming, "Dictionary English and the Female Tongue," in *Enclosure Acts: Sexuality, Property, and Culture in Early Modern England*, ed. Richard Burt and John Michael Archer (Ithaca, N.Y.: Cornell University Press, 1994), 290–326, esp. 313–14 n. 3.

3. David Hume, "Of Simplicity and Refinement in Writing," in *Essays: Moral, Political, and Literary*, ed. Eugene F. Miller (Indianapolis, Ind.: Liberty Fund, 1985), 192.

4. See Judith Butler, *London Review of Books*, letter-response to T. Eagleton, cited in James Miller, "Is Bad Writing Necessary?" *Lingua Franca* (Dec./Jan. 2000): 34. See also Theodor Adorno's comments on language that is "baldly functional," "merely communicative," in *The Jargon of Authenticity*, trans. Knut Tarnowski and Frederic Will (Evanston, Ill.: Northwestern University Press, 1973), 58; and Fredric Jameson on the idea that "thinking dialectically means nothing more or less than the writing of dialectical sentences" ("T. W. Adorno," in *Marxism and Form* [1971; reprint, Princeton, N.J.: Princeton University Press, 1974], esp. 53).

5. Cited in Miller, "Bad Writing," 35.

6. See Pierre Bourdieu, *Language and Symbolic Power*, ed. John B. Thompson, trans. Gino Raymond and Matthew Aronson (Cambridge, Mass.: Harvard University Press, 1991), 47, citing Furetière's *Dictionary* of 1690. Renée Balibar notes that the terms *dialectes*, *patois*, and *idiomes* were confusingly interchanged in nineteenth-century French usage and are still not well distinguished today. See her *Le Français National: Politique et Pratique de la Langue National Sous la Revolution François* (Paris: Hachette, 1974), 32.

7. *The Greek Grammar of Roger Bacon*, Distinccio 1, capitulum 1; cited in J. D. Burnley, "Sources of Standardisation in Later Middle English," in *Standardizing English: Essays in the History of Language Change in Honor of John Hurt Fisher*, ed. Joseph B. Trahern Jr. (Knoxville: University of Tennessee Press, 1989), 32. The Baconian formulation invites comparison with Raymond Williams's discussion of how a "virtually metaphysical notion of the language" comes to subtend distinctions between "standard" English and "dialects" of English. By this projection "of a concept of English as existing metaphysically, in other than its actual variations, there comes to be a singular *English* and then *dialects of English*" (Raymond Williams, *Keywords: A Vocabulary of Culture and Society* [New York: Oxford University Press, 1976], 106 [Williams's italics]).

8. Giles de Rome, *De regimine principum* (1285), 2.2.7; cited in Latin and French in Serge Lusignan, *Parler Vulgairement: Les Intellectuels et la Langue Française aux XIIe et XIVe Siècles*, 2d ed. (Paris: Librairie Philosophique J. Urin, 1987), 43 (my translation).

9. George Puttenham, *The Arte of English Poetrie* (Kent, Ohio: Kent State University Press, 1970), 156–57.

10. Tullio De Mauro, *Storia Linguistica dell'Italia Unita*; cited in Jonathan Steinberg, "The Historian and the *Questione della Lingua*," in *The Social History of Language*, ed. Peter Burke and Roy Porter (Cambridge, U.K.: Cambridge University Press, 1987), 198.

11. All citations of the *De Vulgari Eloquentia* refer to the third (bilingual) edition by Aristide Marigo and Pier Giorgio Ricci in volume 6 of the *Opere di Dante*, general editors Vittore Branca, Francesco Maggini, and Bruno Nardi (Firenze: Le Monnier, 1968). The quoted passage is from book 1.1.2–3, 6–8. Citations will henceforth be given in parentheses with book, chapter, and passage number followed by the page numbers of Marigo's edition. My translations are based on those of Robert Haller, *Literary Criticism of Dante Alighieri* (Lincoln: University of Nebraska, 1973), and on those of Marianne Shapiro, *De Vulgari Eloquentia: Dante's Book of Exile* (Lincoln: University of Nebraska Press, 1970).

12. See C. T. Davis, "Dante and the Empire," in *The Cambridge Companion to Dante*, ed. Rachel Jacoff (Cambridge, U.K.: Cambridge University Press, 1993), 67–79; see also his *Dante and the Idea of Rome* (Oxford: Clarendon Press, 1957).

13. Dante also uses the metaphor of the sieve in *Paradiso*, canto 26.1.

14. Interestingly, Dante gives the name of the mother first in his examples of *puerilia*: "nec puerilia propter sui simplicitatem, ut *mamma et babbo, mate et pate*" (2.7.4, Marigo ed., 228). For a provocative discussion of the rather contradictory perspectives on baby talk in the *De Vulgari* and in Dante's epic—which latter appears to

offer a more favorable estimate of baby talk than the treatise does—see Robert Hollander, "Babytalk in Dante's *Commedia*," in *On the Rise of the Vernacular Literatures in the Middle Ages*, ed. R. G. Collins and John Wortly (Winnipeg, Canada: University of Manitoba Press, 1975), 73–84.

15. For a fuller discussion of this point see Margaret Ferguson, *Dido's Daughters: Literacy, Gender, and Empire in Early Modern England and France* (Chicago: University of Chicago Press, forthcoming), chap. 3.

16. Quoted in Kathleen Lambley, *The Teaching and Cultivation of the French Language in England* (Manchester, U.K.: Manchester University Press, 1920), 28.

17. See Patricia Parker, "A Virile Style," in *Premodern Sexualities*, ed. Louise Frandenberg and Carla Freccero (New York: Routledge, 1995), 199–222.

18. Cited in and translated by Walter Mignolo, *The Darker Side of the Renaissance: Literacy, Territoriality, and Colonization* (Ann Arbor: University of Michigan Press, 1995), 38.

Hume's Learned and Conversable Worlds

> They that content themselves with general ideas may rest in general terms; but those whose studies or employments force . . . closer inspection must have names for particular parts, and words by which they may express various modes of combination, such as none but themselves have occasion to consider.
> —Samuel Johnson, *Idler*, no. 70 (1759)

SAMUEL JOHNSON denied the possibility that the language of common life could be sufficient to provide all the "terms of art," the expert terminologies, necessary for specialized studies and employments. In the *Idler* essays and the preface to his *Dictionary* (1755) he describes this lexical divide as a consequence of the pursuit of advanced knowledge, accepting with regret the professional isolation that inevitably results. Although Johnson confronts the issues concerning specialized language that we address in this essay, the degree to which general languages could speak to expert needs seems more settled for him than for other writers, whether before or after.

British philosopher, historian, and essayist David Hume characterized the conflict between specialized and public languages as a split between the "learned" and the "conversable" worlds. *Learned*, for Hume, signified the idiom of university-trained specialists, *conversable* the conversational vernacular of a broadly educated public. In his 1742 *Essays, Moral and Political*, Hume imagined himself as an ambassador moving between these worlds. Such an emissary was needed, Hume noted, because philosophy in particular had suffered much by its disengagement from common life, losing any claims to "liberty and facility of thought and expression" and becoming "chimerical in her conclusions as she was unintelligible in her stile and manner of delivery."[1] Hume's advocacy of a more conversational style in philosophical writing came in the wake of the popular failure of both his own, highly learned *Treatise of Human Nature* (1739–40) and John Locke's earlier efforts to make philosophy better suited for "well-bred company" and "polite conversation."[2] Locke's push to conjoin the expert pursuit of knowledge with rational communication in society, here reiterated by Hume, resembles concerns raised in our own time about the accessibility of academic writing. And, as Hume shows, although questions about the intelligibility of a discourse are, on one hand, about linguistic choice, they are, on the other, about the values we attach to technical humanistic studies. Then as now, they are loaded questions.

Our subject here is neither the role of the modern university in the heritage of these debates nor the debates' genesis in the eighteenth century. Rather, we examine how the ideal of conversational language endorsed by Locke and his successors was differently deployed in scientific and humanistic contexts in the eighteenth century. In so doing we speak genealogically across time to the methodological divides facing today's academic writers. We treat the case of David Hume because his career, although unusual in its trajectory, crystallizes our concerns: in response to the mistakes he perceived in earlier metaphysical systems, he began life as a professional philosopher looking for a scientific method, one that would allow him to achieve a revolution in morality and epistemology analogous to the one Newton achieved in physics. However, in publishing the *Treatise* he ran up against the fundamental difference between disciplines that do their work on and in natural languages and those that work on physical objects or through mathematical representations.

The precondition of describing the findings of physical science in ordinary languages is that such formulations inevitably will be incomplete: the essence of the work is given up in the transition from mathematical to linguistic representation. The vernacular description of the work is acknowledged as a series of metaphors that can be shaped to conform to the level of understanding of the projected audience without affecting the original results. Thinking in language comes after the mathematical or experimental fact and is, or is presumed to be, radically autonomous from science itself.

By contrast, in the humanities and social sciences findings and their representations to an audience are bound up together in one and the same language. This entanglement between the work itself and its linguistic presentation gives rise to the assumption that because one can understand a vernacular language, one should be able to understand all things written in it. But the problem with this assumption is that it discounts the histories, traditions, and methods that develop in expert discourses and their constituent terminologies. Although specialized vocabularies are intertwined with the language of common life (if indeed such a common-life language exists as such), they are not identical to it. The oft-voiced prejudice against disciplinary jargons likewise adumbrates a host of suspicions. Such wariness is founded on a hazy but nonetheless powerful anxiety that texts written in expert idioms are hiding important knowledge from the vernacular culture for diabolical or at least potentially exploitative purposes. The widespread distrust of legal language is the paradigmatic example, but other disciplines have likewise long contended against similar misgivings.

The sciences and humanities thus have long displayed asymmetrical relationships to natural languages. This asymmetry confounds modern readers no less than it confounded Hume when he assumed in his early work that the audience for philosophical prose was coextensive with the generally educated reading public. When his early effort at a scientific philosophy in the *Treatise* was met with general incomprehension and was largely ignored, he moved toward a more sociable, collegial style, adopting the language of coffeehouse periodicals for metaphysical ends. He simultaneously discarded the technical, epistemological pursuits that could not be represented in nonexpert languages.

Language and Specialization

We frame our own investigation with a polemical question: Why does the claim that science can only be incompletely represented by ordinary language descriptions make the work done by scientists seem all the more important because all the more incomprehensible to the lay reader?[3] And why does the pressure work in the opposite direction in the humanistic disciplines: the more specialized humanistic language becomes, the readier the reading public is to discount or suspect its value? Ordinary, or conversational, language figures centrally here because the eighteenth century witnessed the movement of specialized, disciplinary knowledge into the public sphere through demonstrations and expositions couched in language readily available to an ever-broadening, nontechnical readership. But why was there a felt need for such knowledge to move into the public sphere, the world of everyday language? If we begin with the case of science, we can find answers in recent scholarship. The new, experimental scientists (Newton, Boyle) differentiated themselves from their rationalist counterparts (Descartes, Leibniz) by conducting their work on and with nonlinguistic materials—prisms, air pumps, telescopes—and through the highly specialized language of mathematics. They fostered a new epistemology based in experimental objects and mathematical symbols. This innovation required justification. Scientists made the empiricist epistemology credible by staging their work in public demonstrations and describing it in publications written in ordinary language. Popular exhibitions of scientific instruments served to show how natural and mechanical objects could be made to speak.[4]

Laboratory work made its way into common parlance through lecture tours and written exegeses that glossed mathematical reasoning in everyday terms. Popularizations of works such as Newton's *Principia* (1687) made their basic claims, if not always their methods, accessible to the lay reader.[5] The fiction guiding these scientists was that their laboratory experiments and mathematical expressions made the facts of nature available to them and that their public demonstrations—when they differed from what was done in the lab or the study—were only secondary representations meant to convince an untrained audience. They were not the thing itself.

In a 1761 lecture chemist Joseph Priestley compared this relationship between fact and representation to the difference between history and fiction. "All true history has a capital advantage [over] every work of fiction," he wrote, because "works of fiction resemble those machines which we contrive to illustrate the principles of philosophy, such as globes and orreries, the use of which extend no further than the views of human ingenuity; whereas real history resembles the experiments by the air pump, condensing engine and electrical machine, which exhibit the operations of nature, and the God of nature himself."[6] Priestley's facts of nature—made available through experimental mechanical devices—were constructed in the belief that "facts were theory-free and value-free."[7] The eighteenth-century scientist's insistence on the separation of the scientific fact from the capriciousness and imprecision of language was crucial. Experimental scientists became publicly credible because they emphasized the limits of the authority of language and the dominance of specialized modes of knowing. Paradoxically, they leaned heavily on visual and linguistic rhetoric to make this distinction clear. Over time the perceived remoteness of science from the world of rhetoric gave it independence and power.

The burgeoning realm of vernacular print culture both expanded audiences and confronted the emerging disciplines with unforeseen demands. If the public sphere was where rational, factual knowledge could be tested and deemed credible, it would seem to be the ideal place to try the claims of any new epistemology. There was thus a parallel impetus for new methods in humanistic studies to make the same move into the public sphere. David Hume thought along these lines, calling his 1739/40 *Treatise of Human Nature* an "attempt to introduce the experimental Method of Reasoning Into Moral Subjects."[8] In it Hume railed against the narrow, Aristotelian logic of his metaphysical predecessors who would cavil endlessly over concepts such as "the self," inventing entities without seeking empirical evidence for their existence. Rather than beginning with general principles, he founded his work on observation, the evidence of his senses, taken individually and collectively. He called his method inductive, directing attention to his procedural distinctions from the deductive techniques of earlier moral philosophers.

Hume thus embarked on a project with the same set of assumptions that Newton or Priestley did: that experiment could make fact—the real thing—available to him through sensory observation. His chosen method obliged him to proceed as if his analysis would produce objective certainty. But following his process through to its logical extreme, he undermined his own operating assumptions. His *prima facie* privileging of our sensorium—our best source of empirical information—was itself deconstructed. He demonstrated that we have no way to prove that our sense organs give us facts about the world. Inquiring into the basis of our notion of what is real, he instead discovered he could not show that what our senses give us are facts; they only offer grounds for strongly held beliefs. He showed that we work from our beliefs in our representations of nature without any assurance that this *is* nature itself. In so doing he revealed that the inductive method, when applied to consciousness, increases our sense of the contingency of our knowledge and thus delimits the claims of the method itself. Hume did not entirely discredit our ways of knowing; rather he pointed to their susceptibilities and qualifications and to the inability of any observation-based procedure to stabilize its object of knowledge.

But Hume presented his struggle with the nature of knowledge through a method difficult enough to keep most readers from grasping what he had done. To Hume's consternation the reading public failed to follow—or to want to follow—him through his own involved reasoning. This outcome should not have surprised him as much as it did, considering the complexity of his analysis and the idiosyncratic precision with which he used ordinary vocabulary. Almost from the beginning he attributed his readers' difficulties to their misunderstanding his use of language. When the third volume of the *Treatise* was published in 1740, he annexed this remark: "I have not yet been so fortunate as to discover any very considerable mistakes in the reasonings deliver'd in the preceding volumes. . . . But I have found by experience, that *some of my expressions have not been so well chosen, as to guard against all mistakes in the readers*."⁹ Hume follows in the footsteps of Locke, who had similarly found that his writing was subject to misunderstandings and miscommunications and had likewise blamed insufficiently attentive readers for the communication gap.

In an effort to untangle his work for the inexpert reader, Hume took it upon himself to imitate the scientists by becoming his own expositor—adopting a second, more public language, writing in 1748 the more accessible and considerably shorter *Enquiry Concerning Human Understanding* and in 1751 the *Enquiry Concerning the Principles of Morals*. Even taken together, these two works leave out many of the most specialized aspects of the *Treatise*. Over the course of his career Hume moved toward increasingly approachable, essayistic forms and left off writing more technical works altogether. Here is where the correspondence we have been tracing between moral philosophers and natural philosophers, between humanists and scientists, ends. In moving from philosophical discourse to more readily available language, Hume eventually abandoned wholesale the most difficult, most technical aspects of his philosophical writing. The technical language went out the window, and he never took it up again. With it he also cast away the set of ideas not responsive to treatment in the language of the essay, the genre of the public sphere.

But even after the successes of Hume's later writings his *Treatise* did not, at least in the public sphere, follow the trajectory of Newton's *Principia* by becoming more valued because more inaccessible. The difference seems to lie in some combination of their respective disciplinary practices and the rhetoric used to present their work. Shortly before he died, Hume penned an advertisement that would be prefaced to his posthumous collected works:

Most of the principles, and reasonings, contained in this volume, were published in . . . *A Treatise of Human Nature*. . . . But not finding it successful, he was sensible of his error in going to the press too early, and he cast the whole anew in the following pieces, where some negligences in his former reasoning *and more in the expression*, are, he hopes, corrected. . . . Henceforth, the Author desires, that the following Pieces may alone be regarded as containing his philosophical sentiments and principles.[10]

Hume locates the difference between the two kinds of writing not in their reasoning, although he says he did rectify a few errors there; rather, he finds it "in the[ir] expression." That is, he represents the two works as differing primarily in their linguistic style. He proceeds as if the difference happened only in the manner and not in the matter. Here Hume's concerns intersect with our own: Hume performs the same critical maneuver on his writings that more recent critics are quick to perform on academic writing when they confer bad writing awards and the like. They insist that difficult writing is a marker of muddled or lazy thinking. They share the splenetic and delusional perspective of the dying Hume, who held the wishful sentiment that all reasoning, however strenuous, could be embodied in ordinary language.[11] Critiques (including Hume's self-critique) that consider difficult writing to be by definition bad writing mask deeper structural divergences that such thinking refuses to acknowledge.

Although untrained readers may not have grasped much of Hume's essay, what they did comprehend were reviewers who suggested they should not read Hume's work at all because it was so pockmarked by the unpleasantness of skepticism, disguised by difficult language. One of the few published reviews of Hume's *Treatise* takes him to task for the trouble to which he puts his readers:

I should have taken no notice of what he has wrote, if I had not thought his book, in several parts, so very abstruse and perplex'd, that, I am convinced, no Man can comprehend what he means; and as one of the greatest Wits of this Age has justly observed, this may impose upon weak Readers, and make them imagine, there is a Great Deal of deep Learning in it, because they do not understand it.[12]

This review's unnamed author exhibits a keen awareness of the power the recondite text may hold over its readership, suggesting itself as holding secrets unavailable to the casual reader. However, he dismisses such an interpretation of Hume's *Treatise* as a red herring. The *Treatise*'s rhetorical complexity is not caused by the immense learnedness of its author—as the weak reader might assume—but rather by its author's linguistic inexactness and faulty reasoning. But as another critic has observed, this anonymous reader was himself not a very careful one, refusing or failing to evaluate Hume's system on its own terms and, instead, holding it accountable to the very rationalist doctrines Hume sought to undercut.[13]

This critical reader of Hume would have agreed in part with the more perceptive reviewer of the *Bibliothèque raisonnée*: "Perhaps it will be found that in wishing to investigate the inmost nature of things, [Hume] sometimes uses a language a little unintelligible to his readers. . . . Metaphysics has its stumbling blocks as well as the other sciences. When it passes certain limits, it obscures the objects that it searches out. Under pretence of yielding only to evidence, it finds difficulties in everything."[14] Hume himself worried over this: if clarity of understanding is the goal, certain philosophical or rhetorical procedures ought not to be employed under any circumstances because they inevitably muddy the water, impeding the view of the very objects they wish to expose. Much of the *Treatise* is devoted to leading its readers into philosophical dead ends, to showing the limits both of received epistemologies that argue for nonempirical sources of knowledge and of experimental methods that rely on experience alone to explain human understanding. Such a procedure is by its very nature difficult to follow. What later academic philosophers have found most compelling about Hume's method lies in these very mazes. It is in the nature of his intellectual maneuverings to leave more questions than answers. However, an appreciation of such a method runs counter to the prejudices of a wider reading public, who tended (and still tend) to believe that what is possible at all in language is possible in commonsensical formulations.

The belief in the power of common language to address philosophical questions was and is still bolstered by a host of eighteenth-century writings on the topic. Authors from John Locke to Hugh Blair have averred that when language is held strictly accountable to the ideas underlying it, both language and ideas will be transparent to their readers. That is to say, critical investigations into subjects not easily made tractable to straightforward (or straightforwardly worded) solutions ran counter to the stated aims of enlightenment. For at least this brief moment in history popular pressure and philosophical epistemology coincided—in theory. Rhetorical clarity was the hallmark of the way empiricist philosophers thought of themselves. When clarity was not possible, inquiry was inadvisable.

But alongside this belief ran another, perhaps articulated best by philosopher George Berkeley (1685–1753), about the difficulty that the nonscientific disciplines faced in sharing the vocabulary of everyday life:

> Herein Mathematiques have the advantage over Metaphysiques & Morality[.] Their Definitions being of words not yet known to [th]e Learner are not Disputed, but words in Metaphysiques & Morality being mostly known to all[,] the definition of them may chance to be controverted. The short, jejune way in Mathematiques will not do in Metaphysiques & Ethiques, for y[e]t about Mathematical propositions men have no prejudices, no anticipated opinions to be encounter'd, they not having yet thought on such matters. [T]is not so in the other 2 mention'd sciences, a Man must not onely demonstrate the truth, he must also vindicate it against Scruples & establish'd opinions w[hi]ch contradict it. In short the dry Strigose rigid way will not suffice.[15]

That is, mathematicians do not have to contend with their audience's preconceptions about their terms because such terms are expressly set apart from and defined in contradistinction to everyday language. In contrast, metaphysicians must defend their language from the claims of common sense. Practitioners of nonmathematical, technical disciplines must contend with the commonplace notion—in Berkeley's time and our own—that language is language is language. The operative belief here is that common speech embodies common sense and that anything worth saying can and should be said in broadly accessible terms. This is the heart of the critique of Hume's *Treatise* by Thomas Reid, the eighteenth-century commonsense philosopher: knowledge is not knowledge if it cannot be comprehended in commonsensical terms.[16] Twentieth-century ordinary-language philosophers have leveled a similar critique at technical disciplines more generally: technical work must have been ultimately—at its origin—based on ordinary understandings of the world.[17] This search for intuitive origins or even a consistent language of common sense entails problems very much like the ones Berkeley spells out, namely that expert languages often operate differently from commonplace usages, even if they had at one time overlapped.[18] Indeed, one of post-Lockean philosophy's—as well as post-Newtonian science's—tasks has long been to point out the assumptions and presumptions lying behind common sense and its unilateral advocates.

Hume confers great value on common sense and habit because they allow us to get on with the business of everyday life. He does not, however, see common sense as the solution to epistemological problems. Hume's achievement in the *Treatise* is to illustrate that our faith in the alignment between fact and its representations is itself a problem, riddled with difficulties implicit in the act of representing. Hume's *Treatise* opens up the fundamental mistake in the insistence on the rhetorical transparency of common sense embodied in ordinary language.

We can thus recognize that reducing the difference between Hume's two kinds of writing to "stylistics" is itself a rhetorical move on Hume's part. Much of his readers' trouble in understanding the *Treatise* did not stem from Hume's language as such (as many critics have demonstrated, his sentences are generally very lucid) but rather from the philosophical method bound up in the language. Hume responds to this level of difficulty by banishing many of the parts of the *Treatise* he had explicitly marked as abstruse to his first *Enquiry*'s appendix and eliminating others altogether. He also provides his readers with suggestions on which sections of his *Enquiries* they ought to skip if looking for light entertainment. In writing the *Enquiries* he both implicitly and explicitly denies the possibility of translating the *Treatise*. Hume hovers between admitting philosophical abstraction cannot be explained without resorting to a highly learned approach necessarily difficult to read and an assertion that he will manage it anyway, by dismissing much of what he had to say altogether.[19]

Lost in Translation

Reading Hume thus raises for us a question: Is it possible for nothing to be lost in such a "translation"? Literary scholar Gerald Graff has argued, "Good academic writing . . . tends to be 'bilingual,' making its point in the complicated language of academese and then restating it in the vernacular (which, interestingly, alters the meaning)."[20] This is a version of Hume's point about the transfer of knowledge between learned and conversable worlds. But, although Graff ostensibly maintains that specialized writings have a certain, if limited, right to exist, his remarks belie a basic suspicion of the value of specialized, "difficult" language. The neologistic denomination *academese* tends to mock the language in which many academics write. The fundamental problem, though, is the metaphor of translation that Graff applies to the process of moving from disciplinary language to everyday language. *Translation* is misleading because it suggests that the operative fiction here is that as little as possible is lost in the move. This is not to disregard recent work in translation theory but rather to suggest that the process of transmutation may be described better by "representation" than "translation." Graff's own parenthetical remark "(which, interestingly, alters the meaning)" is a recovery effort, an acknowledgment that *translation* may be inadequate to describe what is accomplished and what is forfeited in moving between two methodologies.

In fact, the alteration of meaning lies at the heart of the move from expert to general language. As Graff suggests, simplification has its value. As admirers of Hume have observed, few people might have ever read the *Treatise* if the better-reviewed *Enquiries* had not called attention to it. In his own time Hume gained widespread approval for his efforts to focus on the aspects of philosophy more compliant to vernacular treatment. His *Enquiry Concerning the Principles of Morals* was the best received of his philosophical works; not coincidentally he also called it his favorite. The January 1752 *Monthly Review* recommended this *Enquiry* for its congeniality to the taste and abilities of the general reader:

The reputation this ingenious author has acquir'd as a fine and elegant writer, renders it unnecessary for us to say any thing in his praise. We shall only observe in general, that clearness and precision of ideas on abstracted and metaphysical subjects, and at the same time propriety, elegance, and spirit, are seldom found united in any writings in a more eminent degree than in those of Mr. *Hume*. The work now before us will, as far as we are able to judge, considerably raise his reputation; and, being free from that sceptical turn which appears in his other pieces, will be more agreeable to the generality of Readers. His subject is important and interesting, and the manner of treating it easy and natural[.][21]

On the one hand, Hume's sacrifice of complexity as he moved from the *Treatise* to the *Enquiries* was rewarded by reviewers who found grounds for praise in both the easy flow of Hume's language and the absence of philosophical difficulty. On the other, critics have remarked almost since Hume's own time that in order to fit the *Treatise*'s ideas into the more conversational *Enquiries*, he left out much of what has most interested professional philosophers in his own time and ours. Far from being stylistic residue, certain methods of inquiry were abandoned because they were not directly amenable to linear expository presentation.

We can easily see how the impulse not to differentiate between philosophical and customary uses of words arises—both technical terminologies and general usage are embodied in one and the same words. An ordinary-language philosopher of the twentieth century might well agree that Hume was on the right track in abandoning problems that did not exist in ordinary language. Hume says as much himself. However, such abandonment still begs the question: Is it possible to talk about the range of difficulties we find in ordinary-language constructions of the world without a technical language? Hume's explicit answer to this question might have been a qualified "yes," but the course of his career after the *Treatise* suggests that the answer is "no." That is, Hume's later writings indicate that when he turned to popular forms, he gave up pursuits deemed impossible for a general reading audience to understand.

Hume's rhetorical strategy differed fundamentally from the techniques of self-presentation used in science, where the scientific experiment itself was put forward as essentially different in nature, not simply in style, from the ordinary language later used to represent it. Science was able to find an epistemology that lay outside ordinary linguistic norms while also receiving public approval for the existence of such ways of knowing. We do not want to suggest that scientists can avoid vernacular language in their writing; scientists today must as a matter of course describe their research for nonspecialists when applying for grants in ways similar to those that the early experimentalists did to gain approval for their labors.[22] Instead, we want to point out that the separation between the work scientists do and the ways they represent it has, from an early point, been clearly demarcated as an act of representation. Vernacular formulations are considered fundamentally different from the *work* itself because the experiments and calculations were neither conducted in nor reliant on the same language used in everyday life. Such thinking persists in our own time. Indeed, in 1988 Stephen Hawking could write that "if we do discover a [unified] theory [of physics], it should in time be understandable in broad principle by everyone, not just a few scientists. Then we shall all, philosophers, scientists, and just ordinary people, be able to take part in the discussion of the question of why it is that we and the universe exist."[23] According to Hawking, public conversation about such findings can and will happen only after the scientific facts are determined and then only in broadly metaphoric terms.

What remains for those of us whose work and the language used to represent it are indistinguishable?[24] The case of David Hume lets us see that attempts to insist that specialized knowledge can be translated into "everyday language" with minimal loss are incorrectly formulated. If we accept the modern point of view that facts, formulae, and statistics are themselves representations, the gap between those representations and ordinary language is the same rift that opens up when one makes a representation of a representation. There is an axiomatic difference between the fiction of translation (what Graff urges) and an acknowledgment of the process of representation (the lesson we take away from David Hume).

Historians have shown that the rhetoric surrounding early empirical science established in the popular consciousness the idea that experimental practice has a claim on a reality not subject to the accidents and ambiguities of conversational languages. We have tried to suggest a backward look at how and why practitioners of what would become the humanistic disciplines sought—unlike the scientists—to avoid marking themselves off into a separate realm of specialized knowledge apart from the public sphere. In the case of Hume we hypothesize that he succumbed to his own reasoning, which called into question all claims to any separate, factual spheres of knowledge that were not contingent on habit and common sense. In the *Treatise* he sought truth and found only belief; in his later writings he stopped looking for shared truth and worked instead from commonly held beliefs. Hume's radical linguistic shift seems thus to have resulted from some combination of his own skepticism about the claims to factuality of any epistemology, including his own, and of the social and marketplace pressures influencing the reception of his writing. Print culture and Hume's own love affair with it disallowed this insulating divide between specialist and ordinary uses of language because it elided multiple audiences into a single one.

In retreating from the *Treatise*'s technicality Hume suggested he was making a decision about a way of life as much as about a philosophical method. Indeed, in the *Treatise* Hume dramatizes the difficulties of pursuing such a methodology. He portrays the problem as a split between a life in society and a life of the mind, a divide between conversational and philosophical ways of regarding the world. In philosophical mode he finds himself "affrighted and confounded with that forelorn solitude" to which his thoughts subject him, imagining himself "some strange uncouth monster, who not being able to mingle and unite in society, has been expell'd [from] all human commerce, and left utterly abandon'd and disconsolate" (264). Hume runs himself ever deeper into his solitary, abandoned realm until his senses call him back into a convivial, social world of "blind submission": "I dine, I play a game of back-gammon, I converse, and am merry with my friends; and when after three or four hour's amusement, I wou'd return to these speculations, they appear so cold, and strain'd, and ridiculous, that I cannot find in my heart to enter into them any farther" (269). The choice is sentimentalized, allegorized, made into a decision between fear and despair, on the one hand, and sweetness and light, on the other. With such a value-laden choice, who could wonder at Hume's eventual adoption of the latter? Hume preferred ultimately to follow in the capacious train of Joseph Addison, the eighteenth-century master of essayistic language, in exerting himself to bring philosophy "out of closets and libraries, schools and colleges, to dwell in clubs and assemblies, at tea-tables, and in coffee-houses."[25] This decision pushed Hume's philosophy away from an emerging intellectual disciplinarity, away from the difficulties of questions that required special exertion, broad and deep reading, and perhaps some suffering. Whatever may be gained herein, it also entails a substantial loss.

Notes

1. David Hume, *Essays Moral, Political, and Literary*, ed. Eugene F. Miller (Indianapolis, Ind.: Liberty Classics, 1985), 534–35.

2. John Locke, *An Essay Concerning Human Understanding*, ed. Peter H. Nidditch (Oxford: Clarendon Press, 1975), 10. Indeed, Locke's student Anthony Ashley Cooper, the third earl of Shaftesbury, took up this cry, trying to develop a truly conversational philosophy.

3. For consistency's sake throughout the essay we use the term *science* in the cus-

tomary modern sense to refer to natural and/or physical sciences. This definition dates from the nineteenth century; these fields of study would in the eighteenth century have been called "natural philosophy."

4. Larry Stewart pursues the distinction between "deeds" and "words" in seventeenth-century science in great and illuminating detail in *The Rise of Public Science: Rhetoric, Technology, and Natural Philosophy in Newtonian Britain, 1660–1750* (New York: Cambridge University Press, 1992).

5. As Stewart has shown, Newton's mechanical principles were illustrated by way of "mathematical analog[ies]" in traveling science shows, in which, for example, (naked) strong men were used to demonstrate how simple machines that took advantage of Newton's discoveries offered mechanical advantages, enabling more weight to be lifted, moved, balanced, and so on. (Stewart, *Rise of Public Science*, 125–26).

6. Quoted by Simon Shaffer in "Natural Philosophy and Public Spectacle in the Eighteenth Century," *History of Science* 21 (1983): 1. Shaffer cites Joseph Priestley, "Lectures on History and General Policy," in *The Theological and Miscellaneous Works of Joseph Priestley*, ed. J. T. Rutt (London: Hackney, 1817–31), 24:27–28.

7. Mary Poovey, *A History of the Modern Fact* (Chicago: University of Chicago Press, 1998), xviii.

8. David Hume, *A Treatise of Human Nature*, 2d ed., ed. L. A. Selby-Bigge (Oxford: Clarendon Press, 1978), xi.

9. Ibid., 623 (our italics).

10. David Hume, *An Enquiry Concerning Human Understanding*, ed. Tom L. Beauchamp (Oxford: Oxford University Press, 1999), 83 (our italics).

11. We cannot take credit for this slur; it comes from Thomas Hugh Grose, Hume's nineteenth-century editor, on whose work most modern editions of Hume are based. M. A. Box calls attention to Grose's remark that Hume's late-life retraction of the *Treatise* was the "posthumous utterance of a splenetic invalid" (M. A. Box, *The Suasive Art of David Hume* [Princeton, N.J.: Princeton University Press, 1990], 63).

12. "Hume's Account of Necessity," *Common Sense: or, the Englishman's Journal* (July 5, 1740): 1–2; reprinted in James Fieser's *Early Responses to Hume's Metaphysical and Epistemological Writings* (Bristol, U.K.: Thoemmes Press, 2000), 89.

13. Ernest Campbell Mossner, "The First Answer to Hume's *Treatise*: An Unnoticed Letter of 1740," *Journal of the History of Ideas* 12, no. 2 (1951): 293. The opposition to learned works on the grounds that they were obscure is a reversal of the Hermetic tradition in place before the seventeenth century, in which knowledge worth having was thought to be knowledge worth concealing. See Edgar Wind, *Pagan Mysteries in the Renaissance* (New Haven, Conn.: Yale University Press, 1958).

14. *Bibliothèque raisonnée des ouvrages des savans de l'Europe* 24 (April–May–June 1740): 328. Translated in Ernest C. Mossner's "Continental Reception of Hume's *Treatise*, 1739–1741," *Mind* 56 (1947): 36; and in Box, *Suasive Art of David Hume*, 74.

15. George Berkeley, *Philosophical Commentaries*, ed. A. A. Luce and T. E. Jessop, vol. 1 of *The Works of George Berkeley, Bishop of Cloyne* (London: Thomas Newlson and Sons Ltd., 1948), 22.

16. See Thomas Reid, *An Inquiry into the Human Mind, on the Principles of Common*

Sense (Edinburgh, 1764), esp. secs. 1.5–1.8, 2.6.

17. See, e.g., J. L. Austin's remarks on the ordinary language conceptions that underlie scientistic models of the world in his *Philosophical Papers*, 2d ed., ed. J. O. Urmson and G. J. Warnock (London: Oxford University Press, 1970), 185.

18. Even the vernacular language of scientific disciplines looks very different from parlance outside the discipline: a mathematician's statement "that's intuitively obvious," or "that's trivial," means that an observation does not have to be proven explicitly in mathematical terms. Such an utterance would decidedly *not* indicate that a nonmathematician would find the observation obvious; rather, it indicates that others inside the discipline would know how to find the solution without having it worked out for them.

19. See esp. the introduction to his first *Enquiry*, the first paragraph of which denies the possibility that moral philosophy could be easy to understand at all times and the second paragraph of which professes that he may have done it anyway.

20. Gerald Graff, "Scholars and Sound Bites: The Myth of Academic Difficulty," *PMLA* 115, no. 5 (2001): 1044.

21. *"An Enquiry Concerning the Principles of Morals,"* *Monthly Review* (January 1752): 1; reprinted in James Fieser's *Early Responses to Hume's Moral, Literary, and Political Writings* (Bristol, U.K.: Thoemmes Press, 1999), 11–12.

22. There is, in fact, currently a closet industry of traveling rhetoric teachers (latter-day Sophists?), mainly university professors trained in humanistic disciplines, who teach scientists to communicate their work to outside readers.

23. Stephen W. Hawking, *A Brief History of Time*, 10th anniv. ed. (New York: Bantam, 1996), 191. This book was a runaway bestseller. A former postdoctoral student of Hawking's has pointed out that he has "sold more books on physics than Madonna has on sex" (vii).

24. To take advantage of what a separate language can offer analysis, in recent years analytic philosophers and linguists alike have increasingly moved toward mathematical representations of their work. For example, in using symbolic logic, practitioners of these disciplines are working toward notational forms that deliberately move away from natural language formulations. Aristotelian logic, grammatical analysis, and mathematics all come together under this shared symbolic system.

25. This quotation comes from *Spectator*, no. 10, first published March 12, 1711.

Bad Writing and Good Philosophy

I BEGAN WORK on this topic for a conference at the University of London on style in philosophy. The organizers suggested that I address the question of what it is for a piece of philosophy to be badly written—no doubt thinking that as a reader of French philosophers, I would have special expertise on this question or at least a lot of relevant experience.

In fact, I was happy to take up this question because I have been intrigued of late by claims made in the world of Anglophone philosophy about bad writing. The journal *Philosophy and Literature*, edited by an Australian philosopher, Denis Dutton, had for several years announced a Bad Writing Award, and since this award had recently been conferred on a sentence by Judith Butler that appeared in *Diacritics* during my stint as editor, I had a personal interest in the concept of bad writing in philosophy and the criteria of selection. What counts as bad writing for this journal? What were the parameters of their Bad Writing Contest?

This contest was conducted for four years, and the prize was always awarded to someone well known, never to analytical philosophers but always to someone involved with Marxist, feminist, or postcolonial theory: Fredric Jameson, Roy Bhaskar, Homi Bhabha, Judith Butler. The contest attempts "to locate the ugliest, most stylistically awful passage found in a scholarly book or article published in the last few years." In an article in the *Wall Street Journal* Denis Dutton explains: "The rules were simple: Entries should be a sentence or two from an actual published scholarly book or journal article. No translations into English allowed, and the entries had to be nonironic."[1] I was surprised to learn that the editor asked only to see a sentence or two. When the *New York Times* phoned me for my reaction to Butler's receiving the award, I said that it seemed to me a matter of bad faith to take a single sentence out of context and charge it with obfuscation; I hadn't realized that this was actually the basis of the contest.[2] What if, for example, the sentence uses jargon that has just been explained?

I confess that it had never occurred to me that one ought to be able to understand every sentence of a work of philosophy in isolation, that every sentence should be clear *in and of itself*, that ugliness and impenetrability can be assessed independently of what comes before. I wondered whether only theorists of a continental persuasion produced sentences that failed this test, and I thought I would take a look, in a negative version of *sortes vergilianae*.

The first book I took down from the shelf was one with a good reputation, which I had always meant to read—Robert Nozick's *Philosophical Explanations*. Although Nozick sometimes writes highly technical philosophy, he has achieved a broad audience, and this book takes on large questions of interest to many people (its chapters are "The Identity of the Self," "Why Is There Something Rather Than Nothing," "Knowledge and Skepticism," "Free Will," "Foundations of Ethics," and "Philosophy and the Meaning of Life"). But the first page to which I turned, in the opening chapter, on the identity of the self, contained this sentence:

We have said that W is a whole relative to parts $p_1, \ldots, p_n$ when the closest continuer of W need not be the sum of the closest continuers of the parts p_i, when (a) it is possible that the closest continuer of W exists yet does not contain as a part some existing closest continuer of one of the p_i's; or (b) it is possible that the closest continuer of W exists and contains some part q that is not a closest continuer of any of the p_i (nor a sum or other odd carving up of these); or (c) it is possible that at some later time no continuer of W is close enough to be it, even though each of the p_i then has a continuer close enough to be it—the parts exist at the later time but the whole does not.[3]

This is certainly ugly, awkward, and hard to follow (a potential prizewinner, I should have thought!), but of course one *can* follow it if one is interested in the project of trying, with elaborate invented examples, to work out what logically would have to be the case for some y to count as a continuation of x and all the conceivable configurations that might complicate such ascriptions of identity. Having found enough sentences like this to assure myself that analytic philosophy is not necessarily more graceful, witty, and comprehensible than other sorts and that looking for sentences that by themselves are ugly and opaque is not a very good way of evaluating philosophy, I happened to glance at the opening page of Nozick's book, to see if he said anything about the kind of writing he was doing, and here is what I found. The book begins:

I, too, seek an unreadable book: urgent thoughts to grapple with in agitation and excitement, revelations to be transformed by or to transform, a book incapable of being read straight through, a book even to bring reading to a stop. I have not found that book, or attempted it. Still, I wrote and thought in awareness of it, in the hope that this book would bask in its light.[4]

Prose that basks in the light of the hope of unreadability. That this might be the goal of an eminent analytic philosopher warns us not to take ease of assimilation and transparency as the hallmarks of good writing in philosophy or difficulty as the necessary sign of bad writing.

With this idea in mind let me turn to the winner of the 1999 Bad Writing Prize—a sentence from a brief essay by Judith Butler called "Further Reflections on Conversations of Our Time." This essay introduced a conversation between Butler and Ernesto Laclau, whose book *New Reflections on the Revolutions of Our Time* provides the basis for Butler's title. Here is the sentence.

The move from a structuralist account in which capital is understood to structure social relations in relatively homogeneous ways, to a view of hegemony in which power relations are subject to repetition, convergence, and rearticulation, brought the question of temporality into the thinking of structure, and marked a shift from a form of Althusserian theory that takes structural totalities as theoretical objects to one in which the insights into the contingent possibilities of structure inaugurate a renewed conception of hegemony bound up with the contingent sites and strategies of the rearticulation of power.[5]

This is not an easy sentence, certainly. Here is what Denis Dutton says about it in commenting on the award: "Kitsch theorists mimic the effects of rigor and profundity without actually doing serious intellectual work. Their jargon-laden prose always suggests but never delivers genuine insight."[6] Then comes Butler's sentence. Dutton continues: "To ask what this means is to miss the point. This sentence beats readers into submission and instructs them that they are in the presence of a great and deep mind. Actual communication has nothing to do with it."

I think this is complete rubbish, actually. I wonder *who* it is who has failed to do serious intellectual work—such as read Butler's three-page article. Her sentence summarizes, in the third paragraph of the article, why she has taken an interest in Laclau and Mouffe's writing. She first became interested when she realized "that I had found a set of Marxist thinkers for whom discourse was not merely a representation of pre-existing social and historical realities, but was also constitutive of the field of the social and of history."[7] Then she saw that

central to their notion of articulation, appropriated from Gramsci, was the notion of rearticulation. As a temporally dynamic and relatively unpredictable play of forces, hegemony had been cast by Laclau and Mouffe as an alternative to the static forms of structuralism that tend to construe contemporary social forms as timeless totalities. I read in Laclau and Mouffe the political transcription of Derrida's "Structure, Sign and Play": a structure gains its status as a structure, its structurality, only through repeated reinstatements. The dependency of that structure on its reinstatement means that the very possibility of structure depends on a reiteration that is in no sense determined fully in advance, that for structure and social structure as a result to become possible, there must first be a contingent repetition as its basis.

This is important, as she explains later, because if what is dominant in a society depends for its dominance on constant repetition and rearticulation, there may be sites and strategies for altering that repetition and effecting change. In these opening paragraphs Butler identifies sources of concepts and introduces key terms such as *hegemony* and *rearticulation*, noting that for Laclau and Mouffe hegemony is something dynamic, depending on repetition and rearticulation, which keep it going. Then comes the prizewinning sentence summing up why she found their work important.

The move from a structuralist account in which capital is understood to structure social relations in relatively homogeneous ways, to a view of hegemony in which power relations are subject to repetition, convergence, and rearticulation, brought the question of temporality into the thinking of structure, and marked a shift from a form of Althusserian theory that takes structural totalities as theoretical objects to one in which the insights into the contingent possibilities of structure inaugurate a renewed conception of hegemony bound up with the contingent sites and strategies of the rearticulation of power.

Hegemony is a term that seems to provoke strong reactions, and when it appears twice in a sentence, as it does in Butler's, that may seem the height of obfuscation; but this sentence has been well prepared, and it is not hard to explain, although, of course, it would help to have some specific examples involving contingent sites and strategies of power. But we are still on page 1. Butler goes on, on page 2, to establish a link between Laclau's work and her own writing on a particular aspect of hegemony: the dominant conceptions of gender in society. "Gender is not an inner core or static essence but a re-iterated enactment of norms, ones which produce, retroactively, the appearance of gender as an abiding interior depth."[8] She stresses two points that mirror what Laclau and Mouffe are doing in their theorization of hegemonic politics:

(1) that the term that claims to represent a prior reality produces retroactively that priority as an effect of its own operation and (2) that every determined structure gains its determination by a repetition and hence, a contingency that puts at risk the determined character of that structure. For feminism, that means that gender does not represent an interior depth but produces that interiority and depth performatively as the effect of its own operation. And it means that "patriarchy" or "systems" of masculine domination are not systemic totalities bound to keep women in positions of oppression but, rather, hegemonic forms of power that expose their own

frailty in the very operation of their iterability. The strategic task for feminism is to exploit these occasions of frailty as they emerge. (14)

This is difficult writing, certainly, although not excessively so once one understands a few key terms and has in mind some particular illustrations of the processes at stake. My undergraduate students quickly become able to handle it. In fact, despite the high level of abstraction, it is quite pedagogic writing. Key points are rephrased and repeated so that if you don't catch on the first time around, you have another chance when they come by again. Butler has a distinctive style, determined in part by the counterintuitive processes she is describing: there is not a set of given entities that produce certain effects; rather, what we take to be the entities are the performative effects of repetition. Since English leads us to assume that the nouns we use have preexisting referents, sentences wishing to argue that these entities are themselves produced through repetition turn back on themselves in ways that may make them hard to read. Thus: "gender does not represent an interior depth but produces that interiority and depth performatively as the effect of its own operation."

Denis Dutton maintains, "When Kant or Aristotle or Wittgenstein are most obscure, it is because they are honestly grappling with the most complex and difficult problems that the human mind can encounter. How different from the desperate incantations of the Bad Writing Contest Winners, who hope to persuade their readers not by argument but by obscurity that they too are the great minds of the age."[9] I do not find helpful the distinction between honest grappling and the desperate production of obscurity, but Butler is certainly grappling with difficult problems.

Dutton's comment indicates, though, the ease with which—depending on whether or not one sympathizes with the philosophical mode—one can praise difficult writing as a heroic struggle with the antinomies of thought or else condemn it as pretentious vacuousness. There is bad writing everywhere, but public complaints about bad writing in philosophy generally seem complaints about a philosophical mode: a mode of thought one finds uncongenial, concerns of which one doesn't see the pertinence, so that the writing seems pointless and pretentious in its flaunting of specialized language (as I found the Nozick passages).

In the hope of avoiding the issue of sympathy with or antipathy to a philosophical mode, I want to approach the problem of philosophical style and bad writing not through texts outside the analytic tradition but through a very interesting and enigmatic figure, Stanley Cavell. A student of J. L. Austin and admirer of Wittgenstein, Cavell is known for his distinctive writing. What is happening philosophically in Cavell's stylish writing?

The reviews suggest that if we wanted a famous philosopher who could be charged with bad writing, Cavell would be an obvious choice. The *Times Literary Supplement*'s review of his most famous book, *The Claim of Reason*, by Anthony Kenny (entitled "Clouds of Not Knowing"), speaks of Cavell's "self-indulgent" style, especially his penchant for gratuitous qualifications and parenthetical interruptions, and concludes that despite "Cavell's philosophical and literary gifts, his book is a misshapen, undisciplined amalgam of ill-sorted parts."[10] Mark Glouberman, in the *Review of Metaphysics*, calls his style "inexcusable";[11] Dan Ducker, in *International Philosophical Quarterly*, writes that "the pattern of withholding judgment, of putting off closure, builds certain frustrations in the reader. There are moments in Cavell's book where one wants to scream, 'Good God, come to the point!'"[12] Even admirers have harsh words for his style. At the beginning of *Stanley Cavell: Philosophy's Recounting of the Ordinary* Stephen Mulhall notes "a feature of his writing which has become increasingly prominent over time, a feature one might call its 'lack of momentum'—a sense that there is no necessity to continue beyond the end of any given sentence."[13] Richard Fleming, in another book-length study, speaks of "the inertia of the many voices expressed in [Cavell's writing] and its constant self-reflections and pondering about self-knowledge."[14] Fleming continues, "It is certainly true that Cavell's way of writing has kept him outside of mainstream philosophy—if only because it has kept him from being read."[15]

Bad writing? Without more ado, here is the opening sentence of Cavell's most famous book, *The Claim of Reason*:

If not at the beginning of Wittgenstein's later philosophy, since what starts philosophy is no more to be known at the outset than how to make an end of it; and if not at the opening of *Philosophical Investigations*, since its opening is not to be confused with the starting of the philosophy it expresses, and since the terms in which that opening might be understood can hardly be given along with the opening itself; and if we acknowledge from the commencement, anyway leave open at the opening, that the way this work is written is internal to what it teaches, which means that we cannot understand the matter (call it the method) before we understand its work; and if we do not look to our history, since placing this book historically can hardly happen earlier than placing it philosophically; nor look to Wittgenstein's past, since then we are likely to suppose that the *Investigations* is written in criticism of the *Tractatus*, which is not so much wrong as empty, both because to know what constitutes its criticism would be to know what constitutes its philosophy, and because it is more to the present point to see how the *Investigations* is written in criticism of itself; then where and how are we to approach this text?[16]

And the first paragraph concludes: "How shall we let this book teach us, this or anything?"

Is it necessary to say that this is deliberate? I imagine that an editor at Oxford University Press might even have red-penciled this sentence and been told to let it stand. It would certainly have been easy to make it easier for the reader. For example: "How should we approach Wittgenstein's *Philosophical Investigations?* We could start on page 1, but the terms for understanding the beginning of the text aren't given with the text itself; nor is the beginning of the text the beginning of the philosophy. Moreover, the beginning of the philosophy is not something we can know at the outset." And so on. The difficulty here is the difficulty of beginning philosophy, where there is in principle nothing that can be taken for granted. This is the difficulty Hegel confronts in the preface to the *Phenomenology* (where there are points similar to Cavell's about the ways in which particular contextual approaches mislead). Hegel's confrontation produces a text thought to be hard to read, though not harder, I think, than this sentence of Cavell's, which seeks not to expound the difficulties but to confuse the reader. The two "if not at . . . " clauses presuppose objections, and the "since . . . " clauses may be taken to embody those objections, but since we don't, until after two hundred words have past, get the question "where and how to approach?" to which the supposed answers are being rejected, the reader couldn't understand the sentence until the very end; and by then, the structure of the sentence has been obscured by the shift halfway through from the negative, "if *not* at . . . since" structure (which would have been comprehensible), to the positive "if we acknowledge at the opening, anyway leave open . . . that," which doesn't talk about a *place* to start or not start and thus leaves readers more at sea. If good writing is that which considers the reader and gives him or her what is needed to follow, this is bad writing, especially since no virtues of elegance or aphoristic elan compensate for the befuddlement generated.

Richard Fleming, who wrote an entire book about Cavell's book, claims that the first sentence shows "the care and high respect that he has for the reader. He writes to someone who has been and continues to be engaged at a sophisticated level by Wittgenstein's struggle with the state of philosophy."[17] I think that is wrong. The sentence isn't any clearer to a sophisticated Wittgenstinean. The explanation lies in a different direction—one indicated by the epigraph to *The Claim of Reason*, from Emerson: "Truly speaking, it is not instruction but provocation that I can receive from another soul." The opening sentence provokes—and thus can, arguably, serve its function of alerting us to the fact that philosophy as Cavell conceives it is not something systematic or even expoundable. The sentence can work this way even if it also makes reviewers write that his style is inexcusable: it makes readers experience what it might *be* for nothing to be given and thus, in a minor way, to live the impossibility of deciding what comes first and how to go about thinking. "A philosophical question has the form: 'I don't know my way about,'" writes Wittgenstein.[18] I imagine this aphorism lurks somewhere in the murk from which Cavell's monstrous sentence arises.

Cavell continues, "I will say first, by way of introducing myself and saying why I insist, as I will throughout the following pages, upon the *Investigations* as a philosophical text, that I have wished to understand philosophy not as a set of problems but as a set of texts" (3). Not "I understand philosophy," but "I have wished to understand." This is the sort of thing that prompts one to call his writing precious or self-indulgent. But that is an interesting charge: "self-indulgent." What does that mean? How is the self being indulged? By contrast with the epistemic standpoint of "I understand . . . " or the impersonality of "Philosophy is better understood as a collection of texts," "I *have wished* to understand" evokes a self with desires and a history. But Cavell's writing is rarely autobiographical, and here, when he might easily take the opportunity to introduce the self, with some substantial remarks about its past and its experiences, we get instead the slim reference to a wished-for understanding of philosophy.[19] He does not seek to explain his views by evoking a past history. "I have wished to understand" marks the fact that an understanding, perhaps especially in philosophy, is not something that can be treated as unproblematically given but consists of inclinations, temptations, possibilities that have been attempted, ways of proceeding. To understand philosophy as a set of texts would be—what?—to try to write in ways that treated philosophy as different practices of writing (not easy to do).

But Cavell makes life hard for those who would justify his style: after this sentence he immediately asks whether this remark about texts is itself to be understood as a text, produces a two-page excursus on the different sorts or lengths of texts, and then continues: "But I was supposed to be saying more, having said something first, by way of introducing myself, and concerning how we should approach Wittgenstein's text. Accordingly, I will say, second, that there is no approach to it, anyway I have none" (6).

This is writing that, first and foremost, calls attention to itself as writing. These sentences do that, with a coyness one can certainly find irritating—as in the gratuitous "second" here. Is this not coyness more than self-scrutiny, or, at best, parody of the idea of steps or method?[20] Why would philosophy call attention to itself as writing? Philosophy is writing not only because that is the form in which we generally encounter it but, most important, because the fundamental philosophical question, for Cavell, is how we understand each other and ourselves. Philosophy and philosophical writing need to seek, and to question in seeking, that understanding. Thus, philosophy cannot be a matter of attempted proofs and well-wrought arguments but of working to find common ground through words that others will feel carry weight, that capture what has remained elusive.

If you give up something like formal argument as a route to conviction in philosophy, and you give up the idea that either scientific persuasion or poetic persuasion is

the way to philosophical conviction, then the question of what achieves philosophical conviction must at all times be on your mind. The obvious answer to me is that
it must lie in the writing itself. But in *what* about the writing? It isn't that there's a
rhetorical form, any more than there is an emotional form, in which I expect conviction to happen. But the sense that nothing other than this prose just here, as it's
passing before our eyes, can carry conviction, is one of the thoughts that drives the
shape of what I do.[21]

Cavell does not answer the question of what in writing might carry conviction. Obviously, there is no recipe for it. But what is involved here? How
is what Cavell does—write philosophy—shaped by the need to write so as
to give conviction a chance to happen? And since Wittgenstein's is the philosophical writing with which he is most concerned, how is Wittgenstein's
writing shaped by this end?

The Claim of Reason is a book focused on the *Philosophical Investigations*,
which Cavell thinks has been approached wrongly, as if, for instance, it contained a philosophy of language to be teased out. "Wittgenstein has no philosophy of language at all," he writes. Wittgenstein is interested in matters of
language because "they are topics in which the soul interests and manifests
itself, so the soul's investigation of itself, in person or in others, will have to
investigate these topics and those interests as and where they ordinarily manifest themselves" (15). Cavell spends a lot of time on the question of the nature of criteria, where his two philosophical mentors and models, J. L. Austin
and Wittgenstein, are at odds. The appeal to what we say and the search for
criteria "are claims to community. And the claim to community is always a
search for the basis on which it can or has been established" (20). Appeals to
criteria expose the fragile agreements on which our relations with others are
based. In the exploration of how such appeals are conducted and of their entanglement with the stream of life, Cavell's Wittgenstein is not seeking to re-
fute skepticism but to explore the problem of the other, of other minds,
which philosophy has been too inclined to treat as a special problem,
whereas in fact it is central to most aspects of life, including doing philosophy, which is writing that must find ways to engage the other.

When he began to study the *Investigations*, Cavell writes, he was struck by
the play of skeptical voices and answering voices. "I knew reasonably soon
thereafter and reasonably well that my fascination with the *Investigations* had
to do with my response to it as a feat of writing. It was some years before I
understood it as what I came to think of as the discovery for philosophy of
the problem of the other; and further years before these issues looked to me
like functions of one another" (xiii). Here again we have that spare form of
self-indulgence, a style shaped by the reference to the temporality of a self
but where the content is not other than philosophical—that is, Cavell is not
trying to ground, justify, or explain a philosophical position by reference to

some other sort of life experience. This might better be seen as confession—impersonal confession: recounting your thoughts in a way that invites readers to consider the possibility of trying out the relation that is narrated. This is different from writing "I intend to show that the text as a feat of writing is a version of the problem of the other." Is the implication that there is no other way to show this than to invite the reader to repeat the passage from one to the other?

Wittgenstein and Cavell write stylish philosophy but in very different ways. Wittgenstein is accused of being maddeningly enigmatic or unforthcoming but not, I think, of writing badly. He is spare, aphoristic, enigmatic, paratactic. Cavell is orotund, expansive, digressive, fussy, hypotactic. But since Cavell regards the *Investigations* as, more than any other text, "paradigmatic of philosophy for me" (xv) and has sought to discover "ways of writing I could regard as philosophical and could recognize as sometimes extensions—hence sometimes denials—of Wittgenstein's" (xv), one might ask whether there are things that Cavell's and Wittgenstein's ways of writing share. What does Cavell point us to in Wittgenstein's writing?

Neither claims to advance philosophical theses, for instance. I quoted earlier a passage suggesting that Cavell had no pretension to formal argument or poetic persuasion. He says, even more strikingly, about Wittgenstein's writing,

There is exhortation ("Do not say: 'there *must* be something common' . . . but *look* and *see* . . . ") not to belief but to self-scrutiny. And that is why there is virtually nothing in the *Investigations* which we should ordinarily call reasoning; Wittgenstein asserts nothing which could be proved, for what he asserts is either obvious—whether true or false—or else concerned with what conviction, whether by proof or evidence or authority, would consist in. Otherwise there are questions, jokes, parables, and propositions so striking that they stun mere belief. (Are we asked to believe that "if a lion could talk we could not understand him"?) Belief is not enough. Either the suggestion penetrates past assessment and becomes part of the sensibility from which assessment proceeds, or it is philosophically useless.[22]

This strikes me as a very significant and acute passage. It is also, of course, a very strong contention: that what does not penetrate past assessment is philosophically useless. That sets high standards for philosophical utility. The goal of penetrating past assessment to become part of the sensibility from which assessment proceeds is a daunting one, a real challenge for philosophical style. But it is clear also that skillful writing is what it calls for: writing that appeals to the other not to persuade but to find an echo and ultimately to receive acknowledgment.

Wittgenstein's writing works out methods for attaining self-knowledge that aspires also to be knowledge of others: posing questions where readers must try out their responses to an imagined situation, seeing what might be said and meant. He makes very heavy use of questions, for example (as does Judith Butler, I might mention); and he goes to much trouble, Cavell writes, "to give them a rhetorical air," as in "What gives the impression that we want to deny anything?" which certainly seems to suggest that he is not denying anything.[23] "He wants to leave that way of taking them open to us, to make it hard to see that they needn't be taken rhetorically, that instead the question is one he is genuinely asking, asking himself, and asking us to ask ourselves. The implication of this literary procedure here is that it is difficult to see that such a question genuinely needs asking, difficult to ask it genuinely" (103). This claim—about the function of making something difficult so that the reader may need aggressively to make an effort to ask a question seriously—may provide clues to some of Cavell's own writing decisions.

Cavell sees the *Investigations* as engaging in the mode of the confession: not because it offers personal information but because in confessing what you would or would not say, what you are tempted to say or resist saying, "you do not explain or justify, but describe how it is with you. And confession, unlike dogma, is not to be believed but tested, and accepted or rejected."[24] The *Investigations* is convincing because its questions and suppositions play out a desire, a willingness to resist the temptations of habitual misunderstandings. Wittgenstein's talk of what "we say" or wouldn't say adduces his linguistics intuitions, his sense of our ways of talking and thinking. "And the fact is," Cavell writes, "so much of what he shows to be true of his consciousness is true of ours (of mine). This is perhaps the fact of his writing to be most impressed by; it may be the fact that he is most impressed by— that it can be done at all" (20). Elsewhere Cavell notes that "skepticism about our knowledge of others is frequently accompanied by complacency about our knowledge of ourselves" but that those who historically have been capable of the deepest personal confession (such as Augustine, Rousseau, Thoreau, Kierkegaard, and Freud) have been those "most convinced that they were speaking from the most hidden knowledge of others" (109). In such cases, of course, the universal bearing of the confession is inextricable from the skill of writers. To write convincingly about the self is to write about others as well.

In Cavell and Wittgenstein the attempt to make suggestions that may have a chance to penetrate past assessment also generates language that attempts to get attention, to stop you, even to make itself memorable, as are Wittgenstein's famous aphorisms: "Why can't a dog tell a lie? Is it because he is too honest?" But Cavell does not attempt aphorism. He is concerned to spell out, inviting participation and recognition, once he has secured attention; his mode is capacious, exfoliating, running to parentheses and qualification. The larger part of *The Claim of Reason* engages in very laborious examination of Wittgenstinian problems, with Cavell imagining questions and questioners, offering discriminations about precisely what concerns him here and what does not, reflecting on the meaning of the various terms we might or might not offer in connection with such dialogues. This is prose that flows on continuously, with passages that go on and on—at the opposite remove, it might seem, from the paratactic paragraphs of the *Investigations*. Yet, in the end, in one way the effect is surprisingly similar. Just as you can't read Wittgenstein straight through but must stop and become involved in the little dramas of questioning and self-questioning his fragments stage, so with Cavell, I find, you can't read straight through to find out what he is saying but have to break the text into short chunks (four or five pages at a time is my limit) and allow yourself to get engaged in puzzling over these matters. You must forget or at least set aside the fact that there are over five hundred pages to this book and read as if it were a series of short scenarios.

Cavell does not, to my knowledge, talk about what might count as bad style in philosophy, but he is critical of philosophy's habit of proceeding by charging other philosophers with mistakes, nonsense, blindness, contradiction, circularity, what have you. Nozick, for instance, reports in *Philosophical Explanation* that he "usually reads works of philosophy with all defenses up, with a view to finding out where the author has gone wrong."[25] This leads to the situation Cavell regrets, where any graduate student can rehearse "how Descartes was mistaken about dreams, or Locke about truth or Berkeley about God or Kant about things in themselves or moral worth, or Hegel about logic, and so forth."[26] But what if philosophers, following Austin's analysis of what is involved in doing something by accident or by mistake (his analysis and not his own conduct in charging other philosophers with mistakes), were to "grant to other philosophers the ordinary rights of language and vision that Austin grants all other men: to ask them, in his spirit, why they should say what they say where and when they say it, and to give the full story before claiming satisfaction."[27] Then just as ordinary-language philosophy ties understanding to the elucidation of underlying consistencies or acknowledgment of commonality, so philosophy might become less of an esoteric battle and more of an enterprise of understanding. Cavell recommends, at least, that philosophy treat criticisms it feels "phenomenologically, as temptations or feelings; in a word, as data, not as answers."[28] In sum, the goal should be not to find mistakes in other philosophers but to understand from within, in the hope of reaching if not understanding and agreement, recognition and acknowledgment.

In something of this spirit, in a fine essay, "Aesthetic Problems of Modern Philosophy," Cavell takes up an issue in philosophy where it is hard to imagine reconciliation. Kant distinguishes the judgment that something is pleasant (canary wine is pleasant—which means "pleasant to me") from the judgment that an aesthetic object is beautiful (it would be "laughable," he says, to justify oneself by saying it is "beautiful to me"). The later judgment demands or claims or imputes general validity. There is thus supposed to be a difference of kind in the judgments involved. "One hardly knows," writes Cavell, "whether to call this a metaphysical or a logical difference. Kant called it a transcendental difference; Wittgenstein would call it a grammatical difference. But how can psychological differences like finding something laughable or foolish (which perhaps not *every* person would) be thought to betray such potent, or anyway different, differences?"[29] Cavell continues:

Here we hit upon what is to my mind the most sensitive index of misunderstanding and bitterness between the positivist and the post-positivist components of analytical philosophy: the positivist grits his teeth when he hears an analysis given out as the logical one which is so painfully remote from formality, so obviously a question of how you happen to feel at the moment, so "psychological"; the philosopher who proceeds from everyday language stares back helplessly, asking, "Don't you feel the difference? Listen, you *must* see it?" Surely, both know what the other knows, and each thinks the other is perverse, or irrelevant, or worse. (90)

Cavell sets out to describe why philosophers like him want to call such differences logical, in responding to the element of necessity felt in them, together with a sense of the ways such judgments are supported and conviction produced—by recurrent patterns of support. And he goes on to argue that Kant's aesthetic judgments, with their "universal" character that does not depend on empirical evidence about assent, are similar to philosophers' claims about "what we say." If you disagree, you don't try to collect data but try to determine why, and if you can't explain the disagreement, you try to find an explanation for that, with different examples.

"The philosopher appealing to everyday language," he writes, "turns to the reader not to convince him without proof but to get him to prove something, test something, against himself. He is saying: look and find out whether you can see what I see, wish to say what I wish to say. . . . All the philosopher, this kind of philosopher, can do is express, as fully as he can, his world and attract our undivided attention to our own."[30]

The reader may well be put off or preoccupied with other things, but language that gets one's attention may also, unpredictably, give conviction a chance to happen. Or rather—since Cavell says that unless suggestion penetrates past assessment, it is philosophically useless—we might speak of the reader "getting the hang of it":[31] coming to participate in a way of thinking that feels right, as something he or she can now do.

It is to give this unpredictable possibility a chance that Cavell writes this stylish, mannered prose designed to capture attention. If it aspires to provocation rather than instruction, it nevertheless instructs, if you take it in small enough chunks that its *longueurs* become occasions for reflection—leading you to see something for yourself—rather than irritation. It can be remarkable philosophy, even though its parts, such as the opening sentence of *The Claim of Reason*, could win any bad writing contest.

Notes

1. Denis Dutton, "Language Crimes," *Wall Street Journal*, Feb. 5, 1999, W11. See also Denis Dutton, "Bad Writing Contest: Results for Round Three," posted at www.miami.edu/phi/misc/badwrit3.htm.

2. I understand that the contest has now been abandoned, perhaps because Dutton realized that this was not a good basis for judgment.

3. Robert Nozick, *Philosophical Explanations* (Cambridge, Mass.: Harvard University Press, 1981), 101.

4. Ibid., 1.

5. Judith Butler, "Further Reflections on Conversations of Our Time," *Diacritics* 27, no. 1 (spring 1997): 13.

6. Dutton, "Language Crimes," 11.

7. Butler, "Further Reflections," 13.

8. Ibid., 14.

9. Dutton, "Language Crimes," 11.

10. Anthony Kenny, "Clouds of Not Knowing," review of *The Claim of Reason*, by Stanley Cavell, *Times Literary Supplement*, April 18, 1980, 449.

11. M. Glouberman, review of *The Claim of Reason*, by Stanley Cavell, *Review of Metaphysics* 32 (June 1979): 913.

12. Dan Ducker, review of *The Claim of Reason*, by Stanley Cavell, *International Philosophical Quarterly* 21 (March 1981): 109–11.

13. Stephen Mulhall, *Stanley Cavell: Philosophy's Recounting of the Ordinary* (Oxford: Clarendon Press, 1994), xii.

14. Richard Fleming, *The State of Philosophy: An Invitation to a Reading in Three Parts of Stanley Cavell's "The Claim of Reason"* (Lewisburg, Pa.: Bucknell University Press, 1993), 10.

15. Ibid., 11. One should note that *The Claim of Reason* is in its seventh printing, but possibly many purchasers quickly stop reading.

16. Stanley Cavell, *The Claim of Reason* (New York: Oxford University Press, 1979), 3. Further references to this work will be given by page numbers in the text.

17. Fleming, *State of Philosophy*, 22.

18. Ludwig Wittgenstein, *Philosophical Investigations*, no. 123, 3d ed., trans. G. E. Anscombe (New York: Macmillan, 1968), 49.

19. Elsewhere Cavell does, I admit, seem to spend more time than other philosophers telling you about the genealogy of his writings—how what you are reading relates to his past writings—and this can certainly seem a form of self-indulgence designed to focus attention on the career and corpus of this self, but I think that what we are dealing with in this passage is different.

20. Cavell says, "If I could set every word down and question the very setting of that word down as I set it down, I would do that to the point of self-excruciation."

James Conant, "Interview with Stanley Cavell," in *The Senses of Stanley Cavell*, ed. Richard Fleming and Michael Payne (Lewisburg, Pa.: Bucknell University Press, 1989), 59. His critics would say this self-excruciation is excruciating to readers.

21. Conant, "Interview," 59.

22. Stanley Cavell, "The Availability of Wittgenstein's Later Philosophy," in *Must We Mean What We Say? A Book of Essays*, by Stanley Cavell (Cambridge, U.K.: Cambridge University Press, 1976), 71.

23. Wittgenstein, *Investigations*, no. 305, p. 102.

24. Cavell, *Must We Mean What We Say?* 71.

25. Nozick, *Philosophical Explanation*, 6.

26. Cavell, "Austin at Criticism," in *Must We Mean What We Say?* 111.

27. Ibid.

28. Ibid., 110.

29. Cavell, "Aesthetic Problems of Modern Philosophy," in *Must We Mean What We Say?* 90.

30. Ibid., 96.

31. See "Austin at Criticism," 103.

The Metaphysics of Clarity and the
Freedom of Meaning

Paradoxes of Clarity

Clarity, as a norm for speech and writing, presents a paradox: although the burden of achieving it falls on the speaker, the achievement itself apparently falls to the hearer. I can labor mightily to produce a clear essay, argument, or sentence. But I have not actually produced it until you agree that I have—if only tacitly, by continuing the conversation. If, by contrast, you tell me that I have not made myself clear, there is no arguing with you about that; all I can do is try again to express what I have to say, in different terms, so that you can understand it. My words are not clear until you have understood what I meant by them.

Other discursive norms are not like this. No one is privileged to judge, for example, whether a given utterance achieves truth. If I tell you something and you tell me that it is false, I can argue with you about that. I can defend my statement, give evidence and reasons for it, and so on—exactly as you can do against it. I am not obliged, just by your reaction, to retract my statement. And it may even be that I am right: that my sentence is in fact true and you were simply wrong to call it false. In any case we are on an equal footing.

To put this into one of the conceptual frameworks that we in the West have inherited, that of Kant: Truth appears to be a cognitive norm, whereas clarity seems to be aesthetic. As a judgment of taste imputes beauty to its object, so I can impute clarity to my words; but this means nothing more than that I expect that others will agree that they are clear. I cannot demonstrate their clarity any more than I can (for Kant) demonstrate that something is beautiful.

But subjecting the paradox of clarity to a Kantian conceptual framework gives rise to another, more daunting, paradox: if clarity is like beauty, then it cannot be defined. We know it when we see or hear it but cannot say in what it consists. For anyone who knew what the nature of clarity was would not need a hearer to tell her if she had been clear on a given occasion: she could simply see for herself whether her utterance matched the criteria for clarity, as codified in its definition. This is a hard place in which to leave clarity, for it makes of it a self-violating norm: what are we to make of a notion of clarity that itself cannot be defined and so is inherently obscure?

A False Solution: Clarity as Unambiguousness

This pair of paradoxes combines into a rather simple dilemma. If, on the one hand, the nature of clarity were clear, then we would know whether we had attained it when we speak, and the first paradox of clarity would not arise. But if the nature of clarity is unclear, we have a sort of practical version of Russell's paradox: a norm that cannot apply to itself. A given sentence or argument or essay might be clear, but the judgment that it is could not.

Many contemporary American philosophers, bobbing along in the wake of logical positivism, have "solved" this dilemma by denying outright its first horn. They would call a statement "clear" not if it accurately conveyed the thoughts of the speaker to someone else but if it allowed for a single and complete distribution of truth values. If we can say, for every object in the universe, whether a given sentence is true of it or not, then that sentence is clear, and we do not need any hearers to tell us so.

This move, it bears noting, subordinates clarity to truth: a sentence is true (according to a famous philosophical tradition) if it corresponds to reality, false if it does not. It is clear if it permits us to assign one or the other of these two values to it: if it is unambiguous. By reducing clarity to the possibility of truth, this view makes of it what Kant would call a "cognitive" matter, amenable to demonstration. I do not need a hearer to tell me whether my utterance is clear, for I can perfectly well decide for myself whether it allows an unambiguous distribution of truth values. If it does, and you as hearer do not think so, you are wrong. The first horn of the above dilemma has now been legislated away—like drug use, and with approximately equal effect: the behavior still continues. In this case people still feel obligated to reformulate their statements when others do not understand them.

The Metaphysics of Clarity

I have now broached two concepts of clarity: clarity as the accurate conveyance of the thoughts of a speaker to a hearer, and clarity as the unambiguous distributability of truth values. Both of these have to do with various sorts of matching or (more mysteriously) correspondence. On the first concept the thoughts in the hearer's head should match or correspond to those in the speaker's. On the second my words should be capable of corresponding, or not corresponding, to reality.

The traditional way to understand correspondence is as a form of similarity. This is what Aristotle does when he defines sentential truth as the connectedness of subject and predicate. Truth and falsity, for Aristotle, depend "on the side of the objects, in their being combined or separated, so that he who thinks the separated to be separated and the combined to be combined has the truth, while he whose thought is in a state contrary to that of the objects is in error."[1] When the separations and connections in my mind match those presented by the objects I perceive, I have attained "truth."

What leads Aristotle to this view is not its epistemological merits alone (whatever they are) but a problem arising from the fact that he views sensation as the passage of a sensible form or quality of an object from the object to the soul of the perceiver of it.[2] The problem arises because the sensible form that passes from an object to a soul, like any form, cannot change—and so cannot be changed by that passage. Hence, as Aristotle puts it in *De Interpretatione*, the things in my soul must be "likenesses" of the things outside my soul (1.16a7–8).

The problem with this is evident: not all sensory qualities are unchanged by their passage from an object into a soul. The cloud I see on the horizon may look smaller than a dime. Sitting across from Coriscus in a gloomy room, I may not perceive his complexion exactly right. The things in my soul are not, usually, exact likenesses of the things outside it but more or less distorted approximations. How, then, can anything in my mind ever correspond to anything outside it? How can anything be true?

Aristotle's answer is that this whole issue does not affect truth, since the likeness involved in truth does not directly concern concrete sensory qualities at all but is strictly a matter of connection and separation. Although the size of the cloud in my field of vision does not match its real magnitude, I can still truthfully perceive the *connection* between that cloud and its color or between it and another cloud. If Coriscus's complexion has been distorted by the intervening air or even by my eyes, that is no matter because my properly cognitive business is not to perceive his complexion at all but to connect whatever color I do see with his other perceived properties and to separate it from other properties that he does not have. Connection and separation, Aristotle's gloss for what more recent philosophers call "correspondence," are thus special cases of sensory form. They are determinate qualities that (unlike color and size) can pass absolutely unchanged from the object known to the knowing soul. Aristotle thus defines truth as correspondence, in part at least, because he is committed to the idea that in cognition form must be transmitted from object to soul without change.

This commitment—I will call it the law of the preservation of form—is more than merely epistemological: it applies to all form as such, which passes unchanged from being to being and only looks different, in different beings, because of the unfortunate accretion of matter. Thus, in Aristotelian genetics the human form passes unchanged from the father to his child, who not only will be conspecific with him but should, as Aristotle rather strenuously insists, actually resemble him: "Any one who does not resemble his parents is already, in a sense, a monster; for in such creatures nature has in some way transgressed the genus."[3] Similarly, although hot water does not feel like hot air, the nature of heat is not changed by being communicated from the fire to the pot above it.

The law of the preservation of form structures not only Aristotle's definition of truth but his view of clarity as well. As Aristotle argues at length in book 3 of *De Anima*, knowledge is a quality or form of a mind. A piece of knowledge cannot, then, be changed by being passed from teacher to pupil. Linguistic communication, such as teaching, is in fact for Aristotle one form of motion, which means that the quality (knowledge) imparted to the learner must already be present in the teacher.[4]

When this is extended to the exchange of information that occurs in all speaking/writing and hearing/reading, we get a demand that the knowledge that comes about in someone's soul as a result of hearing the words of someone else should always be formally identical with the knowledge in the speaker's soul; and this is the first of the two concepts of clarity broached above. An utterance is clear if its words, as the material vehicles of its meaning, convey that meaning without change from the mind of the speaker to that of the hearer. All utterances should be clear because knowledge is a determinate quality, or form, in a soul. Form must be transmitted without change from one mind to another because it is the nature of form not to change, and that in turn is a metaphysical thesis.

The logical positivists, like all moderns, were more Aristotelian than they cared to be: they threw Aristotelian form out of nature but retained it as the universal structuring principle of the human world.[5] The second, "positivist" concept of clarity broached in this paper is, predictably, also rooted in what I call the law of preservation of form—and so in metaphysics. On that view clarity means that the sentence is like a clean, flat mirror: it is ready to convey the properties of things well enough for us to be able to tell what is an image of, or true of, what. The "image" of reality that it presents, in other words, should be undistorted.

This concept of clarity thus also goes back to Aristotle's view that language is a matter of resemblances or matchings, that is, of efforts to observe the law of the preservation of form. His own categories, basic or derivative, are validated, he thinks, as such: they are valid because they (somehow) resemble objects outside the mind. The more they do this—the more they provide headings that group together only things that actually are alike—the "clearer" they will be.[6] The main change from Aristotle to the moderns is the replacement of connection and separation by the much more mysterious, and hence more easily fetishized, relation of "correspondence."

Thus, the category of "slave by nature," which Aristotle discusses in *Politics* 1.5 and which does so much work in legitimating vicious structures of the ancient economy, is valid (in Aristotle's view) because there really is a group of people who have passive but not active reason: they can recognize the right thing to do when someone else tells them but cannot come up with it for themselves. A similar passivity characterizes the seemingly different category of "slave by law," which includes people taken captive in a just war (and their descendants). There really were people in Aristotle's world who had been enslaved on such grounds, and they reached that pass because they chose to surrender rather than to fight on to their deaths—that is, because they really lacked courage. There will always be wars and people deficient in the courage to fight them to the death, so "slave by law" is an eternal kind—very like a natural kind.

Solving the Paradox: Clarity as a Transitional Property of Discourse

It is important to see that the idea that all discourse should be clear is new with Aristotle. This is not always recognized. Martha Nussbaum, for example, has written that "ever since Socrates . . . [philosophy] has been a discourse of equals who trade arguments and counter-arguments without any obscurantist sleight-of-hand."[7] Although Nussbaum was originally trained as a Greek scholar, it is hard to detect in this observation any knowledge at all of Greek philosophy or its development. True, the Presocratic philosopher Parmenides is no Hume; and Heracleitus was famously nicknamed *ho skoteinos*, the obscure one. But things did not exactly get clearer with Socrates: has Nussbaum never heard of Socratic irony? The honest, even yeoman-like argumentation to which she reduces philosophy is, in Plato's dialogues, only the occasional basis of a much more complex series of moves and strategies, as is noted by the author of the "Seventh Letter" (that is, by Plato himself or an associate). It is as if Nussbaum watched a basketball game, saw only dribbling, and denied that the numbers on the scoreboard were rising.

True to his metaphysics of form, Aristotle himself claims that "language to be good must be clear." But he makes the claim in his *Rhetoric*, not in a treatise on philosophical method such as the *Analytics* (where clarity is required only of definitions).[8] And even Aristotle seems to have honored clarity very much in the breach. Anyone who has struggled through even a page of the central books of his *Metaphysics* knows that he dispenses with clarity when it comes to really basic thinking. As Herman Bonitz put it, "Is enim ut est diligentissimus in cognoscendis rebus singularibus . . . ut est acutus et ingeniosus in redigendas his singularis rebus ad summas, quas distinxit, omnium entium categorias; ita quum de iaciendis altissimis doctrinae fundamentis et de confirmandis interque se conciliandis principiis agitur, plurimum relinquit dubitationis."[9]

This discussion of ancient philosophy, although perhaps interesting, has not been a mere diversion. Seeing how clarity, both as the accurate conveyance of the thoughts of a speaker to a hearer and as the unambiguous distributability of truth values, is rooted in the law of the preservation of form enables us to solve rather than deny the paradox with which I began. For clarity is not, it seems, a property of my thoughts, or my words, for if it were, then you would not be its privileged judge. Nor does it reside merely in your understanding of my thoughts or words, because then if my words were unclear, you would have failed and I would not be required to reformulate my views. Clarity is, in sum, a property of the transition between my mind and yours: if my meaning has not changed when it reaches you, the words that conveyed it were clear.

Clarity in speech thus requires both a speaker and a hearer. (It may be worth reflecting on the social conditions that allow something that in its basic nature is cooperative to appear paradoxical. Those conditions may even overlap with those that make it seem plausible for logical positivists to legislate the paradox away altogether.)

What if Matter Speaks?

The instatement of clarity as a necessary condition for good thinking, speaking, and writing is thus grounded in metaphysics—in the law of the preservation of form. Certainly the facts of discourse, as we know them, do not justify it. For there misunderstanding—my meaning not entering someone else's head precisely as I intended it—is more the rule than the exception. Indeed, we would often prefer to have our words creatively applied rather than merely accurately repeated, even if such creativity always involves some degree of what Aristotle would call misunderstanding. Nor need we turn to ancient philosophers to see that unclarity is not only pervasive in learned discourse but even desirable. David Hull has argued both points in the case of contemporary science: "When new ideas are introduced they are rarely expressed with sufficient clarity. Scientists do not know what they intended to say until they find out what other scientists think they have said. . . . But distortion is more than routine in science. It is a traditional mode of argumentation, and a mode that is not entirely counterproductive. It forces scientists to commit themselves."[10] Whether forcing scientists to commit themselves is the only productive role for "distortion" will be discussed shortly. For the moment it seems that the law of preservation of form cannot be grounded in empirical givens. Unclear discourse has had important roles to play in thought, from Greek metaphysics to postmodern science. Nor is it grounded, today, in metaphysics; for Aristotle's metaphysics of unchanging form has long been discredited. Why, then, is clarity still regarded by some people as an indispensable condition for good speech and writing? Why is the law of preservation of form still in force for discourse today? From what can it derive its legislative force?

Could it be that the word *unchanging* is the key? That the demand for clarity is *nothing more than* a demand for unchanging meaning (which in turn implies an unchanging domain of realities to which our words should remain "likenesses")? That this whole effort at universal clarity is nothing more than (yet another) expression of what Heidegger called the "metaphysical" effort to see anything and everything as "something which constantly stands at one's own disposal"?[11]

Aristotle himself seems to have thought so, for in the passages I have cited—as well as in his *Poetics*—he associates clarity with familiarity and ordinariness: a discourse will be clear if it uses standard words in their standard meanings or else works them up carefully by a process that moderns would call "induction" and that remains faithful to the particulars from which it begins.[12] If so, then the privilege of clarity in Western discourse is simply a demand that discourse avoid innovation.

So understood, this demand not only has metaphysical roots but grows from sociopolitical soil. The crystalline clarity of Aristotelian form, after all, is not the whole of his ontology. If it were, there would be no places for form to leave behind and transit to. Also ingredient in the Aristotelian world is matter. The metaphysics of form in terms of which the norm of clarity is historically grounded is one that maintains, and therefore abets, what can only be called the "domination" of matter by form.[13] In cognition this domination proceeds to the point of effacement: matter is unknowable, and all we can know of a thing are the various forms that we can receive in our souls. (Much of the unclarity of Aristotle's *Metaphysics* results from the fact that he is trying there to talk of the relation of form to matter and so—somehow—of matter itself.)

Two things, then, are forbidden by this metaphysics of form and clarity. One is newness: all form is eternal and preexists; the meanings of words, like the forms in the world of which they are likenesses, are eternal. All we can hope to do by way of improving our language is to capture them more adequately in our words (for example by defining *human* as "rational animal" rather than, say, as "animal with earlobes"). The other thing forbidden, and much more stringently, is the possibility that matter itself could ever speak, ever generate meanings. For meaning is form, and matter is—not.

What might we be entitled to expect, then, if matter were somehow to speak—to cease in any traditional sense to be "matter" at all, spontaneously to exceed this most basic of Western dichotomies? Certainly not the conceptually precise discourse of a preestablished set of forms or meanings. More like sighs and groans, at first—the emissions of a body in pain or ecstasy. Then, perhaps, an unrelenting and frustrated struggle to give pattern to the groans, to gain articulation for what is provoking them. Such a struggle may take any number of paths.

And it is taking them, because the speech of matter is the most important global event of the last half century. That period has seen large numbers of beings formerly relegated to the status of mere matter—people who had been thought to be mere bodies, mindless or almost so—stand up and start to talk: gay men, lesbians, people of color, women, groups formerly colonized in a variety of ways. This development is as important to thinking people in the twenty-first century as the triumph of science was to those in the first half of the twentieth and for the same reason: on the one hand, it has the capacity generally to enrich every human being (and not only spiritually). On the other, it has the potential utterly to destroy the world in which we think we live.

As a mere observer of this stupendous upheaval (although a sympathetic one), I can offer here only a few observations about where it may go with respect to the ancient norm of clarity, so suspect in its foundations and so tenacious in its grip.

Aristotle, Hegel, and Anonymous

Any attempt to articulate a life experience that has previously been relegated to the unheard opacity of mere matter can, it would seem, end in one of three ways: in an Aristotelian or Hegelian manner or in one that has no name.

The Aristotelian ending would be one in which the speaking matter, searching for an adequate vocabulary in which to articulate its pains and joys, would find one already familiar and—so to speak—well formed, which needs only to be taken over and used as it stands. The original unclarity was a mere contingent confusion, for the speaking matter could just as well have known from the start that the requisite words existed.

It is unlikely that such faith in the readily available conceptual frameworks is justified. First, it is a fact that the West by now contains a variety of what Richard Rorty calls "basic vocabularies."[14] These are sets of systematically interconnected, very basic, words or concepts to which people appeal for their understanding of themselves and others and in which they formulate their basic goals and plans of action. One generic name for these basic conceptual systems is "philosophy," and we could mention Platonism, Aristotelianism, Thomism, Kantianism, Hegelianism, and Marxism as a few examples of final vocabularies now available in the West. These vocabularies have now diverged from each other to such an extent, thinks Rorty, that communication among them is impossible.

This very plurality suggests that none of the available basic vocabularies by itself has been adequate to articulate everyone's experience up to now. Why, then, should it be assumed that any of them will be adequate to the newly speaking bodies of the third millennium? Moreover, most of the available final vocabularies have in fact been around for at least a couple of centuries, so if any of them were adequate for articulating the experiences of women and minorities, it would have done that job long ago.

None has, and this extraordinary fact suggests something else. To what do the available final vocabularies owe their common inability to articulate the experience of women and minorities? Is there some fault they all share, a core common to all that explains why all of them have, without exception, installed and legitimated the oppression of women and minorities?

In that case Rorty's claim of radical divergence among the final vocabularies available in the West today would be overblown. The various conceptual frameworks that we find around us today would, on a deeper level, be truly at one. Their arguments, however vicious, would be about secondary matters: about means, not ends. Their mutual incomprehension, however genuine, would be superficial: a matter of fashion, not essence. If such is the case, there is even less reason to think that the newly speaking bodies of the third millennium will ever come to rest comfortably and intelligibly within any of the currently prevailing final vocabularies.

And it *is* the case. What I earlier called the "domination" of matter by form is a leitmotif shared by all the philosophies I mentioned above and many others besides. It was first codified by Aristotle in a famous appeal to nature: "In all things which are composed out of several other things, and which come to be some single common thing, whether continuous or discrete, in all of them there turns out to be a distinction between that which rules, and that which is ruled; and this holds for all ensouled things by virtue of the whole of nature."[15] In other words, the domination of matter by form is universal and natural; in every association there must be a ruler (form) and a ruled (matter). The only question left is that of who will be which.

Aristotle's own account of the domination of form by matter was the first such account in Western philosophy, but as I have argued elsewhere it was not the most extreme or oppressive.[16] Modern versions of such domination, freed by empirical science from the constraints of nature, have been even more absolute. For all his jibes at Aristotle's natural philosophy, for example, Thomas Hobbes's subtitle for *Leviathan* is *The Matter, Forme, & Power of a Common-Wealth Ecclesiastical and Civill*. Hobbes means the first two words in their traditional, that is Aristotelian, senses; but his deployment of them is a tyranny far beyond anything Aristotle ever envisioned.

Any attempt of matter to speak thus flies in the face of one of the most basic and dominant themes in Western thought: the domination of matter by form. Matter which speaks, then, can hardly expect to be familiar—or clear.

Aristotle's appeal to nature is basically an appeal to unchanging natural kinds, the general form of which is a form actively controlling some patch of matter. His view of natural kinds, however, does not survive the opening pages of Hegel's *Phenomenology of Spirit*, and its demise, in turn, allows a Hegelian vision of the speaking of matter that is very different from the Aristotelian one. In "Sense-Certainty," the *Phenomenology*'s opening section, experience is presented as a random flux so that a creative effort of the mind is required to gain any purchase on it at all. And as the rest of the book shows, our creative efforts always go astray eventually (that is what makes them *our* efforts), so no category can be eternally valid: all are in principle open to revision. (This is why, instead of transcending time at the end of the *Phenomenology*, consciousness's final, suicidal move is to embrace it).[17]

Since no category will be valid for all time, Hegel would be quite comfortable with my suggestion above that the categories basic to Western thought have reached their limits. Yet every time such a limit is reached in the *Phenomenology*, consciousness attempts to revise its categories in order to express what it has newly discovered. Applying this to the speech of matter suggests that such speech will eventually come to some sort of clarity but only in the terms of a new conceptual framework invented by the newly speaking bodies themselves—not one (or several) that are already available. This framework may be entirely new, or (more congenially to Hegel) it may be one that has been remodeled from previously available ones—but even in the latter case the remodeling may be so extensive as to obliterate any sense of derivation.

In such a case the new conceptual framework may be intelligible only to those who have shared the inarticulate joy and anguish from which it came. Like musical notation or quantum physics—indeed, like any conceptual framework at all—it will not make sense to those who engage it without the requisite prior experience. Yet for all that, it will be clear, at least in that it enables those who *have* had those experiences to think and work together. So this Hegelian outcome would not completely abjure clarity. As with Hull's scientists it would recognize unclarity not as a mere contingent confusion but as a necessary prelude to clarity.

But there is a third possibility, one that (I suggested) has no name. It involves abjuring, rather than seeking, clarity altogether. In such a case, many think, common action will also be abjured, leaving us with what so many on the cultural right see as postmodern: a group of people who perversely choose to express themselves in ineffectual whines.

But there are different ways to "abjure" something. The previous paragraph trades on an absolute sense in which we "abjure" something by rejecting it altogether. But when something has had absolute status, that is, has been canonized as the indispensable goal or necessary precondition of some practice, we can "abjure" it simply by beginning to look on it not as absolutely valid but as merely one among a number of alternatives, thus situating it in a wider spectrum of goals and practices. This would leave room for discourse that is not only not clear from the start (as Aristotelian views hold discourse should be) but that is also not trying to make itself clear (as discourse should on Hegelian views).

Utterances in such discourse would not be merely ambiguous, because ambiguity can be resolved through the available conceptual repertoires. They would have to be so genuinely strange as to mean not more than one thing but fewer than one: utterances whose component elements, for example, cannot be put together in the accustomed ways. An example, recently given fame by Judith Butler, is Adorno's "Man is the ideology of dehumanization."[18]

I have elsewhere developed an extended theory of such discourse[19] and will content myself here with merely pointing out that such a statement may well provoke a proliferation of meanings, when the hearer responds to the unclear statement by extrapolating a new meaning for it—a meaning of her own. In that case we have (at least) *two* meanings: the speaker's original one and the one the hearer comes up with (which may, of course, overlap with the other to some degree).

Thus, Adorno's "Man is the ideology of dehumanization" is transformed when Butler expounds it to mean "the way the word 'man' was used by some of his contemporaries was dehumanizing."[20] For that is not the only possibility. Adorno may have had not merely his contemporaries in mind but the entire philosophy of the Enlightenment, with its constant talk of "man" when it should say "argumentatively trained intellect." He may even have targeted, à la Heidegger, all modern philosophy. And by *man* Adorno might also have meant more than a word: he could have been talking about "man" as a socially functional illusion, such as that of American invincibility prior to the Vietnam War.

My aim here is not to point out deficiencies in Butler's admirably lucid gloss, which elegantly makes her point that Adorno's seemingly unintelligible words can receive a perfectly clear interpretation. But part of the way those words work is to be susceptible of more than one possible meaning; alternatives cannot be ruled out.

Thus, the original meaning Adorno intended when he wrote his sentence and the meaning that Butler gives it overlap but are different. Different again is the meaning that I give it here, as a case of what I elsewhere call "abnormal poetic interaction." In each case the sentence transits into a new conceptual environment, where (as in Derridean iteration)[21] it does new work, and provokes new thoughts in the minds of its hearers. In the process its meaning is transformed—or, better, trans-formed—at every stage.

When things like this happen, we—the speech community—are provided with new meanings and categories, such as Butler's category of "[linguistic] challenge to common sense." Our dependence on the previously available repertoire of meanings and categories is lessened, and our verbal capacities are increased. This process, then, deserves to be called emancipatory. And it is an emancipation we often wish for and sometimes seek; for who does not hope that her words will be taken up by hearers and used in productive ways of which she has not dreamed?

If to engage in such discourse is to abjure clarity, it is also to commend oneself to a complementary set of values—playfulness, improvisation, and freedom itself.[22] It is to forswear the Aristotelian law of the preservation of form in favor of what his wiser teacher, Plato, called the "leaping spark" of philosophical insight: an unpredictable, and so joyful, passage from soul to soul.[23] And it is to forswear the vain project of immortalizing one's thoughts; for even if one's words survive, their meanings will not.

When basic issues are settled and newness is not on, the habitual suffices and our speech can observe the law of the preservation of form in its linguistic sense: we can expect and demand clarity from those who address us. But history—even, as we saw, the history of science—teaches that those conditions do not always obtain. Simple common sense—of all things— shows us that they certainly do not obtain right now. Many people today find that the current conceptualities do not do justice to their experience, and new ones are needed. Breaking free from the old words—always, as Rorty teaches, a delight[24]—is now a necessity for those people, in ways that, if they are allowed to stand as what they are, will enrich everyone.

So we see, finally, the terrible price paid by those who, siding with form against matter, would make clarity an indispensable condition of serious thought. Trapped in a misguided effort to obtain immortality for their own current world, they would force us all to remain in ancient and oppressive habits of thought. They set themselves against time itself—and against the creativity and joy that are our privilege, as the mortal creatures that we are.

Notes

1. Aristotle, *Metaphysics* 9.9.1051b2f; also *De Interpretatione* 1.16a11.

2. Aristotle, *De Anima* 2.7.418a33seq and, more generally, *De Anima* 3.2.425b225–426a1, 416a6–11; also cf. Aristotle, *On Dreams* 459a27–60a32. On the origins of this view in Aristotle's account of form in matter see also Edwin Hartman, *Substance, Body, and Soul* (Princeton, N.J.: Princeton University Press, 1977), 175–80.

3. Aristotle, *De Generatione Animalium* 4.3.767b7f.

4. See Aristotle, *Physics* 3.3.202a31–32, 202b6–8, 8.5.257a1–3, 257b3–4; also *Metaphysics* 2.9.1065b19.

5. On this general characteristic of modernity see my *Metaphysics and Oppression* (Bloomington: Indiana University Press, 2000), 105–8.

6. See Aristotle, *Posterior Analytics* 2.13.97b33–39.

7. Martha Nussbaum, "The Professor of Parody," *New Republic*, Feb. 22, 1999, p. 38; available at http://www.tnr.com/archive/0299/022299/nussbaum022299.html.

8. Aristotle, *Rhetoric* 3.2.1404b1–5; *Posterior Analytics* 2.13.97b30–37.

9. Roughly: "However diligent [Aristotle] is with regard to the knowledge of individual things, and however acute and ingenious he is in bringing these individuals to the highest categories of all beings, which he distinguishes; yet, when it is a matter of laying the foundations of the highest doctrines and of confirming them and reconciling them with one another, he leaves a great many doubts" (Hermann Bonitz, *Aristotelis Metaphysica*, 2 vols. [Bonn, 1848] 2:29; quoted in Irwin, *Aristotle's First Principles* [Oxford: Clarendon Press, 1988], 640 n. 4). Nussbaum says the same thing about Butler: "one is bewildered to find her arguments buttressed by appeal to so many contradictory concepts and doctrines, usually without any account of how the apparent contradictions will be resolved" (Nussbaum, "Professor of Parody," 41). This is high praise from so famous an admirer of Aristotle as Nussbaum. Perhaps it is unintentional.

10. David Hull, *Science as a Process* (Chicago: University of Chicago Press, 1988), 288–89.

11. Martin Heidegger, "Über Nietzsches Wort: Gott Ist Tod," in *Holzwege*, by Martin Heidegger, 4th ed. (Frankfurt: Klostermann, 1963), 221.

12. Aristotle, *Poetics* 22.148a18–20.

13. See Judith Butler, *Bodies That Matter* (New York: Routledge, 1993), 27–55; and the first two chapters of my *Metaphysics and Oppression*.

14. Richard Rorty, *Contingency, Irony, and Solidarity* (Cambridge, U.K.: Cambridge University Press, 1989), 9.

15. Aristotle, *Politics* 1.4.1254a28–32.

16. See my *Metaphysics and Oppression*, 105–93.

17. G. F.W. Hegel, *Phenomenology of Spirit*, trans. A.V. Miller (Oxford: Oxford University Press, 1979), 563.

18. Judith Butler, "A 'Bad Writer' Bites Back," *New York Times*, March 20, 2000, op-ed.

19. John McCumber, *Poetic Interaction* (Chicago: University of Chicago Press, 1989).

20. Butler, "A 'Bad Writer' Bites Back."

21. Jacques Derrida, "Signature Event Context," *Glyph* 1 (1977): 172–97.

22. It is thus no wonder that Martha Nussbaum attacks Butler for "unclarity," as well as for lacking immediate political relevance (of the single kind Nussbaum desires), and that she does so in an angrily dictatorial tone: the absolute installation of clarity brings absolute hatred for creativity and freedom. See Nussbaum, "Professor of Parody."

23. Plato, *Seventh Letter* 341d1. I am assuming here that Plato was the author of the letter; but even if he was not, it clearly expresses an ancient and respectable view of philosophy.

24. Richard Rorty, *Contingency, Irony, and Solidarity.*

PART 2

Institutions, Publics, Intellectual Labor

Feminism's Broken English

You have learnt something. That always feels at first as if you had lost something.

—George Bernard Shaw

THE ARGUMENT of this paper is ostensibly simple: that, in the name of politics, academic feminists need to defend a theoretical humanities. Readers aware of contemporary debates in academic feminism will know that such an argument runs counter to a great deal of feminist sentiment about the relationship between theory and politics. Indeed, in many quarters today the political has been distinctly opposed to the theoretical, in part (say some) because poststructuralist discussion eliminated the imperative to explicate *women's oppression*. At several recent conferences on the future of women's studies, for example, scholars from a variety of disciplines called for a return to the field's origins in social movement as a strategic response to what is characterized as the antimaterialist elitism of theoretical forays into *discursive* subjectivity. This call to remember where we come from is somewhat striking in the midst of the will to forget not only poststructuralism's interest in language as a material force but feminism's own disidentification with political slogans as the critical content of an analysis of power.

But let me not linger on remembering what has been for many academic feminists necessary to forget. Forgetting is, after all, part of the work of politics; when done well, it can aid the process of learning because learning, like politics, is not linear or accumulative but erratic, even—indeed importantly—unpredictable. To forget enables us to learn again, which is not the same thing as discovering what we already know; learning again is not necessarily learning something over.

What might we learn again, then, if we considered what poststructuralism meant to an academic feminism pushed to exhaustion to make the words of social movement critically useful: patriarchy, oppression, resistance, revolution, experience? This is the question that I want to pursue to create a different history of the present from the one that currently writes academic feminism's interest in poststructuralism as the end of its public political commitment. Most generally, I seek to rewrite the conceptualization of knowledge and politics that figures the work of feminism in the academy as political only in relation to a social formation defined as wholly outside of it by exploring how the theory/practice divide is intrinsic to the organization of the disciplines and not, as the current discussion suggests, the effect of a theoretical humanities unable to apprehend a world of real material political struggle. My argument is that, within the broad frame of the human sciences, the relation between scholars and the material real is never simply a matter of political commitment but is part of the order of disciplinarity itself. My point, however, is not to defend the humanities as any more necessary to feminism than other disciplinary domains but to demonstrate how academic feminism's conceptualization of the university, its culture of professionalization and expertise, and its disciplinary organization are not exterior to but foundational for academic feminism's understanding of its own politics today.

By focusing on how current academic feminists write the *academic* against *feminist* in order to define their political commitment, my contribution to this collection on the problem of theoretical language and the growing demand for uninhibited communicability makes three interrelated moves. First, I consider what it is that poststructuralist theory currently stands accused of doing to feminism by surveying recent arguments by prominent academic feminists, with special attention to the work of Lynne Segal, whose 1999 *Why Feminism? Gender, Psychology, Politics* offers one of the most compelling and complex renderings of critical analysis and political life along the theory/practice divide. Then, I examine the unacknowledged ways in which disciplinary authority is exerted in her argument, with the effect of disavowing the university's disciplinary management of the "real" through the methodological and conceptual divides between the humanities and social sciences. Finally, I return to the question of the political need for a theoretical humanities as a necessary part of academic feminism's own critical interrogation into the social organization of knowledge and its power effects. Much of my argument is aimed at defining how the demand for communicability in contemporary academic feminism—cast against theoretical language in the name of reviving the utopian affect of twentieth century social movement—is contingent on a will to forget both what poststructuralism might have meant for feminist analysis and what disciplinary organization currently (de)means.

In calling this essay "Feminism's Broken English" I hope to indicate at the outset something of the way language, discipline, and nation—as they function as references for "English"—are collectively central to the current conversation about communicability, theory, and the deployment of the political in the U.S. university. Although none of these references can be fully pried apart from the others, their relationship is not static, and it is toward current transformations in the ways that language, disciplinary domain, and national culture are linked to the structure and state-based function of the humanities that my discussion will eventually turn. In particular, I will situate the emergence of poststructuralist theory in the context of the disestablishment of the cold war apparatus of the university, which conferred on the humanities in general and English in particular the strategic function of producing citizens within a homogeneous understanding of national culture. Although the current "crisis of the humanities," as it is routinely called, often equates the rise of theory in the humanities with the loss of the humanities' status, I am more interested in understanding, as a kind of positive politics, the ways in which the nation-state has ceased to manage humanistic inquiry in its name. To bring the question of theoretical language into the orbit of the political articulated here is to offer a different and hopefully useful way to understand "academic feminism" today.

Theory as Failure, or the End of Common Language

I own two copies of Adrienne Rich's 1978 collection of poetry *A Dream of a Common Language*. One is paperback, its cover so tattered now the title is reduced to the first four letters: *A Dre* it says, before the heavy beige paper gives way to a stained and messy edge. For several years after its publication I carried this copy in my backpack. More important than a wallet or a set of keys, it provided a necessary sustenance for my then recent entry into feminism. The other copy I own is hardback; I bought it in the mid-1990s secondhand—"Kent R. Johnson" is stamped in the top right-hand corner of the inside page. I remember being startled that he had abandoned it, even as I knew that my nostalgic impulse to buy the book came from my earlier rejection of it. By the 1990s Rich's poetry had become too idealist for me; her dream of a common language was too committed to literary humanism's vocabulary of beauty, pain, and love. Where once her poetic refusal to "make a career of pain" had resonance for me in the alternative sites of community building—study groups, coffeehouses, shelter projects, reproductive rights collectives—the repetition of familiar failures (the loss of trust, the mismanagement of funds, the abandonment of some women for others) undermined my attachment to collective aspirations for utopian completion. Still, I like to say, thinking back on Rich and the sensibility of utter outrage and care that her poetic language evoked, that *I am a seventies feminist*. I don't get to say that sentence very often, in part because I have become something that phrase is not supposed to mean: a feminist academic or more precisely and, for many people, more negatively, an academic feminist.

In characterizations of feminism's recent history some feminists define the space between being a "seventies feminist" and being an "academic feminist" as a political fall, with "academic feminist" serving as a code phrase for poststructuralist theory and theory serving as the categorical designation of the loss of a public political intent. Susan Gubar, for instance, finds the specialized "jargon" of critical theory a "debilitating rhetoric," echoing in a different way Tania Modleski's warning at the outset of the 1990s that poststructuralism might rob feminism of "women," the very centerpiece of feminist politics.[1] Other critical laments focus on academic feminism's institutional success. Ellen Messer-Davidow's recent *Disciplining Feminism: From Social Activism to Academic Discourse* offers a long meditation on what she casts as the political costs of academic institutionalization, in which the battle for legitimization in universities, constituted within the hegemonies of poststructuralist theory, prevented feminists from adequately countering the right's well-funded demolition of all forms of progressive social movement by pushing "debates to a more abstract level . . . [sending us] into the metadiscursive stratosphere."[2] As Naomi Schor wrote before her, "[A]cademic feminism became a victim of its own success . . . weaken[ing] what many of . . . my generation . . . had treasured about feminism: a sense of commonality, of participating even as a footnote in perhaps the most successful peaceful revolutionary movement of our era."[3]

Lynne Segal's *Why Feminism?* takes up these and other criticisms of the contemporary formation of academic feminism. But unlike Schor, who reads the success of feminism in the university in relation to the loss of the literary as a specific feminist focus, Segal, a social scientist, finds the disciplinary proclivities of the humanities part of the reason for feminism's public decline. "[A] feminism which begins with . . . textual practice," she writes, "is one which is incommensurate with, as well as distanced from, the perspectives and practices of Women's Liberation."[4] Segal, to be sure, does not dismiss either cultural studies or discursive analysis; indeed, she is quite forceful in her insistence that feminist analysis requires a range of interdisciplinary inquiries, especially those that cut across the epistemological divides among the disciplines. She thus calls for both the discursive and the material, the cultural and the economic, and the psychic and the social structural. But her analysis retains the distinction of these divisions even as it calls for their analytic integration. As she writes in the first chapter:

[P]ost-structuralism . . . has provided feminists with fresh conceptual tools for problematizing identities and social differences. . . . But in a world of intensifying inequality, any concern with either gender injustice or the fate of women overall must also engage us in social struggle for economic redistribution, alongside (and inevitably enmeshed with) issues of identity involving cultural recognition and respect. . . . [We need] theorizations sufficiently complex to embrace the intricacies of personal life, while refusing to give up on struggles for social justice and equality. (33, 34)

To make this point, Segal devotes the second chapter to queer theory's deconstructive challenge to heteronormative binaries of gender. Although she extrapolates in detail the "tensions between those who stress the psychic life of difference, and those who study the social dynamics of the gender order," the chapter ends on a striking contrast between academic discourse and a politically charged "real" world of struggle (43). She writes: "Just when queer theory and transgression gained academic modishness . . . the most significant, most modest, most easily bestowed choices which might have been made available to young women entering adult sexual arrangements were being systematically withdrawn. . . . Now is not the time for us to be forgetting gender" (73, 76).

Segal's emphasis on time is an important one; the title of her chapter "Gender to Queer, and Back Again" reiterates a now pervasive idea in academic feminism that the future is contingent on a return, in the aftermath of poststructuralist theory, to feminism's political origins in social movement and, with it, to the analysis of and struggle against structures of domination. Segal cites this political origin as "a socialist imaginary, combined with feminism, which has always stressed the sufferings caused by the material exploitation, deprivation and social marginalization of women and other oppressed groups around the world" (34). The return to a socialist feminist imaginary can counter, she posits, the temporal stasis of contemporary feminism, which, through poststructuralism, has grown "distrustful, when not dismissive, of traditional forms of collective action and reformist political agendas" and which thus "faces an uphill task . . . [in] bring[ing] women together in any widely shared transformative feminist project" (35). For Segal "some wider political project" is what separates academic feminism today from its originary impulses in the 1960s and 1970s. Hence the return to an earlier political vision is in a sense a return to the future, to the utopian making of another world. In this nexus between past and future the poststructuralist present of academic feminism is placed outside of, if not implicitly against, feminism's revolutionary place in historical time.

Elsewhere I have used the term *apocalyptic* to categorize such accounts of academic feminism since it is the theoretical present that functions consistently as a form of interruption, dissolution even, of feminism's political future.[5] With my own feminist attachments to theory and politics borne in the increasingly abjected site of the academy, I have generally thought it important to mount a defense against the apocalyptic formulation not simply of poststructuralist theory but of academic feminism, which is far more diverse and institutionally interventionist in its various sites—the classroom as well as research, governance as well as public performance—than the apocalyptic narrative tends to allow. I have thought it important to challenge the assumption that feminism as a political movement and feminism as an academic project could be, even *should* be, coherently related, in language, strategy, and/or goal. I have even found the apocalyptic formulation that posits poststructuralism as a displacement of the pressing concerns of material reality a troubling form of discipline, as it places all feminist thought within a specifically defined understanding of social change, political progress, and collective aspiration. Most crucially perhaps, such a narrative functions, albeit unconsciously, to produce an "authentic" feminist subjectivity in which the acquisition of feminist consciousness in the academy and especially through theoretical discourses is a degraded and apolitical formation. Far from opening feminism's political future to *old and new* debates, subjectivities, and utopianisms, this kind of generational discipline flattens distinctions in order to make equivalences across analytic, institutional, historical, and subjective domains that I would argue actually require more creative vocabularies, more rigorous historical contextualizations, and more finely nuanced formulations.

This is not to say that I disagree with those scholars urging us to attend to social justice goals or to seek new ways, especially in the context of globalization, of understanding structures of domination. My concern arises instead from the pervasive assumption in the apocalyptic narrative, even those as nuanced and critically important as Segal's, that theory belongs to the academy and social struggle is both its anterior and now excluded outside. Indeed, the critique of poststructuralism in the name of social struggle can only be neatly made by refusing to acknowledge the university's own management of social movement and political change as objects of study now legible, because they are themselves institutionalized, in the disciplinary divide between the humanities and social sciences. It is my contention that academic discourse as a set of knowledge divisions authorizes the very critique that has come to define discourse and social struggle as fundamentally opposed—with *discourse* as the theoretical term and *political* the privileged language of a material real.[6] From this perspective the desire to "return" to the political imaginary of 1970s feminism is less a turn outside the academy than a failure to account for the ways in which the history and politics of social struggle have their own disciplinary homes.

Disciplinary Affect

I am saying that the use of the language of political struggle to escape the seeming enclosures of academic institutionalization for feminism is itself a disciplinary move, and not just of the generational kind. It is also, importantly, a form of institutional disciplinarity, part of the war of method and critical apparatus that inhabits academic feminism, itself the conglomerate term for the collective activities of feminist scholars trained in a variety of disciplines. To the extent that these disciplinary identities are competitive elements of the defining terms of feminist knowledge, it is not possible to assume that contemporary feminism's relation to the contents of the categories of discourse, culture, social struggle, materiality, or the political are disciplinarily innocent. My own use of Adrienne Rich clearly demonstrates how academic training in literary languages was instrumental to my earliest relation to feminism—much as my rejection of it was part of my later doctoral training that emphasized rethinking the modernist foundations of U.S. feminism's romance with humanism. To a great extent it is the institutional incorporation of these (and other) differing, indeed contradictory, modalities of feminist subject formation that constitutes much of the struggle today within academic feminism over its terms, political affect, historical vision, and future orientation.

Nowhere is this struggle more intense and pointed than in the critical understanding of the political possibilities and limitations of the various identity-based studies that now focus on gender, race, and sexuality as their proper objects of study. Take, for instance, women's studies. At their most cynical, scholars will claim that women's studies plays the role of wife to the disciplines, offering unpaid labor in the management of the specific needs of female students (psychological counseling and mentoring) and producing a variety of studies for the nation-state that explore the strategies of women's political organization and resistance. At their most optimistic, scholars will argue that such knowledge projects make possible a reformulation of the histories of gender, sexuality, and race that inform the modern organization of the disciplines, producing new historical subjects and providing the means for reconnecting the institutionalized alienation of the social (economics, politics, the state) from the cultural (representation).[7] The cynical view reads the incorporation of identity-based studies into the university as purely appropriative; the optimistic view emphasizes the agency of the subjects of knowledge, finding in the articulation of subordinate social status an epistemological critique (understood by many as a standpoint method) that casts as an intervention identity as a domain of study.

I take a position somewhere between these two readings by understanding the history of identity studies as a dynamic activity. Although the utopian narrative of identity's academic becoming celebrates the social movements that brought women's studies, ethnic studies, and gay and lesbian studies into being and made possible their reshaping of disciplinary definitions of proper methods and objects of study, it is also the case that the disciplines have authorized specific understandings of the meaning, force, and history of both identity and social movement. In this authorization social movements and activist projects, along with racial and gender identity, are not simply studied but constituted by disciplinary formations, and *that constitution is as much within as against* the relations of realness and abstraction, empiricism and interpretation, and experience and representation that have come to characterize the common sense of specific disciplinary domains. This is not to say that the disciplines of the human sciences are static formations always knowable as on one side or other of such methodological and critical divides. In literary study, for instance, the focus on identity served to undermine the formalist poetics of New Criticism to such an extent that today critics must defend the project of studying the aesthetics of texts by minoritized writers against the disciplinary demand to read their narrative productions as sociological expressions of minoritized experience. The struggle over textual forms and social meaning, over the status of the literary object vis-à-vis identitarian aspirations for both political and historical subjectivity, forges an intervention to be sure, but it does so at the cost of establishing as a disciplinary proclivity identity's proper place as a solo referent for injured experience.

The emergence of certain forms of poststructuralist theory in literary studies might be understood as a critical challenge to such discipline. This is especially the case with queer theory, which has harnessed deconstructive techniques to rethink the normative function of the hetero/homosexual opposition so necessary to sexuality's identitarian sedimentation. At the same time, queer theory's use of Foucault to analyze forms of power and its interest in the psychoanalytical significance of language and subjectivity have contributed to a general undermining of the sovereignty of the canonical humanist subject, "he" who could see the world whole and represent it grandly in various forms of language-based expression. Such decentering of the privileged agency of the humanist subject has generated attention in queer theory's humanistic inquiry on (among other things) performative identities, public cultures, intimacy, premodern sexualities, "the psychic life of power," and the language of desire.[8] The theoretical valence of these inquiries has challenged the extension of racial and gendered identity models to sexuality and thereby revised the notion that although there are different identity forms, they all operate similarly as categories of social difference.[9] For literary study this has meant rethinking the assumption that the political import of difference can be registered by more inclusive canonical constructions, as it has raised to the level of critical visibility the impossibility of constituting sexual identity as the definitive term for an alternative literary tradition. Indeed, the political effect of queer theory on literary study as a discipline has rendered the traditional canon inherently queer.[10]

The point here, however, is not to champion queer theory but to demonstrate through it how the question of the politics of poststructuralism cannot be measured apart from the disciplinary domains in which poststructuralist theory has been put to use. When Lynne Segal castigates queer theory for its political failure in *Why Feminism?* she explicitly notes its interest in "the diverse tools of discourse theory, deconstruction and psychoanalysis," but she does not explore the ways in which such tools operated within the protocols of either literary study or humanistic inquiry in general. Instead, queer theory is applauded for its "brilliant outpouring of texts" at the expense of its tragic political effect, "the final trashing of gender" (55, 56). Such a conclusion is based on viewing queer theory's interest in subversion—identitarian, textual, public, and psychic—as "stylish," a form of "cutting edge fashion" that indulged the postmodern fantasy that queers could "at last radically free themselves from the constraints of gender" (57, 58):

No longer simply the object of medical and social surveillance and management . . . the body became the site of resistance for those who felt newly empowered to engage in self formation and self-fashioning. . . . Transgression can be part of a wider culture of oppositional consciousness. . . . But that broader struggle has become less and less visible in recent lesbian and gay texts, which, in the context of the withering away of left alliances and principles, are more concerned with post-modern literary theory. (60, 65, 67)

Segal's chapter ends by contrasting the seeming self-fashioning of the queer theoretical subject with the real world of sexual constraint, where issues of pregnancy and reproductive choice, sex education, sexual violence, and sex segregation in the workplace all stand as evidence against the "flexible" obsessions of a textual queer theory.

Segal's argument reconstitutes against her own stated wishes familiar disciplinary divisions between discourse and materiality, knowing and doing, subjectivity and social structure, and hermeneutics and experience. Although she emphasizes, as I have noted, that feminist analysis requires all forms of knowledge for its long-standing dream of interdisciplinarity, she nonetheless defines humanistic practices as subordinate to the struggle for social justice and social justice as the only viable destination of feminist knowledge production: "the grassroots movements for social justice which women are leading today require a variety of types of scholarly servicing, some of which are increasingly absent from the most esteemed forms of feminist theorizing, as it has moved from its earlier stronghold in sociology and the social sciences into English and the humanities" (222). Indeed, in her terms the very strength of feminist studies in the humanities is the sign of the left's political weakening: "the move in academic fashions from sociology and the social sciences to English and the humanities was itself, at least in part, a sign of the decline of left politics after the close of the 1970s" (222–23). With disciplinary divisions between humanities and social science functioning to narrate the loss of feminism's public political commitment, the very content of "social transformation" emerges in alignment with those objects of study most accessible as such in social science disciplines: welfare, reproductive rights, sexual divisions of labor, and gendered violence.[11] Significantly, it is through their centrality as the definition of a politically engaged academic feminism that Segal's socialist feminist political imaginary can be revived, one that will focus its attention "on actually existing social relations" (222).

What I find most striking in Segal's interpretation of academic feminism today is the way she constructs social scientific inquiry as coterminous with a leftist politics at the same time that the humanities are posited as a knowledge domain wholly *internal* to the university.[12] Indeed, by the end of her study-text-based inquiry comes to bear the entire burden of feminism's incorporation into the academy, as it is the primary evidence for "the academization of feminist politics" (222). For instance, she writes that although feminist studies "began as a genuinely *interdisciplinary* field . . . the current pressures of the academy are such that it is almost impossible to maintain genuinely cross-disciplinary interests and knowledge, so harnessed are we to ever narrower channels of disciplinary career and publication. . . . Indicatively, the conference *At the Millennium: Interrogating Gender* . . . reflected the predominance of English and cultural studies in the vanguard of academic feminism. Indeed, I was the sole speaker from the social sciences" (221). With original interdisciplinarity aligned more with the social sciences than the humanities, Segal casts the humanities *as* "academic feminism," thereby extracting the social sciences from the depoliticizing order of the disciplines. In this way her own disciplinary identity is preserved as outside "narrow channels of disciplinary career and publication" and hence consistent with and not deformative of feminist politics. This disciplinary hierarchy that underwrites the academic/feminist divide operates in contradiction to Segal's own repeated assurance that feminists need cultural as well as material analysis, that symbolic orders matter as much as economic ones. "I am not endorsing those academics now making a name for themselves through an anti-theoretical populism. Least of all am I trying to jettison cultural analysis for what is often falsely posed against it as 'materialist'" (223). Yet her analysis consistently arrives, often after great critical nuance and generosity, at a determination of where "reality" must be politically and definitively located: not in the critical armature of a humanities-resistance theory but in the rock-solid evidence of material lives: "The more flexible and volatile our identities, lives, and bodies are conceived to be in academic discourses deconstructing genders and sexualities, the more predictable social constraints and pressures . . . manifest themselves in the lives of many women" (229–30).

For many feminists this is as it should be because lived experience and the continuing assault on women worldwide *is* the necessary target of feminism's political intention. My point is not to dismiss the sense of urgency that drives Segal's desire to reconvene a kind of utopian political vision: that mobilizing affect that enables people to feel connected to the possibility of social change, not in a distant future but in the emergency of our ongoing present. Rather, I am interested in the way that an authentic feminist politics that is anterior to the academy has its own disciplinary dimensions. For feminist scholars there is no political "before" that can be revived intact, ever unburdened by the consequences of feminism's academic institutionalization, for there is today no discourse of the political produced within the academy that is not defined by, even if in contradiction to, the order of the disciplines. When Segal uses humanities scholarship as evidence that the political has been weakened in feminist studies (as opposed to the field's "interdisciplinary" origins in "sociology and social science"), she has not escaped the disciplinary enclosures of the academy; she has inadvertently confirmed them. This is especially the case because the imperative for the "scholarly servicing," in Segal's words, of "grassroots movements for social justice" brings with it a series of methodological priorities: privileging the live subject, categories of agency and resistance, and social transformation based on interventions in the state.[13] Thus, far from engendering an escape from the enclosures of the university by defining a public in whose name academic feminism can speak, such servicing establishes a *disciplinary* structure for academic feminist knowledge production, providing both its rationale and its epistemological guarantee.

It is this use of the political as a form of disciplinarity for academic feminism that most concerns me. When taken up as the goal of doctoral training in women's studies, for instance, the emphasis on producing activist researchers increases the professionalized relationship between academic feminism and social change now ascribed to humanistic inquiry. When the question of the international becomes the political horizon of these critical activities, women's studies can be understood to play a management role, offering accreditation by the university for the academy's own generation of a professional class to negotiate a global human rights agenda that simultaneously extends and supplants the welfare structures of First World nation-states.[14] Under the conditions of these kinds of changes in capital and corporatism, discourses produced by feminism in the academy about the political *must* interrogate the institutional forms that already inhabit it, thereby resisting the consolidation of how the political might be thought in order to address its deployment within and across social domains. This will by necessity bring the university into question as an important mediating site for the struggle over the language, structure, and symbolic life of the political today.

Does this mean, then, that I share no sympathy with *Why Feminism?*'s desire to critique the effects of institutionalization on feminist politics? After all, academic feminism has witnessed success in the midst of what we might otherwise understand as the "meantime"—the time not of revolutionary beginnings or historical completions but of the endless demeaning of the grammar and affect of social transformation. In the meantime is the time of U.S. feminism's public political decline: in the end of welfare, in the tightening of antiabortion laws, in the legal affirmation of white males as an injured class. The question for me is not, however, what have academic feminists been doing to allow things to go so terribly wrong. *"We" are not, "academic feminism" is not, the solo referent for feminism as a political discourse and world-building force, nor is social transformation as a historical process synonymous with social justice goals.* Indeed, it seems to me necessary to recognize, so as to make politically useful, the differences within and between various modalities of social transformation, not to pit them against one another but to articulate the temporal processes, affects, and languages of institutionalization, grassroots organization, movement politics, and other transformative social forms. Such an agenda does not canonize a particular definition of the political as the disciplinary guarantee for academic feminism's productivity. Nor does it equate the political effectivity of feminism with its critical interventions into the academy's organization of fields. Rather, it tries to engage the utopianism of various deployments of the political and to reimagine what the ongoing project of feminism's academic institutionalization might politically yield.

A Theoretical Humanities

To focus on academic feminism as it negotiates (or fails to) the methodological divides that currently write a theoretical humanities against the urgency of the political present may seem in the end unfair to feminism. After all, it is not the only leftist politics that finds itself at the beginning of the twenty-first century struggling not only to account for its loss of a generative public presence but to do so from within the institutional space of the university. My own sense is that academic feminism is both a case in point and an exception to the general rule. It partakes in the broader discourse about the loss of the left, absorbs that discourse into its own self-assessment, and comes to disavow the project of institutionalization that seems to leave it out of revolutionary time and ensconced instead in the temporalities of the bureaucratic in which the utopian affect of social change overtly vies with the contradictions and complicities of professional culture. At the same time (and this is the exception), academic feminism is perhaps the most successful institutionalizing project of its generation, with more full-time faculty positions and new doctoral degree programs emerging each year in the field it inaugurated, women's studies. The autonomy that this field now seeks and its subsumption of feminism as both its referent and epistemological guarantee generate an extensive and troubling disciplinary imperative on the nomination *academic feminism*.[15] Hence the situation I have been both diagnosing and critiquing is one in which the discourse of political loss that functions as a compensatory narrative about the effects of institutionalization becomes the means to institutionalize an activist origin story as the disciplinary foundation of feminism as an academic field. In this canonization of an originary political imaginary as the content and definition of feminist knowledge production, activism is finally, fully, instrumentalized to the domain of academic professional culture; and the contestations about the meaning, time, practices, assumptions, and future of feminism as a political force are rendered already known as the organizing principle of the field.[16] I am motivated by questions that turn in different directions. In the context of the relationship between the public and politics we might ask, What are the costs for social movement and for critical considerations of politics and social change in founding the autonomy of an academic field on the political origin story of any particular national scene of struggle? Can the difficulties encountered by a First World U.S. feminism be adequately addressed by generating a tradition of knowledge production that takes the Anglo–American context as its political beginning?

In this context the present functions as the scene of abjection, and the utopian gestures that have been possible during the meantime are made to stand as evidence, if not agency, of the demeaning of the past. Here, as we have seen, queer theory, for instance, is read as a flexible obsession that inhabits in a mirroring form the force of postindustrial capital production—a critical move that links notions of subjectivity with relations of production through "flexible" as a prevailing metaphor. But if the language of theory has this kind of power, to quite literally stand in for, as the equivalent to, material forms, then how can queer theory's deliberations over the materiality of language be so roundly disdained as a self-fashioning avoidance of the everyday real? It would of course be much more useful, as well as more critically difficult, to think about queer theory as itself a form of utopian striving whose success cannot be measured in the terms of the present as the horizon of either politics or the real. Segal's determination that queer theorists are in the end delusional in their attempt to "at last radically free themselves from the constraints of gender" (58) closes the book altogether on theoretical language as a means of occupying the difficulties of the "meantime." Most crucially, it raises as a requirement of both political commitment and utopian articulation the finalization of thought in a set of confirmed practices that define the future as continuous with a retrospectively coherent notion of the political past.

My argument for a theoretical humanities in the name of feminist politics arises here: first, as an interruption into this demand for the applicability of feminist thought and, second, as an insistence that a deeper consideration of the knowledge practices of the university be forged. This is not to dismiss the necessity of the kinds of practices that Segal and others call for as part of "concrete" political struggle, but it is to suggest that academic feminism needs that which its anxiety about institutionalization has come to foreclose: ideas without definitive evidence, critical thought without immediate actualization. That the humanities today are one of the only domains in the university that operate without suturing knowledge production to an instrumentalizing function (of whatever kind) makes them not the antithesis to feminism's political aspirations but a critical site for occupying a different (and currently unruly) set of disciplinary demands. Why this is the case has nothing to do with any intrinsic or essential aspect of humanistic inquiry and everything to do with transformations in the status of culture, language, and literacy currently underway in higher education as an institution central to the formation of the nation-state. For some observers, in fact, it is precisely the disestablishment of a generalizable notion of a homogeneous national culture and the transition from ideals of national to transnational citizenship forms that underwrite what has been called, in a variety of venues, the "crisis of the humanities." In this context it is the dissolution of the cold war university and its reliance on the specificity of national culture as the pedagogical means for inculcating citizen subjects that *politicizes* the loss of the humanities as a privileged mode of inquiry in general and literature as a valued object of study in particular. The turn to theory, especially in departments of English, might thus be understood as a form of opportunistic occupation of the vacated sites of disciplinary control.

This is not to say that poststructuralist theory has escaped producing its own disciplinarity, nor can it be applauded for resisting hierarchical reinvestments in the authority of the signature that the critique of literary canonicity raised. But issues of identity and the psychic economy, if you will, of language as the representational apparatus for human subjectivity have enabled feminist scholars to elaborate on the political in domains that had not been pressured to consider it as such. The very "fact" that the state, as the legislative body governing higher education, expresses its deep ambivalence about the status and purpose of the work of the humanities today indicates, if perversely, the political possibilities opened up by its lack of an incorporating vision.[17] In the name of feminist politics we need to engage such possibilities, not to save the humanities as such from their massive defunding but to wrestle with their (tenuous) failure to be instrumentalized to the U.S. nation-state, itself undergoing realignments in the context of geopolitical transformations. This wrestling will by necessity require the critical armature of postcolonial and subaltern studies, not in their utilization as the liberal inclusion of minoritized bodies from the peripheries of Western modernity but as critical frameworks for challenging both the historical organization of humanistic inquiry into the discrete provinces of Euro-American nation-states and the reconfigurations currently underway.[18] Academic feminism must do more than reference this critique; it must inhabit it in the way it articulates a critical history of its own, resisting the desire to make First World struggles for democratic completion the originary political moment in its academic sojourn. To think of "broken English" in this context, as my title proffers, means articulating academic feminism's relation to national discourses of the "political" as they have been organized both across and within disciplines and as they have come to define, if only implicitly, the critical horizons and epistemological foundations of new interdisciplinary identity sites.[19]

It also means considering the ways in which the relationship between language and governmentality is critically at stake in recent demands on the humanities for public communicability. As Rey Chow discusses in her contribution to this collection, many critiques that pit poststructuralist theory against politics tend to render language instrumental to modernity's own historic march toward technocratic utopian goals.[20] The humanities have borne the brunt of demands for linguistic accessibility, as liberalism's ideal of collective personhood (no matter how contradictory in its application) shapes the category of the human itself. Thus, as Chow demonstrates, communicability for the humanities is indistinguishable from the belief in the expressibility of human subjectivity, which in turn serves as the internal logic of modern governmentality as an ideology of social perfectibility. From this perspective, to refuse the demand for communicability is to challenge, at least provisionally, the linkages that have rendered the human foundational as both agent and vehicle for the perfectibility of the liberal democratic state. This is of course the destination of so much debate about poststructuralism: the moment at which we must assess the possibilities (or not) of human agency and the utopianism (or not) of democratic governmentality. To the extent that poststructuralist theory, especially as articulated by feminist scholars, has consistently tried to interrupt permanently this point of arrival, it might be read as a form of political intervention in the equation linking humanism, expressibility, and perfectibility. That such a refusal is experienced socially as well as intellectually as a loss is not a surprise, as it places into doubt *that which we do not know how not to want*. But the operation of this *want* as something more than *the truth* of the political is necessary, not to poststructuralism per se but to feminism's own political articulation of its historical ties to discourses of both the human and liberal governmentality in Western modernity.[21]

In advancing a distinction between the temporalities, if not temperament, of feminism's social movement and its academic enterprise, I have been insisting on the importance for feminist politics of a theoretical humanities. I have done this for a number of reasons, not the least of which is the necessity of challenging the equation that casts feminist politics solely on the side of the subjective, everyday, or concrete once again. That my argument is not original I surely grant: it retraces some of the plotlines and political anxieties that haunted the feminist movement as it struggled to negotiate institutional interventions on epistemological as well as distributive levels. To the extent that the epistemological has been taken up most centrally by the humanities—and turned against itself, we might say, by poststructuralism's critical interest in the unconscious as a form of social language and mediation—feminism has indeed been disciplined.[22] But my point has been this: any call for a return to the economic and material as a function of a pointed agenda of social change, cast as a reclamation of movement sensibility, indeed as a resurrection of public commitment, cannot rescue feminism from institutionalization's disciplinary effects: it can only confirm them, this time from a different position vis-à-vis disciplinary divides. In academic feminist debates about theory and communicability, then, a disciplinary engine is, I venture to say, *always* at work in the production of what is cast as a simple, even commonsense, opposition between the theoretical inside and an exterior public and hence seemingly politically committed sphere. This is not an argument against academic feminism's contemporary desire to think about its obligation to either social movements (past or present) or to a public social sphere in which "feminism" as such has been politically demeaned. Certainly, much more attention needs to be paid to the ways in which academic feminism's institutional position, indeed its power, can be organized in relation to struggles that cut across various domains. But it may not be strategic, finally, to cast academic feminism as the ultimate agent or arbitrator of the deployment of the political, as if its own disciplinary function is to define what the political will come to mean.

If my argument is an attempt to rescue the possibilities of a theoretical humanities, it is not, then, to give it priority in a political configuration that would render academic knowledge production continuous with the temporalities and affect of social movement. Indeed, I have argued the contrary, foregrounding discontinuity in order to pay critical attention to the specificity of institutional politics in which language, disciplinarity, and nation have been definitively linked. It is in this context that I have wanted to learn again what poststructuralism might have meant for academic feminism and hence what it might mean in today's academy for feminism to support, in the name of politics, a knowledge domain not contingent on the immediate, the live, the empirically real. This is one way of registering my own fear that the demand for communicability, cast against theoretical language, will come to stand as compensation for academic feminism's sense of a lost connection to social movement and that, in that compensation, we will lose a way of thinking about the political that we absolutely need.

Notes

1. Susan Gubar, "What Ails Feminist Criticism," *Critical Inquiry* 24 (summer 1998): 878–902; Tania Modleski, *Feminism Without Women* (New York: Routledge, 1991). See also my response to Gubar, "What Ails Feminist Criticism: A Second Opinion," *Critical Inquiry* 25 (winter 1999): 362–79.

2. Ellen Messer-Davidow, *Disciplining Feminism: From Social Activism to Academic Discourse* (Durham, N.C.: Duke University Press, 2002), 213.

3. Naomi Schor, *Bad Objects: Essays Popular and Unpopular* (Durham, N.C.: Duke University Press, 1995), xiv.

4. Lynne Segal, *Why Feminism? Gender, Psychology, Politics* (New York: Columbia University Press, 1999), 14.

5. See my "Feminism's Apocalyptic Futures," *New Literary History* 31, no. 4 (autumn 2000): 805–25.

6. This is not to say that the structure of the disciplines I am noting here is static. Mary Poovey's *A History of the Modern Fact* (Chicago: University of Chicago Press, 1998) is an important intervention in current discussions that seem to take the domain of fact "factually," which is to say as a domain that is stable and not a rhetorical and argumentative technology through which its own claims to ontology are made. In this context it becomes crucial to recognize, as Bill Maurer pointed out to me, that recent feminist moves to recoup a materialist claim as a political/moral discourse of justice often rely on the "factual" and not the argumentative—the empirical demonstration of women's exploitation and oppression serves to ground politics. From within this framework that equates the economic with the factual, poststructuralist insistence that knowledge claims, including the numerical, are argumentative are recast as elitist disregard for justice.

7. See, e.g., Lisa Lowe, "The International Within the National: American Studies and Asian American Critique," *Cultural Critique* 40 (fall 1998): 29–47.

8. On performative identities see Judith Butler, *Bodies That Matter* (New York: Routledge, 1993); on public cultures see Michael Warner, *The Trouble with Normal: Sex, Politics, and the Ethics of Queer Life* (New York: Free Press, 1999); and José Muñoz, *Disidentifications* (Minneapolis: University of Minnesota Press, 2000); on intimacy see Lauren Berlant, *The Queen of America Goes to Washington City* (Durham, N.C.: Duke University Press, 1997); and Kath Weston, *Families We Choose: Lesbians, Gays, Kinship* (New York: Columbia University Press, 1991); on premodern sexualities see David Halperin, *One Hundred Years of Homosexuality and Other Essays on Greek Love* (New York: Routledge, 1990); and Carolyn Dinshaw, *Getting Medieval* (Durham, N.C.: Duke University Press, 1999); and on the psychic life of power and desire see Judith Butler, *The Psychic Life of Power* (Stanford, Calif.: Stanford University Press, 1997); and Philip Brian Harper, *Private Affairs: Critical Ventures in the Culture of Social Relations* (New York: New York University Press, 1999).

9. See my "Queering the Academy" for a more lengthy discussion of the difficulties of articulating sexuality as a term of equivalence with race or gender ("The Gay 90s: Disciplinary and Interdisciplinary Formations in Queer Studies," ed. Thomas Foster, Carol Siegel, and Ellen E. Berry, *Genders* 26 [1997]: 3–22).

10. See, e.g., Eve Kosofsky Sedgwick, *Between Men: English Literature and Male Homosocial Desire* (New York: Columbia University Press, 1985).

11. This is not to say that these issues, as objects of study, were not constituted in social science through a great deal of disciplinary struggle by feminist scholars. Indeed, feminist social scientists continue today to fight for the legitimacy of certain kinds of practices as objects of study and to revise methodological protocols that would render the agents of such practices more than mere informants (as participants). My point here is not to critique the social sciences per se but to demonstrate how the various issues that Segal defines as central to a social feminist imaginary—and to a feminism committed to something more than academic professionalization—have greater disciplinary legibility in some places than in others.

12. Segal also fails to identify the ways in which Marxist paradigms lost their critical currency within social science fields throughout the 1980s, giving way to economic analysis drawn to formal modeling. The location of the loss of the political, then, in the humanities displaces a critical account for the ways in which the real has been tethered to a formalist economics in that domain defined, nostalgically, as the foundation of "genuine interdisciplinarity."

13. See Jane Newman's "The Present in Our Past: Presentism in the Genealogy of Feminism" for a discussion of the ways a constricted notion of the political generates an eternal present as the temporal framework for feminist knowledge production. Her concern, specifically, is how such presentism operates in women's studies curricula in ordering a narrow relation to the study of the past (*Women's Studies on Its Own*, ed. Robyn Wiegman [Durham, N.C.: Duke University Press, 2002]). For a discussion of the constriction of the political on poetics see Elaine Marks, "The Poetical and the Political: The 'Feminist' Inquiry in French Studies," in *Feminisms in the Academy*, ed. Domna C. Stanton and Abigail J. Stewart (Ann Arbor: University of Michigan Press, 1995), 274–87.

14. Inderpal Grewal and Caren Kaplan have written at length outlining the importance of critiquing global human rights discourses as they are taken up within feminism. See "Introduction: Transnational Feminist Practices and Questions of Postmodernity," in *Scattered Hegemonies: Postmodernity and Transnational Feminist Practices* (Minneapolis: University of Minnesota Press, 1994), 1–33; "Warrior Marks: Global Womanism's Neo-Colonial Discourse in a Multicultural Context," *Camera Obscura* 39 (September 1996): 5–33; and "Transnational Feminist Cultural Studies: Beyond the Marxism/Poststructuralism/Feminism Divides," in *Between Women and Nation: Transnational Feminisms and the State*, ed. Caren Kaplan, Norma Alarcón, and Minoo Moallem (Durham, N.C.: Duke University Press, 1999), 349–63.

15. Women's studies scholars might object to my use of the term *discipline* here, arguing instead that the field has always defined itself as an interdisciplinary domain. But my point rests on understanding the national move toward autonomous doctoral degrees in women's studies as a reproductive mechanism that cannot *not* accede

to the protocols of disciplinarity. I do not believe that women's studies should avoid
doctoral programs because of this; rather, it needs to grapple with what it means to
establish a disciplinary structure for what it repeatedly takes as a prototypically political, as opposed to academic, project. See Wendy Brown's "The Impossibility of
Women's Studies" (*differences* 9, no. 3 [winter 1997]: 79–101) for an incisive analysis
of the tension between the academic and the political in the curricular agendas of
the field.

16. One can surely object to this interpretation for a number of reasons, not the
least of which might be my use of *instrumentalize* as a negative formulation of the relation between academic feminism and the political. After all, why would academic
feminism not want to make its knowledge applicable to a social movement outside
the academy? Why would it object to the implication that it instrumentalizes not for
capital or the state but for progressive social change?

17. Sheila Slaughter has done a great deal of work that tracks the transformation
of higher education at the end of the twentieth century. See especially Sheila Slaughter and Larry Leslie, *Academic Capitalism: Politics, Policies, and the Entrepreneurial University* (Baltimore, Md.: Johns Hopkins University Press, 1997).

18. I am thinking here of the way that European studies is emerging on some
campuses not as an alternative to the nation-based departmental sites of French, Italian, and German studies but as their expansion, even as the whole of Asia continues
to be taught in area studies configurations where, quite often, Korea, China, and
Japan are organized collectively in a single Asian studies department.

19. It is important here as well to consider the ways interdisciplinary identity
sites, as they produce and often affirm discourses of identity formed by "community," function to mediate the crisis that a theoretical humanities evokes around issues of social subjectivity and governmentality. Where the question of politics has
been formulated on the side of visibility and the articulation of suppressed histories
(and insistently produced as the counter to the theoretical dismantling of the ontological subject), there is something increasingly too cozy between identity studies'
reliance on community as its lingua franca of countergovernmentality and the market's reliance on identity and community as the replacement strategy of the citizen-
function of higher education. From this perspective the nationalist discourses of inclusion and democratic completion that resonate as originary discourses in women's
studies and other identity-based sites are temporally dislocated from the political effects of institutionalization in the present. This does not mean that identity studies
are simply conservative actors, as too many commentators of the left now assume;
but it does point to the kinds of issues that most constructively constitute the internal critique and political complexity of understanding the present—and I would say
future—of interdisciplinary identity studies today.

20. The contemporary order of the disciplines speaks to this general ideological
and instrumental function, although the ways in which knowledge domains are instrumentalized varies. In law, for instance, the unintelligibility of its discourse to a
general readership is itself a condition of the culture of professionalization and expertise, but that illegibility in no way hampers law's instrumentalized relation to the
state. Rather, law is instrumentalized for the state precisely in relation to its lack of

generalizable intelligibility. Disciplinary modes of instrumentalization are thus inconsistent across domains, which is one way of saying that it is important to understand how communicability as an ideal is never simply the same thing.

21. In this vein academic feminism needs a theoretical humanities in order to reassess its own critique of abstraction as Western modernity's methodological inscription of masculinism, which has had the effect of aligning both women and feminism with the experience, the subjective, and the partial seemingly once again. Debates about sentimentalism in the nineteenth century have retraced the perpetual dilemma we encounter here where the necessity of citing women's resistance, if not liberation, often returns us to a celebration of the very forms of their social abjection. If abstractions, like both objectivism and universalism, have been understood as modes of masculine power, why must academic feminism authorize, in the name of politics, the gendered binary that gives these to "them" again? This question is really rhetorical in the sense that there is no escape from the conundrum in which feminism, academic or otherwise, finds itself: where its emergence is always a form of belated and hence contradictory originality.

22. Some commentary is necessary here to challenge the way in which debates about the fractured identity of *academic feminism* tend to align disciplinarity fully with the university's knowledge production, leaving the public formation of feminism as both outside and resistant to disciplinary forms. But certainly a great deal of the process of feminism's public political demeaning has been wrought through the forms of discipline that adhere to the public sphere. I am thinking especially of commodification. Although I have limited my discussion to knowledge-based organizations of disciplinarity, it is important to an overall consideration of the history of contemporary U.S. feminism to consider how political affect has been publicly disciplined and hence how the sphere of the public, so often heralded as the realm of political commitment, has come to be managed by disciplinary forms. For critical insight into this issue see Berlant's *Queen of America*.

The Resistance of Theory; or,
The Worth of Agony

The Compartmentalization of Knowledges

In the controversy over contemporary critical writing it has become somewhat commonplace to attack poststructuralist theory for being an elitist, privileged phenomenon that is oblivious to reality.[1] Indeed, it is often surprising that the impassioned debates that took place with the emergence of poststructuralism back in the late 1960s and 1970s—debates that problematize long-cherished and naturalized notions of language, subject, text, and meaning—continue to reinstate themselves today, at times in the pages of the most prestigious academic journals. Although the contents of critics' complaints have become more elaborate, so that the evils of poststructuralism are now compounded by those of postcolonialism, especially the voices of women of color,[2] the issue that has remained contentious is that of the role of language.

In the theory-attacking ritual language is typically regarded as a device for communication. The implicit assumption is that such a device needs to remain clear and transparent even when the subject matter it is communicating is extraordinarily difficult. Language exists, in other words, only in order to be a conduit, whose function is to transmit information about the world, its events, and its problems but never to convey anything about language itself.[3] This is by no means a new assumption, and debates about the difference between what is considered common sense (and clear language) and abstract thought (and obfuscated language) have been a regular feature of modernity. Once we locate this controversy in the context of modernity, however, it will have to be quickly added that these demands for language to be clear and transparent are, in fact, selectively placed on certain kinds of knowledge production and not on others. In higher education it is typically disciplines in the humanities, in particular those that deal with things that everyone supposedly understands—such as storytelling, novel reading, writing, and so forth—that are designated the areas on which such linguistic demands are to be made. Disciplines built on opaque, impenetrable languages that are admittedly incomprehensible to the layperson, but that are based in science and technology (such as medicine, computer technology, engineering, and biochemical research), or in law, seem not to have this continual stigma attached to their obviously specialized linguistic usages. In the case of these other disciplines the inaccessibility of their languages is regarded as a sign of their practitioners' professionalism rather than as a sign of their obscurantism: if a scientist, doctor, or lawyer writes in a manner that everyone can understand, this logic goes, well and good—but that would be a bonus, one that he or she is not expected to provide.

This polarization of assumptions—between the humanities, on the one hand, and the sciences and trade professions, on the other—about how language ought to be used is part of the larger historical picture in which we must place the smaller, although no less critical, controversy in the late twentieth and early twenty-first centuries over so-called theory and theoretically informed critical writing. If language has been reduced to instrumentalism (as it undoubtedly has been by those critics who complain of theory's "corruption" of language), such instrumentalism itself is already a product of the modernist progress that transforms the production and dissemination of humanistic knowledge by default into a kind of "communication." In this process, against an increasingly specialized world, it is nonetheless expected that humanistic knowledge should continue to be universally available and relevant in the sense that everyone should be *entitled* to it (whereas the sciences and the trade professions are allowed to have much more stringent membership qualifications). This unequal compartmentalization of knowledges means that the use of language also becomes hierarchically divided: if one happens to be pursuing the humanities—writing about novels, let's say—one does not, however profound one's knowledge might be, have the right to speak in the manner a rocket scientist does. Humanists should not have a technical language because the humanities are not about anything technical; they are about general human things. Indeed, the language at a humanist's command must remain the same language that is *shared* by everybody human. If one is not a scientist, a doctor, a lawyer, or a high-tech guru, one must speak and write in such a way as to remain comprehensible to the masses.

Once the historicity of the demand for "clear" language is foregrounded this way, it becomes possible to understand the moral self-righteousness that often accompanies the hostile criticisms of poststructuralist theory. In a manner that inadvertently aligns them with those instrumentalist forces that have led steadily to the demise and degrading of humanistic knowledge as such, the critics of theoretically inflected writing tend to stereotype theory not merely as bad writing but also as a kind of morally degenerate dismissal of the real world out there. Their reprimand of those who write theoretically is issued on behalf of the disenfranchised masses, who, according to these critics, derive no benefit from such elitist uses of language. In their acceptance, tolerance, and practice of the equivalent of (what in the sciences and trade professions would simply be) a complicated because specialized language, theoretical writers are thus portrayed by antitheory moralists more or less as enemies of the people, whose sufferings they appear not to be attempting to resolve. In sum, poststructuralist theory, like much abstract thought, is for such moralists something to resist—in the name of an altruism called common sense.[4] (In the age before poststructuralism philosophy was typically branded as perpetuating a user-unfriendly and impractical language.) The irony lies, of course, in the fact that these self-appointed guardians of the people are often themselves securely situated in privileged institutions, in career positions that are no less remote from the wretched of the earth than those of the theorists they attack.

The Resistance of Theory and the Point of Agony

In the midst of the oft-repeated commonplaces about high theory's elitism, especially the rather misleading polarization between common sense and abstract thought, the radical intentions that lie at theory's foundations tend to be more or less forgotten. Whether or not we suppose that such intentions are or can ever be realized, any responsible evaluation of the impact of theory in the late twentieth century and beyond would, I believe, need to take them into consideration.

Insofar as it began by fundamentally challenging the generality of the Western logos, poststructuralist theory, in particular, emerged on the epistemological horizon as the writing of a special kind of alterity, an irreducible metaphoricity that insists on having its own autonomous status from within Western thinking itself. As Paul de Man writes:

Literary theory can be said to come into being when the approach to literary texts is no longer based on non-linguistic, that is to say historical and aesthetic, considerations . . . when the object of discussion is no longer the meaning or the value but the modalities of production and of reception of meaning and of value prior to their establishment—the implication being that this establishment is problematic enough to require an autonomous discipline of critical investigation to consider its possibility and its status. (7)

When poststructuralist theory calls attention to the materiality of language, then, it is to point out that language embodies a concrete kind of labor. To this extent, poststructuralism shares important affinities with Marxism: the oppressed who is called on to rebel from within Western society, to problematize the stability of the cognitive field (that ranges from logic and grammar to rhetoric), and thus to reclaim the products of her labor, is none other than language itself. In the hands of poststructuralist theorists, language tenses its muscles and breaks the chains of its hitherto subordination to thought, throwing into question all old illusions of symbolic plenitude and epistemological self-sufficiency and refusing the customary erasure of language-as-language. What is restored by this theoretical revolution, accordingly, is what might be called an originary difference intrinsic to the Western logos. Hence the status of language is—to complete the comparison with Marxism—not unlike that of a guest worker, an exploited "alien" who has been indispensable in helping to hold together the host society with her hard work but whose existence continues to be disavowed. "The resistance to theory," writes de Man, "is a resistance to the use of language about language. It is therefore a resistance to language itself or to the possibility that language contains factors or functions that cannot be reduced to intuition" (12–13).[5]

In order to honor their commitment to linguistic materialism, those who pursue poststructuralist theory in their critical writings find themselves permanently at war with those who expect, and insist on, transparency of language as a mere tool of communication. To counter this kind of "common sense," poststructuralists charge that it is precisely such an expectation that perpetuates the denial of the materiality (the work) of language. In order that such materiality no longer be denied, it is essential for them to adhere to certain principles:

1. The work of language is never finished and cannot be separated from the slow but certain movement of *time* (and, by implication, difference).

2. Any assumption of language's transparency must be systematically *demystified* as an unexamined ideological manner of thinking.

3. Any attempt to deny the work of language and to co-opt us into believing in the likes of "nature," "essence," "identity," "origins," and so forth, must be vigilantly *deconstructed*.

4. Any resistance to (poststructuralist) theory as such is symptomatic of a certain blindness to one's own theoretical assumptions ("The attack [on theory] reflects the anxiety of the aggressors rather than the guilt of the accused" [de Man 10]).

In retrospect, it is important to acknowledge the specific nature of the force carried by poststructuralist critical thinking. This force is most detectable at the points at which such thinking exerts its greatest energies, and it tends to be preponderantly negative—albeit self-confident—in its charge: a profound distrust of literal, naturalized meanings; a persistent refusal or de-

ferral of reference; a determined unmasking of any use of language that
seems devoid of semiotic self-consciousness; a ready dismissal or debunking
of those who challenge any of the above as themselves being the prey to
their own mystifications.[6]

This powerful force, it should be added, is also a force of resistance.

In poststructuralist theory's heroic—if Sisyphian—efforts to obstruct the
path of a sweeping global instrumentalism that has led to the demotion of
language, we see the compelling legacy of a romanticist high modernism
with its avant-garde political-aesthetic programmatic intentions. (Consider,
in this regard, the importance of the English and German, as well as French,
romantics for de Man, and the works of Nietzsche, Heidegger, Lévi-Strauss,
Artaud, and others for the early Jacques Derrida.) Linguistic opacity, obscurity, impenetrability—these qualities that are characteristic of high modernist
works of art and literature, with their aversion to realist and mimetic representation—are also descriptive of much deconstructive critical writing. In
the case of poststructuralist theory, such qualities serve less as markers of an
alternative poetics and aesthetics than as signs of a dissident politics based, as
were many other social movements of the 1960s in the Western world, on
consciousness raising. At the same time, precisely because it can indeed be
seen in this regard as the late twentieth century's version of high modernism,
the practice of poststructuralist theory is likewise shot through with high
modernism's self-contradictions. Like high modernism, we might say, poststructuralist theory wants to be of the masses yet ends up speaking and writing in such ways that few of the masses will ever understand. The radical
events of reading and writing that began as acts of subversions of an unbear-
able regime (Western logocentrism and its many "ideological aberrations," to
use a phrase from de Man),[7] that strove toward a liberating, democratic order that would truly reflect the actual ways in which language (the prole-
tariat) works, fail precisely on the very issue (language) on which poststructuralism has waged its most intimate battles, turning poststructuralist writing,
in a manner quite opposite to its philosophical premises, into the enemy of
the people.

Insofar as it is invested in this permanent contradiction, this unresolvable
agony engendered by the rift between its egalitarian aspirations and their
"elitist" execution, poststructuralist theory may perhaps be described, ultimately, as being driven by a kind of Christian promise. To those who have
faith, it seems to declare, "Never mind the tortuous path you have to go
through now. Believe (in the work of language), put your belief in practice,
and you will be saved (someday, or in an afterlife). Pleasure derived from all
worldly things in the present (read: linguistic accessibility) is a delusion you
must learn to forgo. Agony, and agony only, is the way to truth—and to salvation."

The Work of Myth

Although we must acknowledge poststructuralist critical thinking for its major interventions, therefore, it is perhaps equally necessary to recognize its own (no less ideological) predicament. This predicament may be effectively grasped through a revisit to Roland Barthes's memorable little book of the 1950s, *Mythologies*.[8] My readers are likely already well acquainted with Barthes's then-novel introduction of the science of semiology in the reading of mass culture—and mediatized—materials. For our purposes, it is thus more important to focus on the interesting reflections on the problematic of language in modernity that underlie Barthes's thesis.

In the theoretical part of his book Barthes offers a systematic analysis of what he terms myth—which in today's language might be called the interfacing of multiple domains of signification, whereby meanings, instead of properly stabilizing in one domain, have the capability to shift and slide among different ones, thus offering endless opportunities for duplicity, ambiguity, and ideological manipulation. For our present argument, however, it is not so much the semiotic analysis Barthes provides as two conflicting moments in his definition of myth that are highly suggestive of the complexities informing the issues at hand.

The first moment is to be found in the lingering romanticism Barthes attaches to nature and the countryside, which are, in a manner of speaking, antitheses of the urban, artificial objects that he analyzes with considerable enthusiasm in the first part of the book. We encounter this moment in the section called "Myth on the Left." Here, despite having demonstrated the all-pervasive and inescapable workings of myth, Barthes nonetheless goes on to assert that there is a kind of language that is not mythical—the language of "man as a producer," who seeks to transform reality rather than preserve it as an image (146). Who is it who usually speaks this political, unmythical language? Barthes's example is revealing: "If I am a woodcutter and I am led to name the tree which I am felling, whatever the form of my sentence, I 'speak the tree', I do not speak about it . . . between the tree and myself, there is nothing but my labour, that is to say, an action" (145). Barthes calls this "the real language of the woodcutter," a real language he also attributes to "the oppressed" (148–49).

This assertion of a language that can remain free of myth because of its own material deprivation and barrenness is intriguing because it is, in contradistinction to Barthes's own semiological readings, a remnant of a structure of feeling that is still invested in a stable, as-yet-uncorrupted origin of meaning. As is characteristic of such structures of feelings, this notion tends to attach itself to certain kinds of figures, such as peasants, proletarians, children, the poor, the oppressed, the subaltern, and so forth. It is hence no accident that Barthes refers to the rustic figure of the woodcutter and his tree. His own analytical insights notwithstanding, it is remarkable that Barthes reads in the woodcutter and the oppressed an *unmediated* relation to language—theirs is, he writes, "a transitive type of speech" (148)—a relation that in turn becomes recoded by Barthes as political resistance (to processes of bourgeois mythification) and as truth.

The second moment I would like to highlight is found in the section entitled "Myth as Stolen Language," in which Barthes clarifies in no uncertain terms myth's capacity to absorb and recontain everything, including acts of resistance against it. "When the meaning is too full for myth to be able to invade it," he writes, "myth goes around it, and carries it away bodily" (132). Of special significance here are, once again, the examples Barthes provides—in this case the languages of modern mathematics and avant-garde poetry:

In itself, [mathematical language] cannot be distorted, it has taken all possible precautions against *interpretation*: no parasitical signification can worm itself into it. And this is why, precisely, myth takes it away en bloc; it takes a certain mathematical formula ($E = mc^2$), and makes of this unalterable meaning the pure signifier of mathematicity. . . .

. . . Contemporary poetry . . . tries to transform the sign back into meaning: its ideal, ultimately, would be to reach not the meaning of words, but the meaning of things themselves. This is why it clouds the language, increases as much as it can the abstractness of the concept and the arbitrariness of the sign and stretches to the limit the link between signifier and signified. . . . Poetry occupies a position which is the reverse of that of myth: myth is a semiological system which has the pretension of transcending itself into a factual system; poetry is a semiological system which has the pretension of contracting into an essential system.

But here again, as in the case of mathematical language, the very resistance offered by poetry makes it an ideal prey for myth: the apparent lack of order of signs, which is the poetic facet of an essential order, is captured by myth, and transformed into an empty signifier, which will serve to *signify* poetry. . . . [B]y fiercely refusing myth, poetry surrenders to it bound hand and foot. (132–34, emphases in the original)

These examples suggest that the process of myth as described by Barthes can be viewed as a process inherent to the experience and politics of language in modernity, wherein we can no longer safely assume that language will always function in the unproblematically transparent manner that some of us continue to presume it should. This heightened historical awareness of language as a source of trouble—on account of its faithlessness and its readiness for co-optation—is what led in part to acts of resistance such as those mounted by modern mathematics and modern poetry. In both cases, resistance is issued in the form of a deliberate *obscurity*, *exclusiveness*, and *impenetrability* so as to guard the contents in advance from the ruthless onslaught of myth and restrict access to them only to initiates. Yet, as Barthes points out, such resistance, however sophisticatedly vigilant and anticipatory it might be, can hardly deter myth, for myth has a way of capturing even—and especially—that which resists it the hardest: "Myth can reach everything, corrupt everything, and even the very act of refusing oneself to it. So that the more the language-object resists at first, the greater its final prostitution; whoever here resists completely yields completely" (132–33).

Barthes's thesis on myth is illuminating for a critique of the fraught relations among language, myth/ideology, and the efforts to resist myth/ideology that remain at the heart of debates concerning theory and critical writing today. Let me put it in a nutshell: if the position occupied by the antitheory moralists is comparable to that of Barthes in his moment of slippage back into a longing for an unmediated truth that can be "spoken" without language, then the position occupied by poststructuralist critical writing is, we may argue, not unlike that of the specialized languages of modern poetry and $E = mc^2$. Although it may be easy to dismiss the first position as theoretically naive and untenable, what Barthes has demonstrated, far more disturbingly, is that the second, theoretically astute, position, too, is in the end a fully assailable and co-optable one.

The Forces of Globalization

Poststructuralist theory's revolution, in other words, is caught in a certain dilemma that may be described as follows: on the one hand, it attempts to speak truthfully in resistance to various types of "ideological aberrations" (including in particular the one that reduces language to a transparent communication tool); on the other hand, it is compelled to recognize at every turn the invincibility and ubiquity of the forces of mythic manipulation.

Much like high modernism, this failed revolution must also be considered in the larger context of the demands placed by modernity on languages and cultures worldwide. If an aesthetically self-conscious, incomprehensible kind of language can be seen in the West as a historical rebellion against the increasing trend toward instrumentalism since the Enlightenment, then elsewhere in the world, in cultures that have had to cast off the burden of the ethnic tradition in order to modernize, the problem of language is, rather, always defined in terms of how it can become more clear, more accessible, and more useable—in short, how it can become more of a viable instrument to assist the developing nation in its progress toward the future. It was in the latter kind of cultural furor about cleansing the native/ethnic language of its past—especially of its obsolete, opaque literary qualities—that a country such as modern China, for instance, found itself in the early twentieth century.[9] Globally, hence, it is as though modernity had, in the early twentieth century, compartmentalized the world into two apparently disjointed but in fact mutually implicated halves: in the industrialized West, an avant-garde linguistic drama, staged first through high modernism and then through poststructuralist theory, driven by a fervently puritanist resistance against progressive instrumentalism; in the developing Rest, a characteristically desperate effort to bring the native culture up to date by reinforcing (rather than resisting) such progressive instrumentalism so as to survive the trauma that is none other than the compulsory contact with Westerners. On the one side, the fate of aesthetic/critical language was to become ever more specialized, unreadable, and thus superfluous (so that it cannot be easily appropriated); on the other side, the practical task faced by politicians, bureaucrats, intellectuals, and culture workers alike was rather that of creating a language that can be properly functional, communicative, and useful—a tool, precisely, for purposes of national and cultural self-strengthening.

At the beginning of the new century, in ways that could not have been foreseen, the forces of globalization have brought these two seemingly incompatible sides of modernity face-to-face. For instance, as Asian countries such as China, Japan, Taiwan, Singapore, and Korea become economically prosperous, with sufficient financial resources to be spared for "cultural exchanges," even the most arcane and linguistically formidable Western theory has found unprecedented channels for burgeoning. As many Western theorists have, under the rubric of globalization, become advocates of the need to spread their theory to various corners of the world, their missionary enthusiasm is being increasingly reciprocated in different places by local culture brokers who welcome it as an opportunity for conducting various types of transactions with established venues in Western countries, in particular the generously funded ones in North America.

Like modern poetry and $E = mc^2$, then, theoretical critical language has, contrary to its own expectations, begun to assume a new mythical life—as a trendy global commodity whose market appeal lies precisely in its near inaccessibility. As the operational logic of myth would have it, the more impenetrable the critical prose, the stronger the suggestion that there is some superior value therein; and the more audiences feel the frustration and intimidation of not "getting it," the more they desire and pursue "it." Witness the innumerable mentions and applications of theory at international conferences across the Pacific as well as across the Atlantic, and from the Northern to the Southern Hemisphere. Is theory still the event of political dissidence that it was in its origins? Has it not become, instead, a thriving entrepreneurship, whose powers for expansion and circulation often have little to do with the resistance against myth that once inspired its refusal to be intelligible?

In the new global trajectories of intellectual exchange, the agony that has earned theory the shameful name of elitism, the agony that accompanies theory's self-conscious mobilization of language to unmask ideological aberrations, has taken on a new kind of worth. The revolutionary defiance of instrumentalist linguistic lucidity has transformed, in practice over time, into a potentially gainful means of generating cultural as well as financial capital. As in the case of the uncomprehending masses' mythic invocation of $E = mc^2$ for "modern mathematicity," many who know nothing about the historical specifics of theory tend exactly to drop such names as Benjamin, Bhabha, Butler, Derrida, Foucault, Jameson, Kristeva, Lacan, Said, Spivak, and Žižek like so many instant formulae, as a way to signify one thing and one thing only—that they've got this thing called theory, that their enunciation is fashionably possessed of *theory-ness*. If, at an earlier moment, the resistance of theory could be analogized to the energy that fuses the traditional Christian promise of otherworldly salvation, such resistance can probably be historicized and recharted, at the turn of the new millennium, as part of the unstoppable momentum of a prosperous multinational capitalism, that "ideological aberration" that will likely continue to diversify, reproduce, and reinvent itself in the decades to come.

Notes

1. The title of this essay was conceived in response to the title originally proposed for this volume, *Worth the Agony?* As my discussion will show, I believe that the notions of worth and agony are indeed significant in this context because they serve to highlight the fraught historical implications of the continuing uses of, as well as debates on, critical and theoretical language in the North American academy.

2. See, e.g., the complaints, voiced as recently as the late 1990s, in Susan Gubar, "What Ails Feminist Criticism?" *Critical Inquiry* 24, no. 4 (summer 1998): 878–902.

3. For a well-known example of such ongoing debates see, e.g., George Orwell's "Politics and the English Language," in his *A Collection of Essays* (Garden City, N.Y.: Doubleday, 1954), 166–77. Orwell attributed the "debasement" of the English language in modern times to the conformity and corruption imposed by politics.

4. See a succinct analysis of such resistance in Paul de Man, *The Resistance to Theory*, foreword by Wlad Godzich (Minneapolis: University of Minnesota Press, 1986), 3–20; hereafter page references are included in parentheses in the text.

5. For another well-known, thought-provoking account, in early poststructuralism, of the status of language in modern literature, one that is predicated on language's self-referential agency, see Roland Barthes, "To Write: An Intransitive Verb?" in *The Structuralist Controversy: The Languages of Criticism and the Sciences of Man*, ed. Richard Macksey and Eugenio Donato (Baltimore, Md.: Johns Hopkins University Press, 1970), 134–56.

6. This passage from de Man offers a characteristic summation of these points: "What we call ideology is precisely the confusion of linguistic with natural reality, of reference with phenomenalism. It follows that, more than any other mode of inquiry, including economics, the linguistics of literariness is a powerful and indispen-

sable tool in the unmasking of ideological aberrations, as well as a determining fac-
tor in accounting for their occurrence. Those who reproach literary theory for being oblivious to social and historical (that is to say ideological) reality are merely stating their fear at having their own ideological mystifications exposed by the tool they
are trying to discredit" (*The Resistance to Theory*, 11).

7. See note 6 above.

8. Roland Barthes, *Mythologies*, selected and translated from the French by An-
nette Lavers (Frogmore, St. Albans, Herts.: Paladin, 1973). Hereafter page references
are included in parentheses in the text.

9. I have offered extended discussions elsewhere of the historical specificities per-
taining to modern Chinese language and literature and will not repeat these arguments here. Interested readers are asked to see Rey Chow, *Woman and Chinese Modernity: The Politics of Reading Between West and East* (Minneapolis: University of
Minnesota Press, 1991), chaps. 2 and 3; and "Media, Matter, Migrants," in *Writing Di-
aspora: Tactics of Intervention in Contemporary Cultural Studies*, by Rey Chow (Bloomington : Indiana University Press, 1993).

Styles of Intellectual Publics

IN THE OPENING SCENE of Orwell's *1984* the horror of totalitarianism is driven home to the reader by—of all things—the experience of writer's block. The main character, Winston Smith, has just sat down under the glare of the all-seeing telescreen, intending to begin a diary. He falters. A tremor goes "through his bowels." He feels helpless. "For whom, it suddenly occurred to him to wonder, was he writing this diary?"[1]

Winston's choice of genre, the diary, is perversely apt to illustrate the problem of audience. Perversely, because the addressee of a diary is that unique individual about whom most is known and whose sympathetic response can be taken for granted: oneself. How could anyone, even in the most ruthlessly totalitarian regime, lack an audience for a diary? But even in a diary one never writes simply to oneself in the present. At the very least one addresses one's retrospective reading at some point in the future. One therefore addresses oneself as a partial stranger, one who will have forgotten, or will have been caught up in a different phase of life and will have become, by consequence, different. And thus oneself comes to stand for posterity, and for a posterity partly brought into being by this act of writing.

It might be that a diary is addressed to others entirely, to an unborn posterity, and this in fact is how Winston mentally answers his question: "For the future, for the unborn." But this, too, he finds unsatisfying:

For the first time the magnitude of what he had undertaken came home to him. How could you communicate with the future? It was of its nature impossible. Either the future would resemble the present in which case it would not listen to him, or it would be different from it, and his predicament would be meaningless.

For some time he sat gazing stupidly at the paper. The telescreen had changed over to strident military music. It was curious that he seemed not merely to have lost the power of expressing himself, but even to have forgotten what it was that he had originally intended to say.[2]

Writing in this scene comes to seem impossible because the diary can have no concretely imagined public, present or future. The totalitarian state, with its godlike control of media, has eliminated the civil-society context without which neither public nor private life can have modern meaning. The diarist's blockage illustrates the lack of both. Winston has no privacy because he is visible to the watching telescreen, and when he puts his notebook away in a drawer, he knows it is useless to hide it. But he is also deprived of publicness. That means not only an audience to write for in the present but, more tellingly, the sense of a future that might be capable of comprehension, but different. "Either the future would resemble the present in which case it would not listen to him, or it would be different from it, and his predicament would be meaningless." What he requires is a near future, linked to him by a chain of continuous transformation. Even a diary, the most private of all forms, requires this hope as its condition of possibility. Finally, at the end of the scene, Winston arrives at a resolution:

He was a lonely ghost uttering a truth that nobody would ever hear. But so long as he uttered it, in some obscure way the continuity was not broken. It was not by making yourself heard but by staying sane that you carried on the human heritage. He went back to the table, dipped his pen, and wrote:
   To the future or to the past, to a time when thought is free, when men are different from one another and do not live alone. (26–27)

The public sphere here becomes purely imaginary or, we might say, internalized as humanity. In order to write even a diary, Winston must imagine the ability to address partial strangers—men who are different and do not live alone. When he turns this ability into an internal freedom and is able to dispense with the need to be heard, he begins to speak directly to humanity in an effect that could aptly be called lyrical, since Winston appears to address humanity only in the absence of any actual context of address.

Isn't the imaginary character of such a general address necessarily its weakness? The diary has no place to go, except into the hands of the police. Its address can only be internal projection. It has no readers, no scene of circulation. It stands for the pure wish that such a scene exist, that it might be oriented—as in fact it cannot be—to a horizon of difference. Its rhetorical addressee is only a placeholder for others and merely marks the idea of a sanity that could be confirmed through the exchange of perspectives. Orwell seems to be trying to imagine a way to get around the chicken-and-egg circularity of publics, which only exist by virtue of the rhetoric that addresses them.

This image of writing as a ghost of freedom is a striking image, tapping into a frustration that I think is widely felt, and not just under authoritarian regimes. Orwell presents *1984* as a dystopia of totalitarianism. But is that what this scene is about? The extreme conditions of the novel would be hard to realize outside the most frozen Gulag. Orwell's *1984* is therefore easier to read as the negative image against which liberal society defines itself than as a plausible critique of existing alternatives. That telescreen in Winston's room is not just Stalin technologically extended. It is also an anticipatory image of mass culture, about which Orwell also worried. Orwell's dystopia stirs readers because the frustration it asks them to imagine is common enough not just behind the old Iron Curtain but here in the land of freedom, under civil-society conditions, whenever the available genres and publics of possible address do not readily lend themselves to a world-making project. Anyone who wants to transform the conditions of publicness, or through publicness to transform the possible orientations to life, is in a position resembling that of Orwell's diarist.

For whom does one write or speak? Where is one's public? These questions can never be answered in advance since language addressed to a public must circulate among strangers; neither can they be dismissed, although the answers necessarily remain mostly implicit. One does not stand nakedly to address humanity. Every entry assumes an already recognizable form, a discussion already underway, a discourse already in circulation, a medium, a genre, a style, and, for what counts as politics in modernity, a public to be addressed. People often say, when they are dissatisfied with extant publics, that they write only for themselves; this can only be at best a lazy, shorthand expression, even for diarists. Every sentence is populated with the voices of others, living and dead, and is carried to whatever destination it has not by the force of intention or address but by the channels laid down in discourse. These requirements often have a politics of their own, and it may well be that their limitations are not to be easily overcome by strong will, broad mind, earnest heart, or ironic reflection. To speak in a certain way is to be typed as a speaker. To publish in a certain venue is to orient oneself to its circulation, as a fate.

It might very well be that extant forms and venues will accommodate many political aims. But what if they do not? What if one hopes to transform the possible contexts of speech? Since such a hope is likely, of its very nature, to be less than fully articulate, I suspect it is more common than anyone imagines. One cannot conjure a public into being by force of will. The desire to have a different public, a more accommodating addressee, therefore confronts one with the circularity inherent in all publics: public language addresses a public as a social entity, but that entity exists only by virtue of being addressed. It seems inevitable that the world to which one belongs, the scene of one's activity, will be determined at least in part by the way one addresses it. In modernity, therefore, an extraordinary burden of world-making comes to be borne above all by style.

Recent interest in the idea of the public intellectual suggests, I think, just such a blocked wish, a desire to transform the available contexts of speech and, indeed, of publicness. So does the ongoing preoccupation, voiced by journalists and academics, with the style of left academic theory. When people complain, as many do, that intellectuals are not writing clearly enough, their yardstick of good style generally turns out to be not just grammatical or aesthetic but political. After all, they do not want elegance of just any variety. They do not wish that academics should write beautifully in the mode of, say, Ronald Firbank or Nietzsche. The incomparable prose style of Michel Foucault—densely suggestive, both technical and poetic—far from being their ideal of rigorous style, is more likely to serve as an example of writing that is too difficult to be efficacious. They want language that will bring a certain public into being, and they have an idea of what style will work. The question of style, at any rate, entails a worry about the nature and duties of the intellectual.

The connection is made explicit by many critics of left academics in the humanities, including Katha Pollitt, Martha Nussbaum, Russell Jacoby, and James Miller. Opaque writing is said by these writers to indicate contempt for those whom one might persuade and thus to result in a hollow substitute for political engagement, no matter how radical the claims of the writing. Katha Pollitt, for one, has argued that when intellectuals write for themselves, the result is "a pseudo-politics, in which everything is claimed in the name of revolution and democracy and equality and anti-authoritarianism, and nothing is risked, nothing, except maybe a bit of harmless cross-dressing, is even expected to happen outside the classroom."[3] Pollitt's principal target here is Judith Butler; hence the reference to cross-dressing—although anyone who takes cross-dressing as a metaphor for harmless and risk-free entertainment has never done much drag in public. For the record, I think there is a significant element of truth in Pollitt's argument, and I'll come back to it; for the moment I am concerned to show how the issue is distorted when it is taken to be one of clarity.

The possibility I would like to raise here is that those who write opaque left theory might very well feel that they are in a position analogous to Orwell's diarist—writing to a public that does not yet exist—and finding that their language can circulate only in channels hostile to it, they write in a manner designed to be a placeholder for a future public. At stake here is the question of how, by what rhetoric, one might bring a public into being when extant modes of address and intelligibility seem themselves to be a problem.

A small irony of the recent polemics is that Orwell himself has often been cited as the example of writing that is, as all writing should be in the view of some critics, oriented to the largest possible audience. In a recent essay in *Lingua Franca* James Miller approvingly echoes Pollitt's attack and points out that it has become common among critics who share this view to cite Orwell as a model. Orwell, as they understand him, represents the idea that the writer is obliged to write with the greatest possible transparency, coming as close as possible to an address to all persons. Style, in this argument, is seen as determining the size of the audience, which in turn is seen as determining the potential political result. Orwell illustrates not only the principle of a clear style but the entire chain of reasoning that leads from style to political engagement. "That he was staggeringly successful in reaching the largest possible public, in a way that very few twentieth-century writers have been," Miller writes, is indicated by the "simple fact" that he "has sold, between *Animal Farm* and *Nineteen Eighty-Four*, more than 40 million books in sixty languages which is, according to John Rodden, 'more than any pair of books by a serious or popular postwar author.'"[4] (You can almost hear the Berlin Wall being brought down, like the walls of Jericho, by the chirping of the cash registers at Barnes and Noble.)

Does Orwell really stand for the idea that accessible style leads to mass markets and therefore to effective politics? He himself emphasizes, in "Politics and the English Language," that his ideal of clarity in thought "is not concerned with fake simplicity and the attempt to make written English colloquial." I have my doubts about his definition of precision: "What is above all needed is to let the meaning choose the word, and not the other way about."[5] It is possible to describe the phenomenon that gives force to this idea without the intentionalist semantics to which Orwell here falls prey. Yet he is making a point about the difficulty of precision and not, as is generally implied in current polemic, about the need for a populist idiom in search of a numerically extensive audience.

The image of forty million copies of Orwell lighting up the UPC scanners of the free world certainly contrasts oddly with Orwell's own image of Winston's diary, hidden in a drawer, with a speck of dust carefully placed on top so that it will be possible to tell when the police have read it. "It was not by making yourself heard but by staying sane that you carried on the human heritage." Somehow Orwell has come to stand for the opposite of this sentiment that carrying on the human heritage requires that one be heard by as many people as possible.

We might also read the diary scene, and its intense melancholy, as an unrecognized allegory of the displacement of the writer by the technologies of the mass. There is something unmistakably nostalgic in Winston's fetishization of the cream laid paper, the nib of the pen, writing by hand—a fetishism echoed in that placement of the piece of dust on the cover and by the materiality of every piece of writing described for the remainder of the novel. This is not the image of writing that Orwell's current advocates have in mind; its desperate fetishism suggests that Orwell himself worries about the estrangement of mass publics, which appear in the novel in drag as totalitarianism.

In response to the polemic against the style of left academic theory, Judith Butler has frequently invoked Adorno's *Minima Moralia*—a much more explicit commentary on the estrangement of mass publics. Her appeal to Adorno is the basis for the conceit of Miller's *Lingua Franca* essay, which discusses the debate over clarity in left academic theory by comparing Orwell and Adorno, contemporaries who, in Miller's view, represent antithetical understandings of the politics of style. Adorno, however, fares no better in this exchange of polemics than does Orwell.

Butler cites Adorno to the effect that common sense is an unreliable standard for intellectual writing. The apparent clarity of common sense is corrupt with ideology and can only be countered by defamiliarization in thought and language. The task of the intellectual is to disclose all the forms of distortion, error, and domination that have been embedded in the current version of common sense. As she points out, views that now strike us as grotesque have often been graced with such immediate comprehension that they hardly needed to be stated at all. The rightness of slavery and the subordination of women are only the most politically salient among many other gruesome examples. Common sense is often enough unjust. Language that takes us outside the usual frame of reference, teaching us to see or think in new ways, can be a necessary means to a more just world. And to the degree that our commonsense perceptions contain distortion, just so far will the effort of reimagining seem difficult, even (to many) unclear.

This is a forceful argument, although one might object that the need for unfamiliar thought is not the same as the need for unfamiliar language. There is a long tradition of argument for both. Dissent from the pressure of unexamined common sense is a cardinal principle of the Enlightenment. For most Enlightenment intellectuals the idea was to create a new, more reflective—and therefore more just—common sense. And at least since romanticism there has also been a long history of skepticism about the possibility of pure and universal clarity, given the arduousness of the vision called for, or about the idea that reflection alone will produce insight.

Indeed, Butler did not need to appeal to so suspiciously foreign an authority as the Frankfurt School on this point; a very similar argument lies at the core of American transcendentalism. Henry Thoreau, who is taken in some quarters to be nearly a byword for epigrammatic clarity, had nothing but scorn for common sense and the journalistic demand that one write for it. "It is a ridiculous demand which England and America make, that you shall speak so that they can understand you," he writes at the end of *Walden*. "Why level downward to our dullest perception always, and praise that as common sense? The commonest sense is the sense of men asleep, which they express by snoring."[6] Thoreau had his own reasons for distrusting common sense and its clarity. The commonsensical legitimacy of slavery was one. He also thought that true perceptions must be poetic, transformative, even transgressive; any true thought must wake one out of common sense. This he took to be a demand on style as well as thought. Thinkers who aspire to expand the realm of the thinkable can hardly be expected to avoid experiments of usage. His call for defamiliarizing language contains both a classic Enlightenment wish (since "men asleep" need to be awakened from the sleep of common sense) and a more romantic conviction that the result could never look like simple clear reasoning, which would address the rational faculties only. Hence the need for literary language.

Adorno distrusts common canons of clarity for reasons that encompass Thoreau's but go further on the strength of a different kind of argument. "A writer will find that the more precisely, conscientiously, appropriately he expresses himself," writes Adorno, "the more obscure the literary result is thought, whereas a loose and irresponsible formulation is at once rewarded with certain understanding." Adorno did not think this was necessarily or always true; it is true under the conditions of mass culture and an idealization of common sense that is based in commodity culture. "Shoddiness that drifts with the flow of familiar speech is taken as a sign of relevance and contact: people know what they want because they know what other people want."[7] In other words, they embrace the idiom that, in its social currency, promises them the widest possible belonging. Commodity culture intensifies this desire and distorts it. The producers of mass culture, for obvious reasons of self-interest, take care to make their commodities intelligible to as wide a market as they can. This is one side of the picture but not what concerns Adorno most. He does not just criticize mass culture as cynical manipulation. He sees the way the expansiveness of mass circulation affects and distorts a desire for social membership on the part of readers; and he thinks this is the root of the problem of style. The wide circulation of language in mass culture is perceived and treasured as a quality of style by those who misrecognize it as clarity and sense.

Adorno is describing the manifestation, in matters of style, of one of the most pervasive and troubling effects in mass society: the phenomenon of normalization. Ideas of the good—and, in this case, the beautiful as well—are distorted, in ways that escape nearly everyone's attention, because they have been silently adjusted to conform to an image of the mass. A good style is a normal style. What counts as normal depends on distribution; the range of variation defines the norm. This is a distinctively modern way of defining value, based in a wide range of quantifying techniques (statistics, demo-graphics, markets) for imagining the social world. The conformity that re-sults is different from, say, conformity to divine law or natural hierarchy. It appears to allow for difference to be generated from the bottom up, so to speak. It does not appear to have any transcendent authority; what is good is inferred from what people happen to do or like. Yet this imagination of value has an authority, and a coerciveness, of its own.[8]

The false aesthetic of transparency, defining *clarity* as that which commu-nicates widely, has a powerful social effect of normalization. One result is that it will naturally privilege the majority over less-familiar views. Equally important to Adorno is that it will distort the judgment of the majority it-self, precisely *qua* majority. The tastes and ideas that become those of the ma-jority do so because people need to believe that their tastes and ideas will be widely shared. The result is a kind of invisible power for dominant norms, even though the people who make these normalizing judgments of taste do so not in order to exercise power (they are not, in other words, simply wielding the tyranny of the majority) but simply to fit in. Adorno implies, with pathos, that people rely on expressions that are precertified for them as common currency out of a kind of defensiveness; they are alienated from the labor of judgment. "Only what they do not need first to understand, they consider understandable; only the word coined by commerce, and really alienated, touches them as familiar."[9]

Now it does not follow that writing, in order to be valid, must be in-comprehensible. Butler, in her op-ed piece in the *New York Times*, comes close to this implication because she stresses the need for defamiliarization.[10] And Miller embraces it outright: "Q.E.D.: The most radical critic of alien-ation will be the most exquisitely aloof thinker, incomprehensible and un-popular by design, as if enraptured by his unswerving address to an ideal au-dience of one: a God who may not even exist."[11] The picture of an Adorno addressing "an ideal audience of one: a God who may not even exist" bears a strong resemblance to the predicament of Orwell's diarist. Yet here Miller shows himself hasty to score points against Adorno. This position is incoher-ent except as caricature. You cannot be incomprehensible by design, espe-cially if your audience is yourself. You also cannot be cynically strategic and yet "enraptured" by an unswerving address.

Adorno does not prescribe incomprehensibility nor unpopularity. He prescribes careful, rigorous, precise expression, whether the result is a popu-lar idiom or not—as, for that matter, Orwell does in "Politics and the Eng-lish Language." In order to present willful incomprehensibility as anyone's considered program, Miller has to present that person as nearly insane. He describes Adorno as "the most exquisitely aloof thinker," as "indistinguish-able from a Prussian autocrat," as expressing "nothing but contempt" (41), and as a mandarin, a foreign and inscrutable nerd. Miller does not scruple to produce a personal pathology as the not-so-hidden meaning of Adorno's thought: "*Minima Moralia*," he writes, in an attempt to sound sympathetic, is "the effort of a sensitive introvert" (36).

One of the most amusing moments in Adorno's writing, by the way, is an episode in his autobiographical essay about the years he spent in a research project on the medium of radio in Newark, New Jersey, just after he fled Nazi Germany. One day he was met by a young American researcher who asked him, in what Adorno calls "a completely charming way," "Dr. Adorno, are you an introvert or an extrovert?" He does not tell us his response. Perhaps he was too dumbfounded to make one. When he told this story later, however, it was to illustrate the spread of reified thinking.[12]

Miller, no doubt unaware of this ironic echo, needs to render Adorno an irrational introvert in order to arrive at the question announced by the title of his essay: "Is Bad Writing Necessary?" The question is a false one, an example of polemic rather than real deliberation. To answer the question in the affirmative—bad writing is necessary—entails a contradiction in terms. Any way of writing that could be said to fit necessity cannot be called simply bad. Having posed the issue this way, Miller is able to ensnare the victim in a paradox: "Does this mean that Adorno's and Butler's most challenging ideas, precisely because of their relative popularity among a not-insignificant number of left-leaning intellectuals, have lost their antithetical use value and, by the infernal logic of exchange, been alienated and perhaps even dialectically transformed—turned into something hackneyed and predictable? If one accepts Adorno's position in *Minima Moralia*, there is no escaping the conclusion" (43).

Actually, this conclusion is very easy to escape. Adorno does not infer alienation directly from the number of comprehending readers. He equates alienation with an imitative style of mass comprehension that defensively resists the unpredictability of thought. Numbers of readers are not the issue. The manner of reading is—although Adorno believes that the problem with the currently dominant manner of reading is that its imagination of value is controlled by people's tacit calculations about the numbers of readers with whom they will be in alignment. So no matter how many people read and comprehend his writing, that in itself tells us nothing about its social meaning. Only when the extensiveness of the reading audience is taken into normative consideration in advance by that very reading audience do we have the phenomenon he describes.

I have taken a detour through this episode in Anglo-American polemics partly because it shows how primitive our thinking about publics is. The assumption seems to be that a clear style results in a popular audience and that political engagement requires having the most extensive audience possible.

This view is assumed rather than reasoned, which is why anyone who dissents from it can only be heard as proposing inanities: that bad writing is necessary, that incomprehensibility should be cultivated, that speech in order to be politically radical must have no audience. In Miller's summary both Orwell and Adorno are made to share the assumption that clarity of style produces large numbers of readers: Miller's Orwell thinks this is a good thing; Miller's Adorno thinks it is a bad thing.

We begin to normalize intellectual work whenever we suppose a direct equation between value and numbers—imagining that a clear style results in a popular audience and therefore in effective political engagement. So deeply cherished is this way of thinking that to challenge it is to court derision, especially in journalistic contexts. Adorno tried to identify a connection between the mass circulation of discourse and the mode of reading oriented to that circulation.[13] He is heard, instead, as arguing against readability in principle.

Given such confusion, it is perhaps better to return to very basic questions. What kind of clarity is necessary in writing? Clarity for whom?

For some, the answer to these questions is too obvious to need stating. Writing that is unclear to nonspecialists is just "bad writing." This general moral position is implied by Miller's title, as it is by the Bad Writing Award cooked up by the journal *Philosophy and Literature*. This idea of clarity as a self-evident morality is the self-understanding of a certain middlebrow public and its paid flatterers in places like the *New York Times*. People who share this view will be generally reluctant to concede that different kinds of writing suit different purposes, that what is clear in one reading community will be unclear in another, that clarity depends on shared conventions and common references, that one person's jargon is another's clarity, that perceptions of jargon or unclarity change over time. (My students have trouble reading eighteenth-century prose that was a model of clarity in its time, but they take as self-evidently clear such terms as *objective* and *subjective*—terms denounced as hideous neologistic jargon when Coleridge used them.) People who think the charge of bad writing is self-evident or universally obvious therefore tend to be naive at best and quite often can be shown to be hypocritical. As Judith Butler rightly notes, for example, the charge is almost always reserved for thinkers in the humanities who share certain unpalatable views. Even conservative academics in the humanities who write opaquely are seldom attacked; the hostility of journalists seems reserved not only for certain disciplines but for left thinkers within those disciplines.

Should writing intended for academics in the humanities aspire to accessibility for everyone when we don't expect the same from writing in physics? Isn't such an expectation tantamount to a demand that there should be no such thing as intellectuals in the humanities, that the whole history of the humanistic disciplines should make no difference, and that someone starting from scratch to enter into a discussion—of, say, the theory of sexuality—should be at no disadvantage compared to someone who had read widely in previous discussions of the question? Any institutional context for discussion inevitably limits accessibility. That is not necessarily a bad thing, unless you are a knee-jerk populist. It allows people to develop a line of thinking cumulatively, without starting at each moment from the zero point of maximum accessibility. Some sloppiness no doubt results; institutions allow people to speak in code and forget questions that might be posed from the outside. Yet when the charge of bad writing comes from journalists, it is hard to avoid the feeling that some hostility to the very idea of scholarly humanistic disciplines is involved.

It is also possible to challenge academic writing for a second set of reasons, precisely because of the ideals that separate the disciplines from journalism. Instead of assuming a self-evident standard of clarity and a moral obligation to follow it, one could argue that the imperative to write clearly is not the same as the need to write accessibly, that the project of an academic discipline requires a rigor of definition, argument, and debate. What would count as clarity, in this view, might remain highly specialized and inaccessible to lay audiences or journalists. Indeed, to the extent that clarity might require conceptual precision of very unfamiliar kinds, it might compete with accessibility. People adhering to this ideal might feel that clarity is endangered not by the isolation or specialization of the academy but, on the contrary, by the failure of humanists to take their own disciplines seriously—either because of the humbug of genteel humanistic piety or because of the fascination with journalistic authority that besets such professions as history or because specialized environments like the cultural studies circuit have led academics to think that rigorous argument counts less than a gestural politics of righteousness. To appeal for clarity in this sense would not be an argument about public intellectuals, nor would it apply to left academics more than to anyone else.

A third line of thinking is that a special standard of clarity should be applied to just those academics who claim political consequences for their work—which would include almost everyone working in cultural criticism these days. On this view there might be no need for accessibility in academic disciplines in general, and "bad writing" awards could be dismissed as grandstanding. Yet when academics claim to be furthering justice through their work, this argument goes, they take on obligations that go beyond their own profession. (This is the way the argument has been advanced by Martha Nussbaum and Katha Politt, among others.) Even on these terms it does not immediately follow that *accessibility* is the issue. Nussbaum's critique of Judith Butler's prose style, for example, does not assume that Butler's work should be written for nonspecialists; her more serious charge is that Butler's work is not written for canons of argument among specialists, either in philosophy or in law, and that only the star system of cultural studies accounts for its form of address.[14] Some of the stylistic tics Nussbaum targets, like the tendency to introduce premises in conditional "if . . . then" clauses and then to treat those premises as givens, have to do with logical argumentation but not necessarily with exposition for nonspecialists such as the presumed readers of *New Republic,* where Nussbaum was writing.

So a further assumption seems to be required to produce the charge that inaccessible writing is irresponsible. One must hold not only that clarity is a special burden on writers with political aspirations but that the kind of clarity they need is the kind found in journalistic or political publics. This demand seems to me wholly unjustified for reasons that I hope to make clear. In all the attacks on the style of left academic theory, I have not seen a cogent defense of this extra requirement. It tends to be taken for granted, especially by journalists. There is a reason for the silence; those who believe most ardently in the power of journalistic publics tend to believe that those publics are like the air—everywhere, invisible, and permeable to light. It hardly occurs to them to wonder whether a public might be a cultural form predisposed to some ends over others.

Notice, too, that the charge of bad writing carries a corollary assumption: that if only left academics would write accessibly for journalistic publics, they would be more politically effective. This does not obviously follow, and experience suggests that it is a mistake. Accessible prose alone gets you nothing if the ideas are unpalatable for other reasons or if the public is structured in such a way as to be substantively prejudicial. There are many arguments that will never find their way to the pages of the *New York Times* no matter how clearly expressed. Just as it is a mistake to equate good writing with accessibility, so also is it a mistake to equate an easy style with effectiveness.

We are drawn into these assumptions so insidiously that they can distort the defense of difficult writing as well. It is all very well to argue that some kinds of difficult writing might be good, even politically necessary. But is difficulty a virtue in itself or an effective strategy for defamiliarizing common sense? To defend academic writing on such grounds is to assume that defamiliarization works all by itself. One falls into the same mistake as those who believe in transparency, saying nothing about context, audience, ways of reading, or mediation by form. How does writing defamiliarize common sense? If it does so only when read by the protocols of academic discourse—where, for example, it is axiomatic that complexity is to be valued over simplicity—then the arguments of Pollitt and others have some force: the political benefits that flow from this strategy of resistance do so only within the restricted zone of academic circulation. Defamiliarization for whom?

Might it not be the case that what might have been defamiliarizing has become, for many in the academy, all too familiar? Many people outside the academy are defensive about using their judgment in the face of difficulty; might it not also be true that many inside it are defensive about giving up the display of difficulty in the surface of writing? There would be nothing surprising in this. Style performs membership. Academics belong to a functionally segregated social sphere, and in the humanities in the United States that sphere is increasingly marginal, often jeopardized. People use style to distinguish themselves from the mass and its normalized version of clarity. Often, those who do so—especially graduate students, whose role is not institutionally secured—are also trying to mark their own somewhat tenuous membership in a fragile but desperately needed subculture. A value on difficulty contributes to the poesis of that social world, just as an ideologized clarity contributes to the poesis of journalistic publics. These social dimensions of style are probably more important to the making of any public than either clarity or defamiliarization considered in the abstract.

At stake in the dispute about style, then, are different contexts for writing, different ways of imagining a public. The issues are obscured, rather than clarified, whenever we assume that a public intellectual is one who writes for large numbers, that an untroubling and familiar idiom is essential to political engagement, that meaningful political work is necessarily performed within what currently counts as politics, that it should bring about changes within the calendar of news, or that political position-taking is the only way of being creatively related to a public. What disappears, in this view of the politics of prose, is the public of writing itself. Publics spring neither from clarity, which pretends they are transparent, nor from defamiliarization per se, which makes opacity private. Publics require a manner of address, a material context of circulation, affective dispositions of reading or witnessing, and a social imaginary that confers significance on performance or literate practice.

So we are back where we began: how could one bring a different public into being, transforming the conditions of speech?

The question is blunted by the very ideology that drives much of the talk about public intellectuals in the first place: the dominant ideology of the public sphere, dating at least from the early eighteenth century, according to which the public sphere is simply people making public use of their reason. Citizens, in this commonsense view (shared equally by high theory after Habermas and by the folk theory of democracy), form opinions in dialogue with each other, and that is where public opinion comes from. Any address to a public tends to be understood as imitating face-to-face argumentative dialogue, or rather an idealized version of such dialogue. Public opinion is thought to arise out of a continuum of contexts ranging from common conversation to PTA meetings to parliamentary forensics, op-ed pieces, polls, or critical essays; and at each step the rules of discourse are the same. One proceeds by airing different views in the interest of understanding, making assumptions explicit, and then reaching some decision. The public sphere is critical discussion writ large. A vibrant scene of public-spirited discussion is the motor of democratic culture.

I have argued that publics do not in fact work that way.[15] But if you believe that they do, that there is a continuum from rational dialogue upward to the realm of public opinion, then it might seem obvious that intellectuals are uniquely positioned to address publics publicly. Critical argument is the intellectuals' metier. If public discourse is to be reasonable, who should be better fitted to lead it than intellectuals? If they fail to do so, the thinking goes, then the failure must lie at their own door.

For many people "public intellectual" has come to mean a quasi-journalistic pundit with a mass following. Older conceptions—such as that of the intellectual as the conscience of the age, adhering to conviction or historical memory whether anyone listens or not, keeping alive an alternative that may be reanimated in some distant future—have faded into the background.[16] Contemporary culture regards any thought of a distant future as archaic. Given the contracted span of futurity in the headline temporality of politics, which increasingly dominates all thought, we think in horizontal terms: public intellectuals are those who seek socially expansive audiences.

Under the sway of such thinking one could easily ignore the difference between intellectuals as a class and citizens as a general category. Both use critical reason and articulate considered arguments. Intellectuals are simply those who are equipped to do this in the greatest degree. John Guillory aptly writes that the idea of an engaged intellectual can be seen as "nostalgia for the very public sphere that functioned historically in the *absence* of a socially identified group of 'intellectuals.'"[17] The wish for public intellectuals leads people to speak as though there were a moral imperative to clarity, and a moral imperative to political position-taking as well. To the extent that these are moral requirements, they can hardly be expected to result in such a specialized status as the public intellectual. If one were really to argue that everyone should write clearly and that everyone should take political positions publicly, one would be arguing in effect *against* the idea of a public intellectual as a special role.

More to the point, this ideology misrecognizes the fundamental innovation of the public as a cultural form. The public sphere never required a widespread culture of rational discussion at all but rather a notion of a public—which is, after all, a fiction. Only this essentially imaginary function—which presupposes a temporally indexed circulation among strangers—allows that scene of circulation to be captured as a social entity and addressed impersonally.[18] Success in this game is not a matter of having better arguments or more complex positions. It is a matter of uptake, citation, and recharacterization. It takes place not in closely argued essays but in an informal, intertextual, and multigeneric field. There is no reason why intellectuals should be specially positioned for public address in this sense, except where they are packaged as experts. And expert knowledge is in an important way nonpublic: its authority is external to the discussion. It can be challenged only by other experts, not within the discourse of the public itself.

The sociologist Nina Eliasoph has recently published a disturbing study of contexts of discussion that should challenge any idea of the public sphere as a continuum of critical opinion making. Eliasoph examined a wide range of public discussions in local community groups and found that public-minded discussion is systematically inhibited in almost every context. As conversations get closer to public topics, where opinions would have a general relevance and others' views would have to be taken into account, people tend to shut up, deflecting currents of conversation. Even active volunteers in civic groups construct their volunteering so as to avoid risky discussion. They choose topics that allow them to avoid dissent. They frame their motives as prepolitical. Journalists and officials actively conspire to limit public discussion, diverting it into testimony that can be viewed as private passion rather than opinion or argument. They solicit people to regard their public spirit as good feeling, compassion, volunteerism, or anything else that can be divorced from the conflict of views. Journalists report on citizens' feelings or interests rather than on their arguments, keeping for themselves the role of the uncontested mediators of publicness. They profile those who speak as moms, acting on behalf of their children, rather than as citizens with general views. Officials who respond to citizen involvement tend to invoke expertise or to steer discussion into bureaucratic speech protocols in which their own authority can be performed.[19]

Interestingly, Eliasoph herself does not question the assumption that the continuum of public-minded critical discussion is what the public sphere has been or should be about. Her book is driven by a sense of outrage that actual conversations fail to accord with the ideal. But the ideal of critical discussion was itself never sufficient to bring the public sphere into being. The endlessly repeated discovery that public politics does not in fact conform to the idealized self-understanding that makes it work—a discovery made by the romantics, by Marx, by Lippman, by Adorno, by Habermas, by Foucault, and de novo by Eliasoph—can never generate enough moral passion to force politics into conformity. The image of discussion writ large is necessary to the public sphere as a self-understanding but not as an empirical reality.

That same image, I suspect, fuels the fantasy of the public intellectual as a necessary function for political change, where the intellectual is seen as one especially adept at framing issues for critical discussions and where change results when discussion encompasses the most extensive possible public in its deliberative agency. This conception of the intellectual's relation to politics relies on a language ideology in which ideas and expressions are infinitely fungible, translatable, repeatable, summarizable, and restatable. To the extent that this is what public language is supposed to be about, attention must be deflected away from the poetics of style, as well as from the pragmatic work of texts in fashioning interactive relations. Publics are conjured into being by characterizing as a social entity (that is, as a public) the world in which discourse circulates; but in the language ideology that enables the public sphere this poetic or creative function of public address disappears from view. Rather than help to constitute scenes of circulation through style, intellectuals are supposed to launch transparently framed ideas into the circulation of an indefinite public. Of course, if intellectuals thought of themselves as involved in world-making projects, it is not clear that intellection would be more effective than, say, corporeally expressive performances. It is not clear that intellectuals would have a naturally leading role in the process at all. Hence it is perhaps not surprising that the professional class of intellectuals should seem reluctant to abandon the conception of public discourse whose inadequacy they continue to discover.

The wish for popularly read intellectuals responds in part to the extreme segregation of journalistic and intellectual publics in the United States. They are segregated not just by attitude and style but by the material conditions of circulation. Publics do not exist simply along a continuum from narrow to wide, specialist to general, elite to popular. They differ in the social conditions that make them possible and to which they are oriented. The United States is an extreme case. The American strain of anti-intellectualism has made intellectuals feel like exiles for the past two centuries; small wonder that many should dream of vindicating themselves through fame, the only currency of respect that really spends in America. The intense capitalization of mass culture here means that the media that matter are those whose scale and scarcity of access are most forbidding. Meanwhile, the saturation of universities by commercial and state interests makes academic work in some ways less than public, insofar as intellectuals there come to be either functionally incorporated into the management culture of expertise or, alternatively, marginalized. And for the past thirty years or so trade and academic publishing have been institutionalized as distinct fields of production to a much greater degree than in any other country, and the decentralization of the American university system prevents it from providing the coherent platform of authority that is to be found in more frankly elite systems such as that of France.

University presses and journals are mulish compromises, half professional and half public. Their products are widely available to any stranger who can buy or borrow copies, and in that sense they address publics. But they also take care to maintain a close fit between their circulatory ambit and the private realm of the professions. They select authors from professions; they vet manuscripts (less and less, it is true) with expert readers within fields; they promote works within professional organizations and academic markets. (This is true even of presses like Routledge that have no formal ties to universities.)

The world of strangers to whom this discourse circulates is a world in which strangers are either directly certified in advance by institutions and networks or indirectly limited by the distributional practices of the publisher. Readers share reference points, career trajectories, and subclass interests. They share protocols of discourse, including things like a preference for complexity. ("Actually, I believe it's more complicated than that" is, within the academic world, an unanswerable shibboleth; it articulates a professional mode for producing more discourse and for giving it an archivally cumulative character. The same gesture falls hopelessly flat in journalistic settings, where the extensive uptake of audience attention is at a premium.) Writers in this world are inevitably involved in a different language game from journalists.

The private circulation of academic discourse could be all to the good in the routine functioning of a discipline. But when disciplines decline or go into crisis, or when members for their own reasons seek to use the academic platform to address a different public, the existing routes of circulation prove unsatisfactory. Circulation is then controlled by conflicting laws. Journalists, who as a class have an interest in mass circulation and the forms of authority based on it, are only too happy to point out the conflict.

These conditions structure the available publics for thought and writing in the United States. They are not to be overcome by a mere change of attitude, any more than Orwell's diarist could have been expected to generate, out of style alone, *a time when thought is free, when men are different from one another and do not live alone.* Academic left theory, mostly from within the jeopardized disciplines of the humanities, has been attempting to reconstitute itself as a public, often with the explicit intention of ceasing to be organized by disciplines. Often enough it seems willing to postulate its own world through idiomatic and topical allusions to mass culture. The result frustrates nearly everyone. Between the academy and the mass, between the disciplines and journalism, the conditions for public circulation do not for the most part now exist.

There are of course many ways in which the effort to bring a public into being, to do world-making work in the public sphere, can go wrong. When Katha Pollitt complains that academic intellectuals postulate their own radicalness in a way that entails no risk and reduces to pseudopolitics, the strong version of her point is that the public of academic work is being misrecognized. Like most academic expertise it circulates only in a well-defined path mediated almost entirely by the university system; but it no longer understands itself this way. It seeks to overcome the separation of academic, trade, and political publics by means of its topical content rather than through its public circulation. Of course, this perfectly valid point can also be turned around. As Adorno points out, the journalistic public itself can fail to be a scene of risk or world making. When journalists denounce academics for speaking in a way that is not already familiar, they too are trying to avoid the risk of truly public circulation.

There are many academics, especially in cultural studies, who distrust the claim of journalists and mass media to represent the only relevant public and who seek public relevance in a different way. Rather than seeking fame or publicity in journalistic publics, they seek to regard all intellectuals as public intellectuals. They aspire to see their own work as politics, either in the general sense of contested culture or even in the narrower sense of having a bearing on common action and state policy. Recognizing that academic disciplines, for better or worse, create a functional gap between themselves and political publics, they wish to eschew their disciplines (many of which are in an exhausted state anyway) as the context for their writing and thinking. Yet they do so not by leaving the disciplines entirely, writing for publics and lifeworlds outside the academy, but by adapting work and career within an academic context as much as possible to a political self-understanding.

This experiment has its own dangers. Among them is a loss entailed by imitating the temporality of politics without recognizing the difference of temporality available in these two contexts for circulating discourse. Politicizing thought tends to mean adjusting it to the urgencies of the headline. Some kinds of thought, essential to politics but not captured within its terms, might require a different space of circulation. The academic disciplines have their own orientation to time, which they elaborate by means of a whole apparatus of futurity. They treat knowledge as cumulative; they require new members to master the field's history and contribute to its archives; they treat research as corrigible inquiry; they are structured by roles of apprenticeship and expertise and by a professionalism that is socially self-reproducing. Cultural studies, which arose partly from a distrust of this structure of expertise, has sometimes attempted a methodical elimination of each element in this apparatus of futurity. Yet so long as such work continues to circulate only within a metadisciplinary academic framework, its aspirations to political time remain blocked. This contradiction gives force to the objections of journalists.

Any public includes strangers, present or future. The quality of *risk* that

Pollitt finds missing in left academic theory is just this orientation to strangers and the submission of discourse to estranging paths of circulation. But that risk can happen over longer as well as shorter durations; it's just that the shorter ones are easier to recognize as politics. Orwell's diarist longs for this risk among strangers when he writes to a time when people "*are different from one another and do not live alone.*" The future scholars of a traditional discipline are also, in this limited sense, semipublic; even quite traditional scholarship is oriented to corrigibility over time by strangers. Neither address to the journalistic public nor the immediate politicization of academic publics, in other words, is the only way to take the necessary risk of publicness. World-making projects require not just intentions, nor the moralized postures that are called "having politics," but rather a set of forms that can articulate the temporality and social space of their circulation. Certainly a public practice oriented to redefining public practice is a paradoxical task, not finally dissimilar to the problem of Orwell's diarist. It is a way of imagining a speech for which there is yet no scene and a scene for which there is yet no speech.

Notes

1. George Orwell, *1984* (New York: Signet, 1981), 10.
2. Ibid.
3. Quoted by James Miller, "Is Bad Writing Necessary?" *Lingua Franca*, Dec./Jan. 2000, 44.
4. Miller, "Is Bad Writing Necessary?" 38.
5. George Orwell, "Politics and the English Language," in *A Collection of Essays*, by George Orwell (New York: Harcourt, Brace, 1981), 169.
6. Henry Thoreau, *Walden* (New York: Library of America, 1985), 580–81.
7. Theodor Adorno, *Minima Moralia: Reflections from Damaged Life*, trans. E. F. N. Jephcott (London: Verso, 1978), 101.
8. I have described this understanding of normalization at somewhat greater length in *The Trouble with Normal: Sex, Politics, and the Ethics of Queer Life* (New York: Free Press, 1999), 52–61. Some will object that I am taking liberties by attributing this understanding to Adorno, when it derives more directly from Canguilhem and Foucault. But I think much of Adorno's thought, especially in his California years, follows these lines, although he does not use the term.
9. Adorno, *Minima Moralia*, 101.
10. Judith Butler, "A 'Bad Writer' Bites Back," *New York Times*, March 20, 1999. Butler's op-ed piece responds to an earlier article by Dinitia Smith: "When Ideas Get Lost in Bad Writing," *New York Times*, Feb. 27, 1999.
11. Miller, "Is Bad Writing Necessary?" 37.
12. Theodor Adorno, "Scientific Experiences of a European Scholar in America," trans. Donald Fleming, in *The Intellectual Migration: Europe and America, 1930–1960*, ed.

Donald Fleming and Bernard Bailyn (Cambridge, Mass.: Harvard University Press, 1969), 338–70.

13. The issues enumerated in this sentence pervade Adorno's writing, but a few key texts can serve as examples in addition to *Minima Moralia*. See, e.g., *The Stars Down to Earth and Other Essays on the Irrational in Culture* (New York: Routledge, 1994); *Introduction to the Sociology of Music* (New York: Continuum, 1989); and "Freudian Theory and the Pattern of Fascist Propaganda," in *The Essential Frankfurt School Reader*, ed. Andrew Arato and Eike Gebhardt (New York: Continuum, 1987), 118–37.

14. Martha Nussbaum, "The Professor of Parody," *New Republic*, Feb. 22, 1999, 37–45.

15. See the title essay in my *Publics and Counterpublics* (New York: Zone Books, 2002).

16. Some of these different conceptions are reviewed in Edward Said, *Representations of the Intellectual* (New York: Pantheon, 1994); and in Bruce Robbins, ed., *Intellectuals: Aesthetics, Politics, Academics* (Minneapolis: University of Minnesota Press, 1990).

17. John Guillory, "Literary Critics as Intellectuals: Class Analysis and the Crisis of the Humanities," in *Rethinking Class: Literary Studies and Social Formations*, ed. Wai Chee Dimock and Michael T. Gilmore (New York: Columbia University Press, 1994), 107–49, 117.

18. This definition of a public is elaborated in my *Publics and Counterpublics*, cited above.

19. Nina Eliasoph, *Avoiding Politics: How Americans Produce Apathy in Everyday Life* (Cambridge, U.K.: Cambridge University Press, 1998).

PART 3

Modernist Poetics and Critical Badness

On Difficulty, the Avant-Garde, and
Critical Moribundity

ANY REFLECTION on the languages and the possible audiences of criticism demands an agile dialectical performance. I want neither to subscribe to dominant current practices in academic writing nor to endorse the generally mindless critique of them. I find it difficult to come to rest in any one position. I hope, then, that what follows will be read as a restless interrogation of the problem rather than a prescriptive conclusion.

One can pick up at random almost any extra-academic cultural journal and find the uncontested assumption that literary and cultural commentary produced by the academy is tendentious, politicized, jargon filled, and generally rebarbative in that it places between the reader and the beauty of the literary or artistic work an ugly and self-regarding prose. Not long ago, for instance, the *New York Times Book Review* had a piece by one Ron Rosenbaum that used a recent meeting of the Shakespeare Association of America to proclaim a reformation of criticism by way of the end of theory.[1] "Theory" in the piece is unproblematically equated with bad writing, and the sample of the latter cited by Rosenbaum—from an essay by Linda Charnes on *Hamlet*—indisputably deserves the label:

Mass culture is being increasingly "quilted," to use Lacan's term, by the *points de capiton* of what I would call the "apparitional historical." It is therefore no accident that *Hamlet* is the play to which contemporary culture most frequently returns. Hamlet-the-prince has come to stand for the dilemma of historicity itself. . . . But the subject of affective time is incommensurable with the order, and the nature, of events. This was one of Lacan's greatest insights, and one of his advances over Freud: his assertion that the true subject of the "impossible real" isn't constituted by her narrative reconstruction of her "story" but rather by the *failure* of that story to "include" its *affective* event-horizon—its epistemological starting- and end-point. As Joan Copjec has recently written about the Lacanian gaze . . .[2]

With apologies to Linda Charnes for prolonging her ordeal as victim of the day—many others could be found for the sacrificial role—one is tempted to make a *distinguo*: this is bad writing not because it is theory but because it is lazy, in-group, sloppy prose that uses allusion to deities and demi-deities of the moment and half-digested theoretical terminology—ripped from context and yoked in half-analyzed ways (see those *points de capiton* conjoined to quilting, for instance)—to make the simulacrum of an argument rather than the real thing.

There is far too much of this kind of writing produced by academics but not because it is "doing theory." On the contrary, it is prose that can't shoot straight enough to be theoretical. And post-theory and antitheory don't necessarily fare any better. Rosenbaum's diagnosis is of course hopelessly out of date; more reliable commentators will tell you we entered "post-theory" at least a decade ago, with the turn to new historicism and postcoloniality, and the same kind of prose is with us.

I want to evacuate the question of "bad writing" and leave it for what it is, bad writing, to get on to the more interesting question of difficult writing. The issue may be stated in this form: must critical writing put certain notions of common sense into question, unsettling the grammatical frame of understanding and reference by which we usually proceed? And if so, what is the relationship of this critical unmooring of common sense to the responsibility that we, as scholars, have to communicate effectively to a wider audience and to those who are not necessarily schooled in the same idiom? These queries suggest that certain ideas and arguments may need to violate standards of decorum, clarity, even grammatical and syntactical conventions, in order to convey, or rather to *do*, something new and unsettling. How can you speak the old idioms if you are trying to make a revolution? Yet, if the revolution is to be effective—reach a wider public—how can you sacrifice the common language?

This question has plagued the avant-garde since its inception. It is part of what Guillaume Apollinaire called the "long quarrel . . . of Order and Adventure."[3] Misunderstandings between the artistic and political avant-gardes have often turned on the issue of language and communicability. Political avant-gardes historically tended to want to promote the language of ordinary men, to make the linguistic sign transparent. The clear moral and political messages of melodrama, delivered in an emphatic rhetoric, suited the French revolutionaries, and it is no accident that after the Bolshevik Revolution Maxim Gorky attempted to revive melodrama as a genre: he knew it was an effective vehicle for mass communication. The artistic avant-garde, however, from Mallarmé onward, chose a hermetic language that required apprenticeship, a novitiate, if one wanted to enter the chapel.

One could argue about which form of avant-gardism has more permanently affected our cultural lives, but it is wrong simply to equate them and to assume the compatibility of their goals. And the assumption one sometimes finds among academics—that practices deconstructive of meanings-as-usual in the world work to subvert the established political and moral order of things—needs critique as well. Subversion for whom, if communication with the nonadepts is lost? And to the extent that the language of the priesthood eventually enters a more public kind of speech, circulates among the laity—witness the term *deconstruction*, which has by now become a journalistic commonplace, applied to everything from architecture to clothing—it is inevitably in a parodistic version of its original contextual meaning and force.

As someone educated when the avant-garde of high modernism still held sway, I was initiated into the belief that difficulty was a positive value in art and that the explication of that difficulty was a worthwhile enterprise. It was worthwhile first of all because unpacking, making perspicuous, and trying to understand the difficulties of a Mallarmé sonnet or Eliot's *Four Quartets* took one to what those poems were "about." They were, among other things, about the difficulty of expression in a language that needed to be made new to be faithful to the new, to the unsaid and unthought. "For last year's words belong to last year's language / And next year's words await another voice."[4] And then it was worthwhile because the explication of difficulty allowed one to exchange the understandings gained with others—they became the basis of a sharing of precious knowledge gained, incipiently the foundation of a community of understanding. (I remember that this sometimes took the form of one of the early Mike Nichols–Elaine May dialogues: "Yes, you've read . . . *Zarathustra?*" "Yes, yes. It was as if the heavens had opened.") So that exegesis was valued—in the classroom, in critical writing—not only because it appeared the royal road to understanding—of things we sensed were important to understand—but because it educated us as finer sensibilities, and indeed created that "us," as partakers in a knowledge worth having.

Northrop Frye could argue in 1957, in his "Polemical Introduction" to *Anatomy of Criticism*: "Everyone who has seriously studied literature knows that the mental process involved is as coherent and progressive as the study of science."[5] And in this belief there is more of a continuity between New Criticism and the French structuralist theories that came to contest its hegemony in American universities than is often perceived. If the notion of a "science littéraire" violated the genteel exegetical traditions of New Criticism, it nonetheless promoted what was essentially another kind of formalism. Both formalisms believed that the patient discernment of literary form and structure were steps on the way to understanding. If New Criticism believed the object of understanding was the poem itself, and structuralism preferred the genre or the overarching notion—such as "narrativity"—they were united in the faith that knowledge of literature, what it meant and how it meant—the conditions for the creation of meaning—was knowledge worth having and worth constructing a curriculum on.

To be sure, our recent culture wars were partly about a nostalgia—on the part of extra-academic cultural commentators, joined by the cultural right within the academy—for a polite, gentlemanly exegesis of great literary works, expressed in a language that didn't need much more technicity than *sestet* and *metaphor*. Whereas the public is perfectly willing to concede that the languages of the sciences—and perhaps even the social sciences—may evolve in response to the imperatives of research, produce new conceptual difficulties and even neologisms, the humanities ought to remain the realm of the true, the tested, indeed of the eternally true. Like "human nature" itself the subject matter and language of literary study and philosophy should not change. Since we humanists still write about Sophocles and Shakespeare, why need we invent new difficulties in the talk about them? Let the humanities remain the place of cultural truisms.

Nonetheless, even if we protest the terms given to the debate by the cultural right, I think we are forced to recognize a true crisis in the notion of difficulty. For one thing, it has lost its moorings in the notion of the avant-garde as a socioculturally valid group and practice and object of attention. It is not that there won't always be art that is misunderstood, that is in advance of public understanding and acceptance—although the recuperative powers of the media and of popular culture have become astonishing, and it now takes precious little time for the challenging art object to be recycled in MTV form. It is that the sociocultural form (should I now say formation?) of the avant-garde now lacks plausibility. The dynamic of the postmodern is such that the expressive media of literature and art no longer have the ability to shock and perplex, at least not in forms that drive those who would understand them—as once was the case—to patient exegesis and explication.

The modernist avant-garde produced criticism as a necessary completion of its artistic practices (Eliot's footnotes to *The Wasteland* might offer the parodic instance of this, and Nabokov's *Pale Fire* its metainstance). Put in historical perspective, the emergence of literary criticism as an autonomous field of practice and then an academic discipline more or less tracks the evolution of avant-gardes from romanticism onward. It responds to the rise of what Charles Taylor calls "the Romantic ideal of self-completion through art."[6] This is foreshortened history, of course, in that there has been criticism from Aristotle on, especially in the form of poetics, which has perhaps been especially congenial at moments of neoclassical revival, where conventions, rules of genre, the grammar from which individual utterances are forged become most evident. The need for exegetical criticism, originally associated with sacred texts demanding interpretation within the moving horizons of history, becomes most clearly marked with the rise of the difficult art of the modern, say from Baudelaire through Woolf. Creative writers themselves become critics, and they spawn exegetes. The relation of exegesis to text is essentially collaborative—by no means always harmonious but nonetheless a recognized commonality of enterprise in the reception and sharing of understandings.

The coming to America of continental "theory" in the 1970s created a new avant-garde of sorts—a genuine one, I think—and a new exegetical enterprise. Yet its fate was different because there was never a public consensus that the work in question constituted art objects whose public exegesis was important. (Witness the almost total neglect by the *New York Review of Books*, founded in the early 1960s, of the work of Lacan, Derrida, Barthes, Foucault, etc.) The need for exegetical criticism, it seems, was linked to poetry and novels. Expository prose of a challenging order could be left to take care of itself. If not immediately comprehensible, to hell with it. Meanwhile, there apparently ceased to be anything identifiable as avant-gardism in poetry and fictional prose (the French "New Novel" of the 1960s is the last example that comes to mind), although the avant-garde impulse continued to manifest itself in the visual arts, especially arts of performance. *Art Forum* for a while achieved a kind of mediatory critical function that literary journals had lost.

It is at least conceivable, then, that the present crisis of criticism derives from a lack of need for criticism in the public perception. Literary journalism of the daily and weekly sort can take care of instructing us what to read and to see and to listen to. There is no longer an imperative to look in the mirror of high art and discuss the reflections one finds there. In this sense the present crisis of critical languages, of how to write criticism, is authentically a crisis of criticism itself. One sits down to write criticism without any sure sense of the audience it might be addressed to, and thus language, tone, and even subject matter become desperately difficult to define. Over my many years as a writer of criticism I have found it increasingly difficult to know what I am writing it for. Who will publish it? Where will it be published? Who, if anyone, will read it? I can no longer harbor a conviction that anyone cares.

The situation of criticism was impressed on me recently when I wrote one of those (agonizing) letters of comparative evaluation of candidates for a professorship at a major university. All the candidates had published original, important, and readable books. Not one of these books has been reviewed in any media one would recognize as "public"—and I don't simply mean the *New York Times Book Review* but such other serious media as *New York Review of Books*, *Times Literary Supplement*, *London Review of Books*, *Los Angeles Times Book Review*, and the nearly moribund quarterlies such as *Partisan Review*. I suppose the commonsense explanation is that there are too many books being published because academic careers demand it. But it's by no means clear there has been a recent increase in publication rates in literary criticism—it has become more difficult than ever to get oneself published. What I think we really see is a failure of discrimination. It's as if the public journals had accepted the view of the cultural right and decided that all academic literary criticism is unreadable and trivial and therefore needn't be bothered with. This was, after all, the position championed by Lynne Cheney when she headed the official organization for our kinds of study, the National Endowment for the Humanities.

But if we have resigned ourselves to the situation of seeing good work go unreviewed (I don't want to be construed as saying that we should so resign ourselves—we need new journals that do serious public book reviewing), it may very well be from a certain weariness with literary criticism itself, which I think derives from a crisis in belief about its usefulness. Most of us who continue to write and publish literary criticism don't particularly enjoy reading it any more—not most of it, anyway. We continue to do so (if we do) out of a sense of duty, because we continue to think it important to learn what's new in the discourse. But most of the fun is gone, since the stakes appear to be diminished, and there isn't much sense of real dialogue about our understandings of texts and issues that matter—that matter in a way on which there is some consensus. Literary criticism gained its broadest audience at a time when literature was taking the place of religion, as a kind of secular scripture—see Wallace Stevens for an extreme statement of the case: "After one has abandoned a belief in God, poetry is the essence that takes its place as life's redemption."[7] It may prove to have been a historically delimited field.

The partisans of cultural studies may claim that they understood this some time ago and therefore have even in some academic settings replaced departments of comparative literature (for instance) with departments of cultural studies. Yes, but: if literary criticism is a dying art, in too much of cultural studies there is no art at all—no hypotheses at least as good as those of the New Critics, or Frye, or the structuralists to account for the conditions of the production of meaning in the field under study. Although recognizing that we all now do cultural studies in one form or another, and applauding the breadth this has given to our inquiries, I also recognize the truth of Geoffrey Hartman's recent strictures:

Literature is becoming less the object of literary study than of an informal sociology or politology. I say "informal" because so few who approach literature this way have actually worked in sociology or political science. They use socioeconomic categories—particularly class, gender, race and property relations—to inspect works of art as "products" of a certain form of social life, which Marx (who is being read) considered temporary or transitional. The motivation of most of these analyses is social justice, and the field established by them is what we call cultural studies. Yet where do we find, together with that social awareness, the inventiveness, playfulness, and art-centeredness of a Kenneth Burke?[8]

It is perhaps unfair, or at least premature, at this point to demand of cultural studies a full-fledged theory of practice. But in the meantime the problem is that so much of it combines a smug assumption that it is on the side of the moral and political angels with a disparate set of critical tools and concepts that never seek justification. Too often it employs a writing style that, for all its gestures toward global inclusion, proves its moral earnestness by in-group allusions. In short, it assumes virtue rather than establishing it.

The solution to all these woes recommended by Rosenbaum—and many before him—is a return to what he calls "aesthetic considerations," by which he really means a "return to questions of value: How good is this passage or play, how do we judge it better or worse than something else in Shakespeare or in the work of other dramatists?"[9] I think it strange that "value" should be evoked in this manner, as if a kind of literary stockbroking could save us—Frye warned us in that same "Polemical Introduction" about the shiftiness of such valuations in the absence of any overall sense of the structure and functions of literature and criticism. This is "aesthetics" only in a narrow and relatively trivial understanding, although one that, alas, is common.

Hartman also wants to revive aesthetics, but he has in mind something more serious, since he evokes Friedrich Schiller's concept of "aesthetic education," which he glosses as meaning "that art is taken to be a serious empirical object of study and a field encouraged to reflect on itself, on its role in human relations. . . . There is no other way to strengthen aesthetic education than to expose students to art itself and those who have written passionately and critically about it."[10] Schiller in fact saw the need for aesthetic education in nearly anthropological terms, as a development of the *Spieltrieb*, that play function that is the essence of human freedom. The aesthetic education of humankind is on this model both an end in itself and a precondition of culture as an active, transformative medium in which people mutually civilize one another and proclaim their sphere of freedom from the state. "There is no other way of making sensuous man rational except by first making him aesthetic," writes Schiller, arguing for the power of fictions to restore people to their humanity.[11]

I think the notion of "aesthetic education" is useful also because it takes us back to pedagogy. Much of the exegetical work of the New Critics, for instance, came in shortish essays that were very much like classroom exercises, and I. A. Richards's "practical criticism," indeed, began as a classroom experiment. That is, to the extent that such criticism was written, and published, it very much limned a certain pedagogical practice. It didn't seek to be an earthshaking new interpretation bound in hard covers. We have placed a premium on "original published scholarship" that leads to a certain critical hyperventilation, the promotion into books of what should not be books, and the claim to significance where one would prefer a modest elucidation.

We all know why this is so. Indeed, I find myself telling younger colleagues that only books "count" any more; articles just don't make the weight. The example of my late colleague Paul de Man, who was appointed to a professorship at Yale on the basis of one slim volume of collected essays (*Blindness and Insight*), seems to me irreproducible today. The decline in prestige of the exegetical article points to another problem: the etiolation of those journals that used to bridge the gap between the academy and a "general public," mainly the famous quarterlies. I doubt if anyone under the age of seventy turns to *Partisan Review* for its literary and cultural commentary, and if the library catalogue didn't assure me of the continued existence of *Kenyon Review* and *Hudson Review*, I would not be aware of it. *Commentary* and the *New Criterion* disqualified themselves as interpreters of culture by becoming public executioners during the culture wars. And nothing has come to take the place of these journals of mediation. (Witness the rise to prominence of *Lingua Franca*, a kind of academic *People* magazine; and even it is now defunct.) But there is perhaps no point in lamenting the decadence of the serious cultural journals since journals of any sort mainly go unread at present.

The decline of the quarterlies of course can be explained as part of a general decline of the literate print media in an age of the "frenzy of the visible," to use Jean-Louis Comolli's phrase.[12] Nonetheless, it participates as well in a loss of faith in the value of exchanged understandings about the meanings and conditions of meaning of literature. I don't think it is simply nostalgia to claim there was once a culture in which serious writers and serious readers were able to meet on the grounds of what to think about Kafka or Wallace Stevens. Now, each new book of literary and cultural criticism must be an individual performance, strenuous, original, self-inventing—and inventive, too, of an audience it hopes to shape and indeed create through its rhetoric. Some of these performances succeed remarkably—as in the work of Judith Butler. Many others simply produce a kind of hypertrophy of rhetoric and alleged significance.

Have I then argued myself into a corner where literary criticism must finally expire and be seen in historical perspective as the acolyte of modernism, rising and falling with the long passage from romanticism through to postmodernism? I think this is a distinct possibility, although not one to which I am currently willing to resign myself. I consider that the writing of literary and cultural critique is still worth the agony. This may be simply the result of years of professional deformation. But there still are grounds to believe that criticism matters. To paraphrase the French poet Paul Claudel, the world is before us like a text to be deciphered. One need not share Claudel's religious commitment to believe that the semiotics of literature and culture are crucial to understanding not only discrete messages and how they affect us but also our very composition as fiction-making animals.

Criticism may need to think more of its pedagogical nature and recreate a closer relation to classroom praxis. I know this sounds like a recipe for superior boredom. But I think most of us—meaning academics—spend a good deal of time making ourselves clear in response to student questions both intelligent and dumb, and intelligibility in response to questions, both real and imagined, is a good test of critical writing. Mikhail Bakhtin comments of Dostoevsky's characters that their "every thought . . . senses itself to be from the very beginning a *rejoinder* in an unfinalized dialogue."[13] If the agony of writing criticism makes it most often seem a deeply monologic enterprise, one can nonetheless keep the dialogic ideal in mind. A dialogic model might conduce to a certain modesty of critical tone. We have come to embrace the notion of the critic as creator, but there is plenty of evidence that the public prefers to see us in the more humble role of reader's surrogate, stand-in, go-between—which is after all the traditional and honorable role of Hermes. We might well recall Diderot's *Paradoxe sur le comédien*, which argued that the actor performs most effectively when he eschews identification with his role in favor of conceiving the performance from the point of view of the audience.

But if literary criticism is in fact a terminal case, what is to be gained from recommendations about its tone and manner? Roland Barthes wrote that "those who neglect to reread condemn themselves to reading always the same story."[14] This of course evokes a kind of mandarin practice, of the leisurely rereading and patient exegesis of texts. Yet I don't see that we have much more to offer. Nor do I think that patient rereading is a negligible enterprise, especially when the notion of text has been expanded to include all cultural discourses, manifestations, artifacts, performances. Here, in my view, the move into cultural studies has been wholly positive. Where it has lost its way is in its all too frequent abandonment of the patient practice of reading in its urge to make heady megaconceptual claims and to construe itself as the teaching of virtue. All of culture offers itself to us for critical decipherment. But the decipherment must be real, not simply a simulacrum in the service of in-group spiritual uplift.

And of course as academics we have a responsibility to work toward the reform of those university practices that have encouraged critical hypertrophy: the demand for ever more publication for hiring and tenuring, the weighing of publications by the kilo, the devaluation of the critical essay, the hyping of the modest contribution to knowledge. If the tenets of high modernism and the avant-garde no longer command allegiance, it may be time to reexamine the kind of value they assigned to individualism and originality. Reconceiving research and critical writing as a collaborative enterprise could move us toward greater dialogism. And, just for starters, I propose that the contributors to this volume persuade some combination of benefactors—perhaps a consortium of university presses along with foundations—to found a new periodical dedicated to serious critical reviews of serious critical writing. I don't see how we can move forward without that.

Notes

1. Ron Rosenbaum, "The Play's the Thing, Again," *New York Times Book Review*, Aug. 6, 2000, 12–13.
2. Linda Charnes, "We Were Never Early Modern," cited in ibid., 12.
3. Guillaume Apollinaire, "La Jolie Rousse," in *Calligrammes* (Paris: Gallimard, 1925).
4. T. S. Eliot, "Four Quartets," in *Complete Poems and Plays, 1909–1950* (New York: Harcourt Brace, 1950).
5. Northrop Frye, *Anatomy of Criticism* (Princeton, N.J.: Princeton University Press, 1957), 10–11.
6. Charles Taylor, *Sources of the Self* (Cambridge, Mass.: Harvard University Press, 1989), 409.
7. Wallace Stevens, *Opus Posthumous* (New York: Vintage Books, 1990), 185.
8. Geoffrey Hartman, *Aestheticide; or, Has Literary Study Grown Old?* Emory Humanities Lectures (Emory University, 1999), 11.
9. Rosenbaum, "Play's the Thing, Again," 13.
10. Hartman, *Aestheticide*, 4–5.
11. Friedrich Schiller, *On the Aesthetic Education of Man*, trans. and ed. Elizabeth M. Wilkinson and L. A. Willoughby (Oxford: Clarendon, 1967), 161.
12. Jean-Louis Comolli, "Machines of the Visible," in *The Cinematic Apparatus*, ed. Theresa de Lauretis and Stephen Heath (New York: St. Martin's, 1980), 122–23.
13. Mikhail Bakhtin, *Problems in Dostoevsky's Poetics*, trans. Caryl Emerson (Minneapolis: University of Minnesota Press, 1984), 32.
14. Roland Barthes, *S/Z* (Paris: Editions du Seuil, 1970), 22–23.

Difficulty in Modern Poetry and Aesthetics

THAT THE NOTORIOUS difficulty of modernist poetry could provide a critical purchase on recent debates over "difficult" academic prose might seem dubious. Or worse, the suggested relationship to poetry might prove congenial to those who overhastily assert that much of contemporary theoretical discourse in the humanities, pretending to describe sociohistorical reality, actually commits egregious crimes of genre with every line it writes: texts that would otherwise be recognized as impressively bad prose poems instead pass for something called theory (or theoretically informed analysis). That is, when liberal and left commentators have criticized the fashion for what is seen as needless obscurity or difficulty, the charge of inappropriate or adolescent literariness is often implicitly or explicitly in play. (I'll leave aside the somewhat different lines of critique found in conservative and right attacks on today's academic discourse.) And at least among liberal and left critics such charges are generally not made from a Socratic-Platonic hostility to the idea that mimesis (artistic representation) might have a right to participate in, or might have a real contribution to make toward, knowledge claims. Rather, what is expressed is an essentially Enlightenment and progressive notion that useful presentations of social, political, historical, and cultural reality should be offered in as clear and communicable a manner as possible—so that the greatest possible number of people can share in such knowledge (and so that they can, should they so decide, attempt to use that knowledge to change the world).

Poetry may be inspirational, but it's usually not been thought to provide objective, empirically verifiable facts that can be shared or transparently communicated. And ever since romanticism, the communicability even of poetry's inspiration has been questioned, precisely on the grounds of whether self-consciously difficult modern art can convey anything of consequence to a broad (and hence potentially world-changing) audience. That was already the crux of a century-long left debate before anyone had ever heard the names Althusser, Lacan, Derrida, Irigaray, Foucault, Kristeva, Benjamin, Adorno, or Žižek. It might thus prove useful, in revisiting that debate and examining its relevance to discussions of contemporary academic prose, to consider a telling literary instance that arises in a decidedly unacademic setting. Although the issue scarcely appears in the film's reception history, Martin Ritt's *Norma Rae* (1979) meditates on, and in subtle ways highlights, the meanings of poetry's difficulty, and it does so while trying to communicate broadly about socioeconomic, political, and cultural struggles. You may recall that *Norma Rae* is a fictionalized account of the effort by the Amalgamated Clothing and Textile Workers Union (ACTWU) to organize the then-largest textile manufacturer in the South, the J. P. Stevens Company. (Years after the film's release, the ACTWU merged with the International Ladies Garment Workers Union to form UNITE, the Union of Needletrade and Industrial Textile Employees.) The film's fictional protagonist, Norma Rae Webster, is a composite of several women workers who had participated in attempts to organize J. P. Stevens, most notably, Crystal Lee Sutton.[1]

One night, after she's thrown in her lot with the union and is working round the clock for its cause, Norma Rae browses through union organizer Reuben Warshowsky's volume of Dylan Thomas's poetry. She asks if Dylan Thomas is "hard to read" and—finding that Thomas *does* seem difficult to understand—asks, "Why should I bother?" Reuben casually but pointedly responds, "Maybe he has something to say to you." Their repartee furthers not only the film's leitmotif of the social import of advanced levels of literacy, of opportunities for education that for the working class have tended to go hand in hand with the conquest of some measure of industrial democracy and economic justice; the conversation also reiterates the film's earlier, insistent focus on the difficulty of understanding *words* (and, in turn, the difficulty of finding words that will communicate ideas that unquestionably need to be communicated): standing outside the plant and passing out union literature early in the action, Reuben had heard a then-uncommitted Norma Rae call out to him, after she had glanced at his proffered leaflet, "Hey, there's too many big words; if I don't understand it, they [her fellow workers] ain't gonna understand it." The next time Reuben had given the still-undecided Norma Rae a leaflet, he'd furthered the same banter and theme: "I took your advice; I think I got it down to two syllables." "One's better," she had parried. Yet finally it will be the two syllables of one word, which she's defiantly written on pasteboard and held high for all inside the plant to see—UNION—that causes the workers to stop their machines and that gets Norma Rae accosted, fired, arrested, booked, and jailed. Terminated and therefore technically no longer an employee eligible to vote for the union, Norma Rae concludes the film standing outside the factory gates with Reuben, overhearing the jubilant shouts that tell of the union's election victory by vocalizing—by *chanting*—that two-syllable word, *union*. The film then ends with Reuben's promising, at their parting, to send Norma Rae the volume of Dylan Thomas; she tells him not to bother—because she's already gone out and bought her own copy.

Now, Dylan Thomas is hardly an exemplar of modernist esotericism. On the contrary, precisely the combination of his perceived accessibility, his able reconjurations of traditional notions of bardic oracularism and lyric mellifluousness, his progressive sociopolitical stances, and, of course, his romantic hard-drinking image led to Thomas's popularity in activist trade union, left, and Marxian circles in the United Kingdom and, to a lesser extent, in the United States.[2] That's why it's so intriguing that Ritt and the film's screenwriters (Harriet Frank Jr. and Irving Ravetch), well aware of this tradition of left Thomas-reception, nonetheless make Thomas into a sign of *difficulty*. As *Norma Rae* retells a classic left-Enlightenment scenario (in this case via an encounter with Thomas's poetry), hard-won literary education or aesthetically articulated insight parallels, or somehow even contributes to, hard-won social struggle. But, significantly, the film's conclusion doesn't erase or resolve the question of why either contest (aesthetic or social) has been hard-won, which is to say that it doesn't erase the question of difficulty. For what ultimately persists is the difficulty—indeed, the seeming impossibility—of the neat integration of realms or levels of experience, thought, and action.

Having given almost everything to the organizing struggle, having been the key activist *in* that struggle, Norma Rae finally finds herself standing literally outside the struggle's central physical and material location. As the film closes, she's outside the factory grounds, banished not by a defection from class struggle to literary delectation but by the company's retaliatory action for her having voiced, written, and inspirationally communicated the union's message; as she speaks warmly of her volume of Dylan Thomas, she now—in a charged inversion of the old J. S. Mill formulation—can only "overhear" the triumphant public celebration of her fellow workers inside the plant. It would be exactly wrong to see this as what is today typically (and, far too often, facilely) stigmatized as "bourgeois, self-cultivated transcendence," wherein a literary or aesthetic "ideology" of autonomous separation supposedly trumps committed engagement with material, sociopolitical reality. Because in the most rigorous, tightly constructed manner the film has ensured from the start that the literary and the sociopolitical constantly articulate, without ever determining, each other. Neither causes the other; neither demands an escape from, or triumph over, the other. Instead, the film manages to do what critical aesthetic semblance—critical mimesis, critical artistic representation—does when it's really working: it makes the audience *feel*, as an apparent intellectual-emotional insight (parallel, here, to Norma Rae's own insight), that the aesthetic and the social necessarily comprehend, translate, or, on some ultimate level of the characters' own experience, voice one another. In that sense aesthetic experience undertakes the difficult task of making or fortifying subjects' felt capacity for transformative relationships with, and to, conceptual knowledge (and to the empirical world to which conceptual knowledge corresponds).

As usual, the issues are more than academic. I first saw *Norma Rae* at the time of its initial release, at a moment of embarking on what I'd assumed would be a permanently postliterary trajectory, one that, as it turned out, *did* occupy the better part of a decade spent in law school and as a fledgling labor lawyer. The fervent debates over *Norma Rae* (its basic authenticity; its decisions about addressing "ultimate" matters of sociopolitical causation; its chosen modalities for representing workers' at-the-machine, in-the-meeting-hall, and at-home experience, not to mention issues of race, gender, and regionalism; its overall approach to the cinematic means and relations of artistic production) that I'd avidly followed in film, art, and political journals in some ways paralleled, and in some ways split off entirely from, the astonishing reception the film enjoyed (immediately and for an impressively long time thereafter) across wide sectors of labor and in the labor movement itself. One could point to various American films that, at least as courageously and perhaps even more militantly, narrate labor's story (*Salt of the Earth* and *Harlan County, USA*, come immediately to mind, although their genre and historical differences from *Norma Rae*—their respectively semidocumentary and documentary character, along with the McCarthyite context informing *Salt of the Earth*'s production and distribution battles—distinguish them from *Norma Rae*). But quite simply, virtually no other American post-McCarthy labor film seems so effectively to have reached its intended potential audiences: namely, people currently experiencing, or likely to experience, organizing drives in their own workplaces.

The rapidity with which *Norma Rae* became a touchstone, and then the ways it sustained that status, not only within the labor movement but also for unorganized workers, was little short of remarkable. An extraordinary number of those who have worked in the labor movement, or in government agencies or independent organizations involved with labor, or in occupational safety and health and related areas, have testified to this phenomenon. Within a year of the film's release the number of workers who began explicitly referring to or riffing off the film's story and dialogue (during union campaigns, all the way to the sort of National-Labor-Relations-Board election portrayed in *Norma Rae*'s penultimate scene) was unprecedented—as, again, countless participating workers, as well as union, management, and Labor Board representatives, have noted. (I vividly recall experiencing this personally and recall hearing scores of labor-movement and Labor Board colleagues from around the country report—in a process that spanned years—about having witnessed near-identical instances of *Norma Rae* invocation, allusion, and applied interpretation, quite frequently on or near the shop floor.) Perhaps more remarkable is the fact that by all accounts this phenomenon continues today, twenty-three years after the film's release. And although Crystal Lee Sutton had vigorous disagreements with the film's portrayal of the character that was based in large part on her, it is also the case that *Norma Rae*'s long afterlife has created successive waves of interest in Sutton's biography and activism; in response Sutton has continued as a notable presence in labor struggles around the country. She was, for example, one of the keynote speakers at a June 2001 march-and-rally in Columbia, South Carolina, that was called to defend the Charleston Five. (The Charleston Five are activist members of a largely African American local union in the International Longshoremen's Association, against whom an extremely conservative South Carolina state attorney general brought Riot Act charges after a Charleston judge had refused to enjoin or otherwise curtail their picketing activities in a 1999 labor dispute.) Meanwhile, in a striking number of cases the *Norma Rae* references made by workers (and by union representatives) have involved the question of the character Norma Rae's *reading*, of the way that her burgeoning literary interest functions as a dynamic sign, so to speak, of her participation in the fight to secure some measure of a simultaneously collective and personal autonomy.

One could say that the powerfully felt significance of Norma Rae's poetry reading is a palpable, yet difficult or complicated, thing for working people to explain; but the truth is that it's an inherently difficult thing for anyone to explain. It bears emphasizing that it's not the matter of seeking to attain factual knowledge in relation to sociopolitical struggles that's so complicated; however hard certain facts may be to come by, and however complicated are the particular facts themselves, the necessity of *getting them*, and the problems caused when they're unavailable, are pretty obvious. What's more difficult to express is why people's own *aesthetic* experience can seem so dramatically to be at stake in social, political, and historical matters. Indeed, this difficulty of stating (let alone in a descriptive and accessible vocabulary and form) just how and why such things can feel like they are so inextricably related is one of the oldest conundrums of literary and aesthetic theory. The enigma is so persistent—and has been so central to politically intended art and criticism—that one begins to understand the paradox of the orthodox Marxian critic Ernst Fischer's inaugurating his most important literary-aesthetic work by quoting, with surprising and disarming approval, the emphatically uncommitted artist Jean Cocteau: "Poetry is indispensable—if

I only knew what for."[3] Well before asking the question of whether difficult *writing* might best present the difficulty of this difficult subject matter, one might observe that there has often enough been a rough consensus about the difficulty *of* the subject matter: the difficulty, that is, of understanding and articulating the aesthetic's status—as individuals and collectivities experience it—vis-à-vis the sociopolitical and the historical.

Precisely such difficulty has been theorized (from the romantic era of Kant's third *Critique* to the modernist period of Benjamin, Adorno, and the Frankfurt School—and beyond) as the central problem of modern art and aesthetic theory. Generally speaking, in these theorizations of what Kant had initially understood as a "reflective aesthetic judgment" paradoxically synonymous with estrangement and defamiliarization, the aesthetic has been grasped as the felt-as-necessary (but notoriously difficult to account for) "bridge" between nature and freedom, cognition and morality, theoretical and practical reason, fact and value. In short, the aesthetic wants to bridge objective-conceptual knowledge (or the objective world to which conceptual knowledge is meant to correspond) and the subjective human capacity for a critical agency that would be more than arbitrary in relation *to* objective knowledge of existing reality. The key notion is that aesthetic thought-experience, although feeling itself to be cast in or aiming for conceptual ("objective" or objectively oriented) thought, is not yet substantively-objectively conceptual. In proceeding via the *feeling* that it is objective (that it is keyed to judgments that could be universally shared), aesthetic thought-experience maintains the form—but only the form—of conceptual thought; this formality in relation to substantive conceptuality makes the aesthetic effectively quasi-conceptual. The inherently experimental exercise of that "formal" experience can produce, to paraphrase Kant, a wealth of thought-emotion that cannot be reduced to any determinate, presently existing substantive concept and that thus can allow for the emergence or reconfiguration of the materials for a subsequent, postaesthetic construction of *new* concepts and the sociopolitical dispensations that would correspond to them.[4]

Why do Benjamin's and Adorno's famously "difficult" Marxian restatements of such ideas so often make poetry—lyric poetry in particular—a special case within this theory or view of how art and aesthetic experience attempt the difficult task of *bridging* and the task of stretching (or stretching past) the bounds of extant concepts (of gesturing toward the construction of new concepts that would be more than instrumental but also more than arbitrary)? (Here I can only assert something that will receive full elaboration elsewhere: contrary to so much of contemporary Marxian and Marxian-inflected theory's "antiaestheticist" hostility to aesthetic experience and aesthetic judgment, Marx himself intentionally marshals the aporetic but by no means paralyzing structure of Kantian reflective aesthetic judgment precisely for the "theory of *praxis*" announced in his *Theses on Feuerbach*.) For the traditions of poetics in which Benjamin and Adorno participate, modern lyric ambition stands as a, or even *the*, high-risk enterprise, the "go-for-broke game" ["*va-banque-Spiel*"], of literary art: the lyric poem must work coherently in and with the medium—language—that human beings use to articulate objective concepts, even while the lyric explores the most subjective, nonconceptual, and ephemeral phenomena. This theoretical or philosophical difficulty, concerning how simultaneously to think objectivity and subjectivity, also arises practically as lyric's great problem of form-construction: How—with language alone as medium—to build a solid, convincing artistic structure out of something as evanescent as subjective song and how, in the bargain, to delineate or objectivate the impressively fluid contents of capitalist modernity? How, spontaneously yet rigorously, to make thought sing and to make song think? For the Frankfurt School critics, lyric dramatizes with special intensity aesthetic quasi-conceptuality's more general attempt to stretch conceptual thought proper; this special intensity arises from lyric's constitutive need musically to stretch conceptual thought's very medium, language—to stretch it quasi-conceptually all the way toward affect and song, but without relinquishing any of the rigor of conceptual intellection.[5]

Benjamin and Adorno go on to argue that high capitalist modernity and its unprecedented acceleration of the abstracting processes of commodification (the "reification" not only of objects, products, and people but of thought and language themselves), along with the concomitant "loss of aura" (the collapse into immediacy of a previously charged, critically enabling, auratic-aesthetic *distance*), require that Kantian aesthetic difficulty—the difficulty of grasping and negotiating the transition between types of knowledge and realms of experience—be supplemented. What, in a later, faster, and technologically more complex modernity, is Kantian difficulty to be supplemented with? Apparently, with a lot *more* difficulty: more difficulty within art, and within the judgment, interpretation, and criticism that art calls forth; and all this for the purpose of accurately conveying the problems bedeviling the attempt critically to cognize an increasingly opaque modernity. And as far as Benjamin and Adorno are concerned, a crucial chapter in this modern aesthetic-social history involves Charles Baudelaire's lyric poetry, where lyric's presumed condition of possibility—the availability of an auratic, reflective experience that in its turn makes possible a noninstrumental, potentially emancipatory capacity for constructing new conceptual-objective knowledge—seems to have disappeared. Hence the Frankfurt focus on Baudelaire: Baudelaire, who for his subject "ch[ooses] the modern itself"; who abjures or scorns an already-known socioliterary language, so that his "lyric poetry is a slap in the face not only to the *juste milieu* but also to all bourgeois social sentiment," yet whose "tragic, arrogant mask" of advanced technique is nonetheless—indeed, is in consequence—"truer to the masses" than conventional "'poor people's poetry'" (and this because Baudelaire's experimentalism proves capable of bringing into aesthetic experience the new historical reality unavailable to a conventional poetics, a conventional poetics effectively if unwittingly determined by reigning concepts of what social conditions are or have been).[6] The much-vaunted Frankfurt preference for modernist artworks of great complexity is the preference for a Baudelairean art still intent on risking experimental enactments of aura together with mimetic reflections on modernity's most advanced technical-productive developments. This is a preference for an art that, while refusing to give up aura's ghost (which is to say, while continuing its attempts to differentiate itself from reification and the reified communicative discourse that have tended to vitiate aura), also views productive and technological modernity as having become part of art's very materials.[7]

To say this much is to say that the Frankfurt School's reputation for difficulty (a reputation that is not the only source but is certainly *a* crucial source and touchstone in today's debates about academic prose) is best understood in relation to the Frankfurters' emphasis on the aesthetic. And although this clearly involves taking up and foregrounding self-consciously difficult artworks of the Baudelairean line—and of a properly aesthetic critical prose aiming stylistically to dramatize the defamiliarizing experience of the artworks at issue—it is not only artworks themselves that constitute the aesthetic sphere. Benjamin's and Adorno's attempts to contribute to Marxian-derived projects that seek historically, sociologically, economically, and politically to grasp capitalist modernity are always to some extent broached through an aesthetic insight that is prior to, or broader than, their experience of individual artworks or of artistic tradition more broadly. This ur-aesthetic inflection informs their criticism not merely because Benjamin and Adorno are from virtually their earliest years profoundly and preternaturally aesthetic thinkers and writers, nor does it occur because of some belief they hold in the sheer superiority of aesthetic modes of thought and presentation.

Rather, the crucial point is that Frankfurt analyses of sociohistorical phenomena tend to concern themselves with human subjects' abilities critically to take in and respond not only to the local but especially to the larger systemic situations that confront them. This capacity for reflective and potentially activating response is conceived as the possibility of an act of understanding that would proceed in a more than merely instrumental, *and* in a more than merely arbitrary, manner; that would proceed, in other words, in a manner directed toward meeting at least the minimal requirements for critical agency. In the quite Kantian tradition that those in and around the Frankfurt School generally share, the precise designation for such thought-experience (where subjectivity itself tries critically to understand its animating, quasi-conceptual relationship to concepts and objective entities like capitalist society) is *aesthetic*. An aesthetically generated or informed approach is by no means the only valid path one could or should take when examining and writing about social phenomena. But for the Frankfurt School the aesthetic *is* by definition the key modality for the investigation and enabling of *subjective*, critical human capacities to process intellectually and emotionally (and to work transformatively with) the overarching *objective* structural realities of modern society.

A number of conclusions would seem to follow. First, Frankfurt School commitments to difficulty do not imply that economics, history, sociology, political science, and the theories attendant on them (and on adjacent disciplines) should be characterized willy-nilly by difficult and/or aesthetically inflected writing. For the Frankfurt School the aesthetic's difficult modalities *can* challenge one-sided positivist analyses in which a crucial subjective element may have essentially been ignored or banished; Frankfurt studies in fact often dedicated themselves to correcting such positivist one-sidedness. But this means that there is no warrant for believing that difficult academic or theoretical writing is inherently required, advisable, or even justifiable, much less inherently progressive or revolutionary. In short, the justification for difficult writing depends on the materials the writing seeks to present and on judgments about one's intended audience for the presentation. (In that light perhaps too little attention has been paid in the United States to the ways in which members of the Frankfurt School—even those most identified with "Mandarinism"—although trying to remain faithful to the complicated concepts and theories they were developing, nonetheless attempted regularly to modulate their discursive registers and to pursue opportunities to address nonacademic audiences via the mass media, most notably, radio and newsmagazines.)[8]

Even where complex modern artworks are not the central concern, if the materials under study nonetheless contain an important aesthetic element—if the materials are in significant part composed of or oriented toward human beings' attempts subjectively to imagine their way into the assimilation and potential re-formation of concepts that correspond to objectively existing social phenomena—then modalities of aesthetic difficulty may well be called for. And if one traces the course of various Frankfurt disputes—even or especially those between Benjamin and Adorno, over technical-mechanical reproducibility and over the need simultaneously to engage the questions of aura, economic structure, and the aesthetically stimulated reconfiguration of materials for the construction of new concepts—it turns out that all those difficult dances with aesthetic subjectivity, quasi-conceptuality, and the not-yet-formed concept are meant to serve an expanded, noninstrumental notion of "objective" conceptuality and reason. This is, in effect, the project quietly hinted at in *Dialectic of Enlightenment* and more explicitly articulated in *Negative Dialectics*: an imagining of the ways in which Enlightenment conceptuality or reason might examine and critique itself and its own tendencies toward sheerly instrumentalist and identitarian thought; an imagining of the ways in which conceptuality might cease to repress those areas of experience and reality left behind after they've been conceptualized; in sum, an imagining of how scientific (or scientistic-objectivist) conceptuality might remain in dialogue with aesthetic quasi-conceptuality, with the thought mode that stands formally for the materials or areas of experience that conceptuality tends to leave behind after having intellectually "dominated" them. As I've shown at length elsewhere, Adorno's and Benjamin's debate over the latter's essay "The Paris of the Second Empire in Baudelaire"—their debate over competing versions and approaches to lyric aura—is actually a debate over the possibility of continuing to expand conceptuality beyond determinist parameters. Significantly, that debate leads Benjamin not only to write his brilliant "On Some Motifs in Baudelaire" (with its animating and fruitful tension between the disappearance of lyric aura and an artistic-critical re-posing of aura precisely in aura's wake). It also—on his own account—directly leads Benjamin to think and write a critique of linear, deterministic "progress" and its presumably unbroken "continuum of concepts," a critique that will be known as the "Theses on the Philosophy of History" [Über den Begriff der Geschichte] and that will become a key source-text for later Frankfurt efforts to understand, critique, and transform Enlightenment conceptuality and reason (from *Dialectic of Enlightenment* all the way to *Negative Dialectics*, *Aesthetic Theory*, and *The Aesthetic Dimension*).[9]

As far as Benjamin, Adorno, and their cohorts are concerned, all these ideas depend in part on a criticism that takes care to write some very precise, concrete, and crackling prose. The desideratum stems at least in part from Benjamin's theorization (which he often repeats and which Adorno constantly echoes) of the *constellation* and *force field*. Contemporary theoretical discourse rightly understands the theory and practice of the constellation as an intellectual attempt nondeterministically to identify and dynamically connect elements (historical, socioeconomic, cultural) that are not initially given as relational but that, when animated—constellated—into conjunction create or reveal a signifying force field. That force field for its part illuminates the larger social reality whose elements have been brought together in affinity and tension (rather than in a misleadingly integrative totalization) to make the force field visible. After our previous discussion it may not be surprising to recall that one of the Frankfurters' key models for understanding *how* concept-expanding constellations of critical thought are made, and for how force fields are created, is art: not least, the "go-for-broke" art of lyric poetry, with its special relationship to conceptuality's basic medium, language. And although Benjamin and Adorno emphasize the need for criticism to learn *aesthetic* lessons from lyric's manner of constructing constellations, they nonetheless inveigh against an aesthetic*ist* identification between criticism and lyric; they caution against self-deluding modalities in which the critic tries to write as if he or she were a poet working (even if dialectically-critically) with aesthetic semblance (*Schein*). From a Frankfurt perspective critical writing that invokes the concepts of the constellation and force field asks to be judged by standards as rigorous as those that Benjamin and Adorno apply to lyric poetry and other forms and genres of art.

In Benjamin's and Adorno's view artworks are to be judged by how well they accomplish their difficult constellative task of formally enacting art's determinate indeterminacy, art's exact but capacious—and sociopolitically enabling—ambiguity (a "precise ambiguity" that must be spontaneously enacted, or forged anew, with each work yet that also springs in some general way from the fact that art pushes toward an expanded conceptuality while itself remaining quasi-conceptual). Criticism likewise seeks, with a matching recourse to experiment and precision, to construct constellations of critical thought; but unlike art, criticism seeks to do this essentially without semblance. Criticism *conceptually* articulates the contributions *toward* an expanded conceptuality that art has generated *mimetically*, nondiscursively. Criticism thus follows art in open-endedly and nondeterministically constructing constellations that are in no way pregiven; but criticism's precisions finally seek to enunciate conceptually what art has, in accord with its own character, quite precisely constructed as quasi-conceptual.[10]

At any rate criticism's profoundly aesthetic dimension, which stems from its affinities with artistic practice and aesthetic theory, becomes ever more evident when one considers Benjamin's often-stated specification of what, within criticism, constellative form requires, of how and why it creates a force field (and this is a specification Adorno will time and again make his own): in writing that seeks to present constellative critical thought each sentence should point back—formally and substantively—to a constantly moving center from which that sentence has all along radiated. That's no small task; in fact, it's pretty damn near impossible, as it perhaps would figure to be, given that Benjamin develops this ideal of exact, imaginative, in-motion form largely through his formidable engagements with the formidable artists of the Baudelairean lyric countertradition. Benjamin's formulation also stands as one of the great modernist, constructivist reimaginings of that familiar old lyric-aesthetic friend whom it thereby radically reinvents: organic form. In Adorno's musical formulation such constructivist reimagining of what is still really organic form appears, in advanced modernity, as the simultaneously dissociative and structural principle of dissonant composition.[11]

This would be the moment to turn from the sketching of overviews and principles toward treatment of concrete examples from Benjamin and Adorno: toward a detailed engagement with their discussions of nineteenth- and twentieth-century poetry and the other arts, and then toward coordination of such a treatment with fuller consideration of contemporary academic prose's attempts to apply or enact Frankfurt notions of difficulty. Limitations of space unfortunately make that impossible here; and they likewise prevent me in this essay from satisfactorily taking up one of the most significant challenges that Benjamin and Adorno set for themselves and others: that criticism about aesthetic or aesthetically informed matters should immerse itself in the problems of contemporary art, including the art of poetry. For now the most minimal gestures in that direction will have to suffice and to serve as a provisional conclusion.

"Baudelaire envisaged readers to whom the reading of lyric poetry would present difficulties."[12] Benjamin took his life within two years after writing that well-known first sentence of "On Some Motifs in Baudelaire"; Adorno, for his part, spent a good portion of the next three decades trying to unpack and trace the meanings of those *difficulties* for—and in—modern art. The two short texts presented immediately below come from later moments of the history Benjamin and Adorno had been investigating; these texts are separated by almost thirty years and are authored by two of the United States' most important contemporary poets, both of whom, although they belong to different generations, are known for their filiations with experimental traditions of modern lyric (and for their more-than-passing interest in what Frankfurt School aesthetics has itself meant for post-1945 poetry). If these texts seem far from mainstream or direct styles of lyric address, they nevertheless take up the very problem that Norma Rae discovers and voices in her fraught initial encounter with the nontransparency of even a Dylan Thomas lyric. First, a passage from Barbara Guest's book-length poem *Symbiosis* (2000), a work made in collaboration with the painter Laurie Reed:

The difficult! the difficult!

                    loosen the ropes that entangle it,
          tear them down from the mast!

          The schooner off its route,

                         adios to the bird of prey,
          flies in another direction,   the nineteenth
century

          wears a plaid cap.[13]

Guest—now in her eighties—is one of the original members of the
"New York School" of poets; the New York School has, of course, been
made almost synonymous with the advent of postmodernism in American
poetry (although it is significant that Guest, often deemed the school's most
aesthetically fearless and formally uncompromising artist, is also thought of
as its most relentless *modernist*). Here, characteristically, she swings with such
grace of musical phrase and gentle backbeat that the gravity of her subject
seems to register only recursively. Playfully and exclamatorily turning *difficult*
from adjectival description into a substantive that is then itself made to signify a quality or state of being, Guest uses both sound values and the sus-
pended pause of the page's blank space to make "difficult!" virtually chime
with "entangle it." She sets the pleasing suggestions of sonic and visual affinity in intriguing tension with the perhaps paradoxical command to loosen
the bonds that entangle "the difficult." (Unentangled, will Difficulty Un-
bound prove more—or less—difficult? Will it move farther from, or closer
to us? What of the fact that the ropes entangling it seem to be made of these
verse-lines themselves?) Meanwhile, the increasingly complicated—yet increasingly mellifluous, sensually serpentine—commingling of pleasure and
problem seems to suggest a triangulation of the present moment (the contemporary perils and beckonings of song and thought) with two crucial earlier moments of history (and of literary history): Homer singing about
Odysseus's self-torturing attempt to know the Sirens' song without being fa-
tally dashed against the rocks; and the death ships' mascot-albatrosses in the
flights of Coleridgean and Baudelairean song.

    If Guest implicitly shades in the Homeric instance as the ancient or ar-
chaic foundation stone in this structure of music-and-dilemma (a structure
that yields, among other things, *musical dilemma* as both artistic and social
problem), her more charged historical gesture casts the Coleridgean and, especially, the Baudelairean instance not just as absurdly outdated ("the nineteenth / century / wears a plaid cap") but as positively archaic in their turn.
Indeed, for the nineteenth-century or Baudelairean flaneur figure, with all
its cool-culture cachet (not least in its repeated rediscovery and celebration
during the last three decades of poetics and criticism), to be pictured *now* in
a plaid cap is playfully but insistently to have the "fli[ght] in another direction" operate to make "the nineteenth / century" (whose very enjambment
conveys its being reduced to pieces of itself) *more* archaic than the *Odyssey*.
Or, perhaps more devastatingly, it is (in line with Benjamin's analysis of what

had once made Baudelaire so modern) *our* moment that is archaic and the Homeric that is modern, whereas the presumably modernist-archaic epoch of *flaneurisme* (so imbricated, in Benjamin's thinking, with the emergence of both modernism and Marxism) has become that trivial thing, the simply quaint or comically outdated: "a plaid cap." The exacting construction of syntactical indeterminacies drives home the poem's exploration of the ambiguous cross-directionality of the phenomena at issue, quite pointedly on the model of ships crossing in the night (is it that "schooner" or "the bird of prey" that actually "flies in another direction" and gives us to understand the plaid-cap nature of a nineteenth century that will apparently last just as long as postmodern celebrations of it—celebrations, that is, of a certain aesthetic-political *flaneurisme?*). In any case Guest's stripped-down but sinuous lyric, reaccessing the oldest and most troubling riddles in both poetic and sociocultural history, works from a long-standing nexus of music, meditation, and difficulty to ask again about what has changed and what is new—and about how to ask that question itself.[14]

And here is the poem "for," from Michael Palmer's 1974 volume *The Circular Gates*:

for . . .

This is difficult but not impossible: coffee
childhood; in the woods there's a bird;
its song stops you and makes you blush
and so on; it's her
small and dead behind the roses
better left alone; we wander around the park
and out of our mouths come blood and smoke
and sounds; small children and giants
young mothers and big sisters
will be walking in circles next to the water[15]

Palmer—one of the most admired poets writing today in English and a member of the Chancellors' Board of the Academy of American Poets—began to come to prominence in the early 1970s as a new voice extending aspects of the experimental lyric practice of the "San Francisco Renaissance" (most associated with Robert Duncan, to whom Palmer was extraordinarily close until Duncan's 1988 death). *The Circular Gates*, with its epigraph from one of the volume's abiding presences, the great left, modernist poet César Vallejo ("Toda la canción / cuadrada en tres silencios [All the song / quartered in three silences]"), was one of Palmer's first books.

"Coffee / childhood" is indeed "difficult but not impossible" to wrap one's mind around; the two don't tend logically or sequentially to go together. Except that they do, retrospectively: in the aftermath of thought-provoking, Madeleine-spiked cups of coffee that fuel the view back toward the past. Such retrospection here moves somewhat eerily, if not surprisingly, into nostalgia for lyric's own vulgar-modern roots; it moves, that is, to echoes of Dante's "wood" and haunted-forest birdsong and common tongue. Yet poetry's historical lyricization of birdsong also appears here as the object of critique, a self-mockery at once gentle and unsettling, as the straightforwardness of Palmer's language not only undercuts any possible divineness in this comedy but also shifts quite explicitly to the language of parody and cliché: "makes you blush / and so on"; and then, disturbingly, we pass from parody to something noirish, violent, troublingly ambiguous (is the "her" of "her / small and dead behind the roses" a girl, a woman, the bird, birdsong in modernity, institutional-cliché birdsong?). In its direct and slightly clipped and then periodically more expansive rhythms and diction the poem moves from enunciations of imagistic strangeness toward full-blooded surrealism: toward "mouths" "out of" which emerge "blood and smoke" (and, only at that point, out of which also emerge audible articulations—"sounds"); toward a pairing of "children and giants" that turns what otherwise might merely be a slightly asymmetrical coupling ("young mothers and big sisters") into a jointure that helps unfold an arresting other-logic.

Progressing through vocabularies of estrangement and parody and dissonant critique, and with an irregular start-and-stop metrics that nonetheless makes felt a coherent rhythmic expansion and contraction of thought, Palmer's almost-deadpan delivery yields weavings and phrasings that stretch from a classic surrealism to his own, remade-again language: of fable, Grimms' fairy tale, philosophical meditation, singsong nursery rhyme, Webernesque condensation. With the final line's return to an expanded length we catch up to find we've all along been treading a homeopathically artificial path, one that has, paradoxically, had us traveling backward-forward toward breath-song's circulations around nature's life source: " . . . small children and giants / young mothers and big sisters / will be walking in circles next to the water."

Much more is at work in these ten lines, and those additional elements could be felt without specialized knowledge of poetic history. But such knowledge *would* help one better describe the virtuosic formal layerings that contribute decisively to the reader's sensing of a charged and ghostly echolalia. For Palmer has pillaged and translated the majority of these lines from Rimbaud's *Les Illuminations*, adding crucial components to them, torquing them differently, and—perhaps most ambitiously—imagining and working out the sedimented form- and content-effects that will carry over or be created when he replaces Rimbaud's already modernist prose-poem passages into still-more-modern *verse lines* (in ways suggesting that, at however subterranean a level, the formal transposition or retranslation is itself crucial in order to convey not only estrangement but also song's self-renewal, melody's altered, stagger-step yet weirdly elegant reemergence from song's wake and its own self-critique). If experimental lyric's re-posing and exercising of such formal aesthetic dynamics and capacities can indeed prove "difficult but not impossible," it may also, through its work, help demonstrate—or stimulate—a critical subjectivity that asks about how to know the coordinates of a much-changed world and about how to refashion knowledge-processes themselves.[16] With such necessary, and necessarily complex, explorations, contemporary poetry rededicates itself to what an earlier stage of modernism had likewise taken from a still earlier moment of art and criticism (a still earlier moment called romanticism): a commitment to the challenge—at once aesthetic and sociopolitical—of what is difficult.

Notes

For their responses to earlier versions of this essay I am grateful to Bill Brown, Adam Casdin, Norma Cole, Jonathan Culler, Geoffrey Galt Harpham, Saree Makdisi, Jocelyn Saidenberg, Arthur Strum, Robert von Hallberg, and Alex Woloch. I am also indebted to numerous former colleagues from a different, sometimes overlapping world, including especially Robert Remar, initially of the National Labor Relations Board and, later, counsel to the International Longshore and Warehouse Workers Union, AFL-CIO; the late Maxine Auerbach, initially of the National Labor Relations Board and then counsel to numerous San Francisco Bay Area unions; Michael Eisenscher, former field organizer for the United Electrical, Radio, and Machine Workers of America; Mary Ann Massenburg, District 65, United Automobile Workers of America, AFL-CIO; and David Borgen, Coummunication Workers of America, AFL-CIO.

1. For a quick rehearsal of the film's background and the labor history it tells see Carlton Jackson, *Picking Up the Tab: The Life and Movies of Martin Ritt* (Bowling Green: Bowling Green State University Popular Press, 1994), 180–93.

2. For a useful, essentially orthodox Marxian recounting of this Thomas-and-the-left history see Victor N. Paananen, "Dylan Thomas as Social Writer: Toward a Caudwellian Reading," *Nature, Society, and Thought* 3, no. 2 (1990): 167–78.

3. Jean Cocteau, quoted in Ernst Fischer, *The Necessity of Art*, trans. Anna Bostock (1957; reprint, London: Penguin, 1963), 7.

4. For discussion see, e.g., Anthony J. Cascardi, *Consequences of Enlightenment* (Cambridge, U.K.: Cambridge University Press, 1999); Frances Ferguson, *Solitude and the Sublime: Romanticism and the Aesthetics of Individuation* (New York: Routledge, 1992); Howard Caygill, *Art of Judgment* (Oxford: Blackwell, 1989); Robert Kaufman, "Red Kant, or the Persistence of the Third *Critique* in Adorno and Jameson," *Critical Inquiry* 26, no. 4 (summer 2000): 682–724; and Robert Kaufman, "Negatively Capable Dialectics: Keats, Vendler, Adorno, and the Theory of the Avant-Garde," *Critical Inquiry* 27, no. 2 (winter 2001): 354–84.

5. See Adorno's quite Benjaminian "On Lyric Poetry and Society," in Theodor

Adorno, *Notes to Literature*, ed. Rolf Tiedemann, trans. Shierry Weber Nicholsen, 2 vols. (New York: Columbia University Press, 1991–92), 1:43, 44; "Rede über Lyrik und Gesellschaft," in Adorno, *Noten zur Literatur*, ed. Rolf Tiedemann, 4 vols. (Frankfurt am Main: Suhrkamp, 1958–74), 1:85, 87.

For more on the history and theory of Benjamin's and Adorno's approaches to lyric see Robert Kaufman, "Aura, Still," *October* 99 (winter 2002): 45–80; and Robert Kaufman, "Adorno's Social Lyric: Poetics, Aesthetics, Modernity," in *The Cambridge Companion to Adorno*, ed. Tom Huhn (Cambridge, U.K.: Cambridge University Press, forthcoming).

6. Adorno, "On Lyric Poetry and Society," 44, 45–46; "Rede über Lyrik und Gesellschaft," 87, 89–90. (Adorno here again seeks to telescope Benjamin's prodigious although largely uncompleted writings on Baudelaire into a few pages.)

7. For sustained treatment of Frankfurt School analyses of the Baudelairean countertradition in modern lyric, and for Benjamin's, Brecht's, and Adorno's surprising later indications that lyric aura might have a renewed, progressive role to play in contemporary poetry and theory (*after* lyric's apparent supervention by mechanical-technical reproduction or reproducibility), see Kaufman, "Aura, Still."

8. Although Herbert Marcuse—and the Benjamin of the mid-1930s—would be obvious instances, the case is perhaps best made by considering the most ostensibly Mandarin of the Frankfurt critics; in that light see, e.g., the May 5, 1969, interview with Adorno that appeared in *Der Spiegel* under the title "Keine Angst vor dem Elfenbeinturm," trans. Gerhard Richter (the literary critic, not the painter) under the title "Who's Afraid of the Ivory Tower? A Conversation with Theodor W. Adorno," ed. and with an introduction by Richter, *Monatashefte für Deutschsprachige Literatur und Kultur* 94, no. 1 (spring 2002): 10–23.

9. See, again, Kaufman, "Aura, Still," esp. 73–74 n. 46. For a valuable consideration of how the triangulated crises of aura, experience, and conceptuality inform an always-implicit ethical theory in Adornian and Frankfurt thought see J. M. Bernstein, *Adorno: Disenchantment and Ethics* (Cambridge, U.K.: Cambridge University Press, 2001). See also Walter Benjamin, "The Paris of the Second Empire in Baudelaire," in Walter Benjamin, *Charles Baudelaire: A Lyric Poet in the Era of High Capitalism*, trans. Harry Zohn (London: New Left Books, 1973), 9–106; and Walter Benjamin, "On Some Motifs in Baudelaire," in Walter Benjamin, *Illuminations: Essays and Reflections*, ed. and introduced by Hannah Arendt, trans. Harry Zohn (New York: Schocken, 1969), 155–200, 217–51; Walter Benjamin, "Das Paris des Second Empire bei Baudelaire" and "Über einige Motive bei Baudelaire," in Walter Benjamin, *Gesammelte Schriften*, prepared with the cooperation of Theodor W. Adorno and Gershom Scholem, ed. Rolf Tiedemann and Hermann Schweppenhäuser, 7 vols. in 14 individual vols., plus 3 supplement vols., (Frankfurt: Suhrkamp, 1972–99), 1.2:431–654. Most of these texts are likewise found in Walter Benjamin, *Illuminationen: Ausgewählte Schriften* (Frankfurt: Suhrkamp, 1961); see also Walter Benjamin, *Charles Baudelaire: Ein Lyriker im Zeitalter des Hochkapitalismus. Zwei Fragmente*, ed. and with an afterword by Rolf Tiedemann (Frankfurt: Suhrkamp, 1969). See also Theodor Adorno and Walter Benjamin, *Briefwechsel, 1928–1940*, ed. Henri Lonitz (Frankfurt: Suhrkamp, 1994), 138 ff., 364 ff., and 388 ff.; in English, *The Complete Correspondence, 1928–1940*, ed.

Henri Lonitz, trans. Nicholas Walker (Cambridge, Mass.: Harvard University Press, 1999), 104 ff., 280 ff., and 298 ff. Finally, see Walter Benjamin, "Theses on the Philosophy of History," in *Illuminations*, 253–64; "Über den Begriff der Geschichte," *Gesammelte Schriften* 1:693–704.

10. For a simultaneously comprehensive and succinct meditation on these ideas about constellative form in critical writing—and for an identification of Benjamin as the greatest theorist and practitioner of such writing—see Theodor Adorno, "The Essay as Form," *Notes to Literature* 1 (1991): 3–23; "Der Essay als Form," *Noten zur Literatur* 1 (1998): 9–49.

11. For an extended discussion see Kaufman, "Aura, Still," esp. 74–79.

12. Benjamin, "On Some Motifs in Baudelaire," 155; ["Baudelaire hat mit Lesern gerchnet, die die Lektüre von lyrik vor Schwierigkeiten stellst"], "Über einige Motive bei Baudelaire," *Gesammelte Schriften* 1.2:607.

13. Barbara Guest and Laurie Reid, *Symbiosis* (Berkeley, Calif.: Kelsey St. Press, 2000), n.p. Guest's recent work also includes the Adorno-invoking *Rocks on a Platter: Notes on Literature* (Hanover, N.H.: Wesleyan University Press, 1999); and *If So, Tell Me* (London: Reality Street Editions, 1999); see also her *Stripped Tales* (Berkeley, Calif.: Kelsey St. Press, 1995); and *Quill, Solitary, APPARITION* (Sausalito, Calif.: Post-Apollo Press, 1996). These and other volumes of Guest's poetry have been published by smaller presses whose books may sometimes prove difficult to find. I should therefore add that most of Guest's work—and that of other poets often associated with experimental traditions—is available through the (nonprofit) Small Press Distribution, the leading such distributor in the United States, at 1341 Seventh Street, Berkeley, CA 94710, (510) 524-1668 or (800) 869-7553, fax (510) 524-0852, orders@spdbooks.org, http://www.spdbooks.org.

14. For more specific treatment of Guest's relationship to the early and continuing reception of Frankfurt School aesthetics in the United States see Robert Kaufman, "A Future for Modernism: Barbara Guest's Recent Poetry," *American Poetry Review* 29, no. 4 (July/Aug. 2000): 11–16.

15. Michael Palmer, "for . . . ," in "The Brown Book" section of Palmer, *The Circular Gates* (Los Angeles: Black Sparrow Press, 1974), 13.

16. For some of Palmer's more recent work see *At Passages* (New York: New Directions, 1995); *The Lion Bridge: Selected Poems 1972–1995* (New York: New Directions, 1998); *The Promises of Glass* (New York: New Directions, 2000), and *Codes Appearing: Poems 1979–1988* (New York: New Directions, 2001). For an example of Palmer's thoughts on the dialogues between Frankfurt aesthetics and contemporary poetry see his "Some Notes on Shelley, Poetics, and the Present," *Sulfur*, no. 33 (1993): 273–81, an essay that might best be read in relation to his *Sun* (San Francisco: North Point Press, 1988) and *At Passages*. For a very helpful discussion of Palmer see David Levi Strauss, "Aporia and Amnesia," review of Palmer's *At Passages*, in *The Nation*, Dec. 23, 1996, 26–29.

Bad Writing

Le Mal—une forme aigüe du Mal—dont elle [la littérature] est l'expression, a
pour nous, je crois, la valeur souveraine.

—Georges Bataille, *La Littérature et le Mal*

The canyons cooled. Indigo darkened,
Oozing out of the earth like ectoplasm,
A huge snake heaping out. "This is evil,"
You said. "This is real evil."

—Ted Hughes, "The Badlands"

IN 1963 ANNE SEXTON composed an elegy for Sylvia Plath called
"Sylvia's Death," in which she wrote, "and I know at the news of your
death, / a terrible taste for it, like salt."[1] This elegy is unusual in that it expresses not loss but sexual jealousy. Sylvia's death has awakened an over-
whelming appetite and envy, a terrible taste.

Critics have often accused Anne Sexton of terrible taste, putting unseemly parts of the female body on display and lusting after death self-
indulgently, even to the point of feeling robbed personally when someone
else commits suicide. But lyric poetry has always been obsessed with death,
and I would argue that in seeing Sexton as all symptom and all body, readers have missed her inventive exploration of more technical questions of
lyric voice. For when she calls Sylvia's death "an old belonging," something
one's mouth opens onto, she is talking about the way in which death's terrible taste has filled poets' mouths for a long time, like salt.

The fact that the history of lyric poetry is so bound up with the nature
of elegy has created the impression that the lyric was invented to overcome
death, not desire it. Poetry, in this view, acts as a consolation, a monument, a
promise of immortality beyond the grave. Yet even the most traditional elegy
contains the guilty secret that desire is not all for life, that poetry offers
something other than life as object of desire. From Narcissus, in love with an
image, and Apollo or Petrarch, consoling themselves with a laurel branch, to
Keats's "half in love with easeful death," Milton's *Lycidas*, or Wordsworth's

"Lucy" poems, the mourned person provides an occasion for poetic performance, not just loss. From there to Sexton's "Wanting to Die" the distance
is not as great as some would have it.

But the conflation of the desire for writing with the desire for death does
not perfectly flow from the fact that both are desires for something other
than biological life. It is true that Narcissus dies from loving an image, but
the critical theory of the "Death of the Author" was not about literal death
but about interpretation and authorial intention. Indeed, it is precisely in the
case of an author who has committed suicide that readers who normally restrict their interest to features internal to a text develop a terrible taste for
biography as a tool for understanding poetry. Readers are unable to resist
asking the poems to tell us why the poet killed herself. The dead author returns to life with a vengeance as the site of an intention to die.

There are two profound taboos threatened when the poet is a woman.
There is something monstrous by definition when a woman chooses death
over life because she has so often been the guardian of the life forces, associated with reproduction, comfort, other-directedness, and maternal care.
When a woman writes about bodies that matter and yet can be accused in
any way of being a "bad mother" or even of being something other than a
counterpart to a man, she is violating the very conditions of her visibility
and is much more likely to be seen as a "bad writer" than to participate in
the culturally valued badness that poetry's job is to hold up to the laws of the
marketplace—or of reproduction.

The cultural prestige of "Le Mal" probably reached its height with
Baudelaire's 1857 publication of *Les Fleurs du Mal*. "Le Mal" is notoriously
hard to translate into English. Is it "evil"? "badness"? "sickness" ["à
Théophile Gautier, je dédie ces fleurs maladives"]? "suffering"? "melancholy" [spleen]? "romanticism" [Mal du siècle]? But sardonic delight in
thumbing one's nose at bourgeois "virtue" was de rigueur for postrevolu-
tionary French poetry. Rimbaud's mother, for example, forbade her son to
read the unseemly writings of "M. Hugot [sic],"[2] and parents threatened to
withdraw their children from their English class when it was learned that the
mild-mannered M. Mallarmé had published poetry.[3] It is perhaps surprising
that the Second Empire courts took literally Baudelaire's poetic celebrations
of evil and prosecuted him for them. But it is even more surprising how surprised he seemed by this. The rise of the bourgeoisie in France was particularly gender divided: women stood for virtue, men for badness of every
sort—so much so that Baudelaire could exemplify his badness through les-
bianism but could disqualify women completely as readers of his book.

Something of Baudelaire's "badness" is lost, I think, when it is translated
by Mallarmé into obscurity alone. Baudelaire explained in an unfinished
draft of a preface that "[f]amous poets had long divided up the most flowery

realms of poetry. I thought it would be pleasant, and enjoyable precisely to the extent that the task was difficult, to extract *beauty* from *le Mal*."[4] This is a defense of difficulty, too, but not in the same sense as Mallarmé's "I say: a flower! and . . . musically arises . . . that which is absent in all bouquets."[5] Contemporary defenses of difficult writing have gone in the direction of Mallarmé's obscurity rather than Baudelaire's evil. The "death of the author," in fact, is prefigured in Mallarmé's famous statement, "The pure work implies the speaking disappearance of the poet, who yields initiative to words."[6] But this is a death without a corpse, without decay, without worms, without *vers*. Mallarmé makes of death a principle of structure so far-reaching that it took the whole twentieth century to understand it. Nevertheless, while making death infiltrate every aspect of signification, Mallarmé is also in some way repressing it, and repressing the badness that no principle can eliminate.

That badness returns, paradoxically, not in the defenses but in the attacks on "bad writing" that have often accompanied obscurity. A sense of such contests at the end of the nineteenth century can be gleaned from Mallarmé's testy defense in his essay "Mystery in Letters":

De pures prérogatives seraient, cette fois, à la merci des bas farceurs.

Tout écrit, extérieurement à son trésor, doit, par égard envers ceux dont il emprunte, après tout, pour un objet autre, le langage, présenter, avec les mots, un sens même indifférent: on gagne de détourner l'oisif, charmé que rien ne l'y concerne, à première vue.

Salut, exact, de part et d'autre—

Si, tout de même, n'inquiétait je ne sais quel miroitement, en dessous, peu séparable de la surface concédée à la rétine—il attire le soupçon: les malins, entre le public, réclamant de couper court, opinent, avec sérieux, que, juste, la teneur est inintelligible.

Malheur ridiculement à qui tombe sous le coup, il est enveloppé dans une plaisanterie immense et médiocre: ainsi toujours—pas tant, peut-être, que ne sévit avec ensemble et excès, maintenant, le fléau.

Il doit y avoir quelque chose d'occulte au fond de tous, je crois décidément à quelque chose d'abscons, signifiant fermé et caché, qui habite le commun: car, sitôt cette masse jetée vers quelque trace que c'est une réalité, existant, par exemple, sur une feuille de papier, dans tel écrit—pas en soi—cela qui est obscur: elle s'agite, ouragan jaloux d'attribuer les ténèbres à quoi que ce soit, profusément, flagramment.

Sa crédulité vis-à-vis de plusieurs qui la soulagent, en faisant affaire, bondit à l'excès: et le suppôt d'Ombre, d'eux désigné, ne placera un mot, dorénavant, qu'avec un secouement que ç'ait été elle, l'énigme, elle ne tranche, par un coup d'éventail de ses jupes: "Comprends pas!"—l'innocent annonçât-il se moucher.[7]

I have permitted myself this extensive quotation because I think it touches on most of the things that come up when one tries to defend obscurity: the division between the crowd and the writer, the crowd's refusal to think there could be obscurity inside everyone, the scapegoating of anyone who suggests otherwise and the paranoid vigilance about it, the accusation that incomprehensible writing is the cause of incomprehension. But the real mystery is why "I don't understand it" should condemn the *author* rather than the *reader* or, at least, as Mallarmé goes on to say, should not amount to a suspension of judgment:

Je sais, de fait, qu'ils se poussent en scène et assument, à la parade, eux, la posture humiliante; puisque arguer d'obscurité—ou, nul ne saisira s'ils ne saisissent et ils ne saisissent pas—implique un renoncement antérieur à juger.[8]

It has become commonplace to allow difficult or transgressive writing to *authors* but not to *critics*. Poetic badness and critical obscurity seem very different, but the condemnation of any writer for obscurity is itself colored with moral indignation. "Don't understand!" becomes an accusation. When what was initially condemned enters into the canon, we can smile with superiority at Rimbaud's mother or Baudelaire's and be amazed at their blindness to poetic genius. Yet in the very act of inventing obscure poetry Mallarmé invented the "poème critique." In other words, it was when he realized that the writer and the reader could no longer be disentangled that Mallarmé became Mallarmé.

The taint of moral unseemliness does not last forever, but literature nevertheless keeps enough of that initial *frisson* to give literary studies a somewhat bad conscience. As Peter Brooks put it: "We teachers of literature have little hard information to impart, we're not even sure what we teach, and we have something of a bad conscience about the whole business."[9] Brooks's remarks come in the context of a defense of studying literature as a specific object. It was written for a fascinating compilation of reports and responses published in 1995 as *Comparative Literature in the Age of Multiculturalism*, in which it is suggested that literature be considered "one discursive practice among many others."[10] Comparative literature, it seems, threatens to dissolve into "cultural studies," seen as the triumph of, as Baudelaire would put it, "bonnes actions" over "beau langage." In fact, none of these slippery slopes are unavoidable, but the best way to make sure that literature doesn't dissolve is precisely to keep that "bad conscience."

Comparative literature as a field seems to need to defend itself against the Scylla of "theory" and the Charybdis of "translation." Although many writers recognize the necessary and irreversible changes each has contributed to the field, they lament the day when comparative literature meant reading several languages and literary traditions in the original. Yet their guilt about "elitism" or "Eurocentrism" leads them to overlook some obvious defenses that no one calls up. They mount, with increasing feebleness, what might be called a "Protestant" defense of multiple languages: it is hard to learn a language; therefore, students who learn more than one have to make more effort and be more talented. Here is how Harry Levin, author of the first report in 1965, put it: "If we profess to cover more ground than our sister departments we should honestly acknowledge that we must work harder, nor should we incur their suspicion by offering short-cuts."[11] This is true only to the extent that languages can only be learned in school. The decline of language teaching therefore makes this way of learning languages even harder. But instead of merely failing to teach languages, the public school system actually *discourages* the use of any language other than English. Education consists, then, of *unlearning* languages, not learning them. Before becoming an elite capable of mastering several languages, children must first pass into the elite of people who speak only English. The number of languages spoken in American homes is everything a dream of multiculturalism could ask for: it is not an idea; it is a reality. If comparative literature could tap into *that* multiculturalism, however, it would tap into the true obscurities and insolubilities of a world that cannot be studied as an object. Every comparatist would already be a part of it.

The "good" object, multiculturalism, would present all the dilemmas of the modern world that its idealization—the "It's a small world after all" refrain—represses. But the "bad" objects, theory and translation, are actually two versions of the same unrepression. It is not just that theory involved a mad impetus to translation but that the theory that transformed literary studies utterly transformed the practice of translation. Translating Derrida or Lacan became an art in itself, and respect for specific effects sometimes became so great that more and more words were left in the original and glossed. Thus, more and more French, Greek, or German words began to have currency in theoretical discourse, which, in turn, increased the anger of beginning readers frustrated at what felt like unnecessary impotence to the point that they felt like slamming down the book, snarling something like, "Take your *Nachträglichkeit* and shove it!"

In 1959 it was still possible to write, as did a translator of Hegel's *Encyclopedia*:

To translate the world's worst stylist literally, sentence by sentence, is possible—it has been done—but it is perfectly pointless; the translation, then, is every bit as unintelligible as the original. But the world's worst stylist is, alas, also one of the world's greatest thinkers, certainly the most important for us in this twentieth century. In the whole history of philosophy there is no other single work that can hold a candle to his *Logic*; a work incomparable in its range, depth, clarity of thought, and beauty of composition—but it must be decoded.

The attempt must be risked, therefore, to rescue its grandeur from its abstruse linguistic chaos. . . . This is like detective work: what Hegel means, but hides under a dead heap of abstractions, must be guessed at and ferreted out. I have dared to translate—not the ponderous Hegelian jargon, which is as little German as it would be

English—but the thought. My "translation," then, is a critical presentation or rendition; it is not a book about Hegel because it faithfully follows the order and sequence of his paragraphs.[12]

After the theory revolution it is no longer possible so serenely to separate style from thinking, idea from language, thought from jargon. The understanding that thought is not separable from its expression—and in that way sometimes escapes the control of the author himself—is what deconstruction found within the structuralism that claimed a panoptic view of meaning making. "As little German as it would be English" indicates that the original is worth translating precisely because it is foreign to its *own* language. When Mallarmé contributed a series of his "poèmes critiques" without translation to W. H. Henley's journal the *National Observer*, a letter from a reader protested that he was ready to accept the anomaly in order to brush up on his French but that Mallarmé was writing in a language that was "as little French as it would have been English."[13] Poetry, for Mallarmé, was that which "de plusieurs vocables refait un mot total, neuf, *étranger à la langue*."[14] For Walter Benjamin, too, translation was "only a somewhat provisional way of coming to grips with the foreignness of languages."[15] Only through translation does the work's foreignness to *its own* language become apparent.

If deconstruction is what is often meant by "theory," whether for good or ill, no one could insist more on going back to the original language than Jacques Derrida. His essay on Plato discovers in the word *pharmakon* an undecidability that all translators—and therefore all Platonisms—have assumed was a decidability. The divide between *poison* and *remedy* happens *in translation*. It is not, however, that such inadequate translations could be avoided if one stayed with the original. It is that an actual history, shaped by a decision that the translators could not choose not to make, makes the original perceptible as resisting it. As Derrida tells his Japanese translator, "The question of deconstruction is also through and through *the* question of translation."[16]

The worry about translation is, of course, always a worry about *bad* translation ("the inaccurate transmission of an inessential content," as Benjamin puts it).[17] But the suspicion is that what is essential about a literary work is precisely what is *always* lost in translation, which is why so many poets have been so intent on *finding* it. That is perhaps why both Baudelaire and Mallarmé wanted to translate the quintessential bad poet of American literature, Edgar Allan Poe. And this takes us back to the badness of literature.

Sometime ago, when I came across a reference to one of my colleagues in the *Boston Globe* as a professor of "comparable literature" (Oct. 20, 2000, B4), I realized that the field itself is oddly named. Why *isn't* it called "comparable literature" in fact? Doesn't the classic version of the field assume that you can take, say, romanticism, and compare its French, German, and English ver-

sions, which are presumed to be comparable? What does "comparative literature" really mean? That what is studied is comparatively (but not absolutely)
literary? Perhaps—but could this have been the original intent? The field
that depends on comparison for its very definition somehow at the same
time opposes some sort of resistance to comparability. Just enough to echo
the irony in the story of Elena Levin explaining to someone why her hus-
band, Harry, author of the 1965 report, was busy working: "The Professors
are here to compare the literatures." It is as if the field defined by comparison unconsciously upholds the adage, "*Comparaison n'est pas raison*," or agrees
with William Blake when, in his poem *Jerusalem*, he has his hero, Los, howl:
"I must Create a System, or be enslav'd by another Mans; / I will not Reason & Compare: my business is to Create."[18]

In order to explore this odd resistance to comparison, I turn to three
more texts that each embody some form of "bad writing": popular culture,
philosophy, and teaching manuals. My three texts are the 1995 film *Clueless*,
H. Vaihinger's book *The Philosophy of "As If"* (first published in German in
1911), and Andrew Boyd's *Life's Little Deconstruction Book* (billed by the publisher as "Po-Mo to Go").

In the film *Clueless*[19] the exclamation "As if!" is used by the protagonist,
fifteen-year-old Beverly Hills high school student Cher Horowitz, to project the frame of reference of other persons into pure fantasy—theirs—and
to expel it from herself. For example, when an unprepossessing high school
boy approaches Cher in an interested manner, she says, "Ew! Get away from
me! *As if!*" In other words, "*As if* I would go out with you!" "In your
dreams!" "You wish!" When another boy, Elton, reveals that he is interested
in *her*, not in the new girl, Tai, with whom she has been trying to fix him up
(this is one of the few places where Jane Austen's *Emma* is recognizable as a
source), Cher exclaims "Me? *As if!* Don't you mean Tai?" In other words,
"*As if* I had been flirting with you for myself!" "*As if* I had been the object
rather than the subject!" Another example: when Cher reports that her
teacher has said that her arguments are unresearched, unstructured, and un-
convincing, she exclaims, "*As if!*"—which I guess means, "Who is *he* to say
such a thing?"

The Beverly Hills high school dialect in the film thus makes use of the
expression *as if* in an interpersonal sense. It is always an exclamation and always casts desire or doubt away from the speaker and onto the addressee. I
don't have time to do a reading of the film as a rhetorical treatise, but as a
study of substitution, transformation (the makeover), and the narcissism of
small differences, it would lend itself very well to such treatment.

For Hans Vaihinger *as if* is an essential mental function enabling people to
use fictions "as if" they were true: religions, philosophies, even mathematical
constructs. As he writes in the preface to the English edition, "An idea

whose theoretical untruth or incorrectness, and therewith its falsity, is admitted, is not for that reason practically valueless and useless; for such an idea, in spite of its theoretical nullity, may have great practical importance."[20] Kant's *Ding an sich*, for example, which can't be proven, is a necessary part of his philosophical system, just as imaginary numbers operate as a necessary part of a system of calculations, even though, in the end, they don't exist.

Life's Little Deconstruction Book is organized as a series of maxims.[21] There are 365 of them—one for every day of the year (I'm not sure what the reader is supposed to do during Leap Year). Maxim 33 reads: "Be as if." I guess that must mean something like, "Ontology is performance" or "Whatever you seem to have in your mind *is* your mind." Or, as Pascal might have put it, "Act *as if* you believe, and belief will follow, or at least, you will have gained everything that you would have gained by believing."

Teaching theory I come up again and again unexpectedly against the problem of belief. In literature I can suspend disbelief, but in theory I feel as if my location with respect to other writers and thinkers is somehow the stuff of the course. Because the writers I am teaching have designs on the most fundamental assumptions I make while I read, I cannot teach them as if they were a subject matter. At the same time, my own relation to the writers has changed over time, and it has changed with respect to that of my students. What is different about teaching theory for me now is the sense of my own historicity. Yet if I look at the theory I teach exclusively from the outside, I am not teaching theory but history. There would certainly be usefulness in teaching the history of theory, but it would not give access to the "Aha!" that ignites an interest in theory in the first place. When Frantz Fanon says about his reaction to Sartre's reading of Aimé Césaire's poetics of Negritude, "I needed *not* to think I was just a minor term in a dialectic," he is saying, in effect, I needed to read *as if* I believed in the Negritude I now take a distance from, in order to get to the next stage in my thinking. *As if* is something that cannot happen right if it happens in the mode of *as if*.

I have found that the way in which students dismiss or take distance from the texts we read in a theory course follows patterns that are quite different from critiques. And that perhaps was true of my own dismissals of their predecessors. But my task is to make sure the students actually *read* whatever is on the syllabus—which may now include some of those predecessors I am reading for the first time. "Bracketing the referent" or "preferring *langue* to *parole*" are important ways of seeing the limitations of Saussure, but they help only in understanding what Saussure *didn't* do, not what he *did* do—not what those limits *enabled* but only what they prevented. Understanding the conceptual breakthrough involved in saying, "In language there are only differences," depends on pausing there long enough (recall Cher's reaction to stop signs—"I totally paused") to see *what Saussure was critiquing himself.* Thought as a *break* is different from thought as a *chain.*

The same is true for elements of a theory—say, female sexuality in Freud—from which one knows one has taken a critical distance, or elements in a theory—say, ethnocentrism in Lévi-Strauss—where one may be critical of a framework of which one is nevertheless still a part. What has been called "political correctness" is something I would prefer to call "double consciousness"—the knowledge that one is viewed, not just viewing. W. E. B Du Bois defined double consciousness, famously, as "the sense of always looking at one's self through the eyes of others, of measuring one's soul by the tape of a world."[22] The strength of those "others" produces double consciousness. But how can white double consciousness or male double consciousness or Eurocentric double consciousness be anything but reactive and defensive, if the power of those "others" is itself what consciousness was defined against? Double consciousness would feel a lot like paranoia. No wonder people might attempt to eradicate it. But in this case, as they say, even paranoids have real enemies. Or perhaps we should say, denying paranoia doesn't make those "real others" go away. What does the necessity of double consciousness have to do with the question of teaching *as if* one believed?

The dangers of representativeness and tokenism are precisely the dangers of losing the "foreignness" of texts to their *own* languages. But to fear such a danger is to forget that what should happen in literature courses is *reading.* Yes, the changes might reflect an unquestioned notion of individualism. And yes, the students will not see that from which a syllabus is departing. But surely the students have imbibed cultural assumptions that will be defamiliarized by some of the texts. Perhaps the use of tokens or of islands of knowledge in a sea of ignorance can homogenize all differences into various versions of the same. But even when something like colonialism attempted to reproduce itself in, say, the Caribbean, it became something quite different from what it started out to be. At the same time, how could a syllabus mark radical change within a culture—and an educational system—that changes much more slowly? If the remedy mirrors the system being questioned rather than the questioning, at least the cognitive dissonance that these contradictory energies embody may correspond to a real conflict in the world rather than the wishful thinking that would seek a more effective critique.

Actually taking seriously the works being read has to become transformative eventually because what is secondary revision for one generation may become primary process for the next. The very transferential process that tends to absolutize the authority of a text (as if it had always been on the syllabus) will deabsolutize the assumptions that are still operative in the teachers who have put those books on the syllabus. On the one hand, if the map isn't being changed in the primary process of thinking, changing it in a secondary revision is not really *thought*. But on the other hand, acting *as if* the map were changing might actually make it so, in the long run.

How does the structure of the *as if* function, then, to allow for a heuristic transference and for a transformative double consciousness at once, even though these two processes draw on the contradictory energies of belief, critique, and defense? Let me end with a quotation from Joan Copjec's book *Read My Desire*, in which a structure she actually designates as "as if" is understood through, and clarifies, the Lacanian notion of *suture*:

Suture, in brief, supplies the logic of a paradoxical function whereby a supplementary element is *added* to the series of signifiers in order to mark the *lack* of a signifier that could close the set. The endless slide of signifiers (hence deferral of sense) is brought to a halt and allowed to function "as if" it were a closed set through the inclusion of an element that acknowledges the impossibility of closure. The very designation of the limit is constitutive of the group, the reality the signifiers come to represent, though the group, or the reality, can no longer be thought to be entirely representable.[23]

What I want to claim here is that the role of academic literary criticism—which is academic precisely because it acknowledges the existence of multiple languages—is always to risk a certain "badness" and to be this suture. It is the field whose only definition is to be the acknowledgment of the impossibility of the field, to be the "as if" of literary closure. Criticism, in other words, is what is *added* to the series of literary signifiers in order to mark the *lack* of a signifier that could close the set. It marks not the *future* of literary studies but the *suture* of literary studies. That is the best way we have of relying on the badness of strangers.

Notes

My first epigraph and much of the framework for this part of my essay are taken from the brilliant article by Deborah Jenson, "Gender and the Aesthetic of 'le Mal': Louise Ackermann's Poésies philosophiques, 1871," in *Nineteenth-Century French Studies* 23 (1994–95): 175–93. ["Evil—an acute form of Evil—of which literature is the expression, has I think supreme value for us."]

1. Anne Sexton, *The Complete Poems* (Boston: Houghton Mifflin, 1981), 126.

2. Arthur Rimbaud, *Oeuvres* (Paris: Garnier, 1960), 357.

3. Gordon Millan, *Mallarmé: A Throw of the Dice* (London: Secker and Warburg, 1994), 144.

4. Charles Baudelaire, *Oeuvres completes*, ed. Claude Pichois, vol. 1 (Paris: Gallimard, 1975), 181.

5. Stéphane Mallarmé, *Oeuvres complètes* (Paris: Gallimard, 1945), 368.

6. Ibid., 366.

7. Ibid., 382–83.

[Pure prerogatives would be, this time, at the mercy of low jokers.

Every piece of writing, outside of its treasure, must, toward those from whom it borrows, after all, for a different object, language, present, with words, a sense even indifferent: one gains by not attracting the idler, charmed that nothing there concerns him, at first sight.

Each side gets exactly what it wants—

If, nevertheless, anxiety is stirred by I don't know what shadowy reflection hardly separable from the surface available to the retina—it attracts suspicion: the pundits among the public, averring that this has to be stopped, opine, with due *gravitas*, that, truly, the tenor is unintelligible.

Ridiculously cursed is he who is caught up in this, enveloped by an immense and mediocre joke: it was ever thus—but perhaps not with the intensity with which the plague now extends its ravages.

There must be something occult deep inside everyone, decidedly I believe in something opaque, a signifier sealed and hidden, that inhabits common man: for, as soon as the masses throw themselves toward some trace that has its reality, for example, on a piece of paper, it's in the writing—not in oneself—that there is something obscure: they stir crazily like a hurricane, jealous to attribute darkness to anything, profusely, flagrantly.

Their credulity, fostered by those who reassure it and market it, is suddenly startled: and the agent of darkness, singled out by them, can't say a single word thenceforth, without, a shrug indicating that it's just that enigma again, being cut off, with a flourish of skirts: "Don't understand!"—the poor author innocently announcing, perhaps, that he needed to blow his nose.]

8. Mallarmé, *Oeuvres complètes*, 383. [I know, in fact, that they crowd the stage and expose themselves, actually, in a humiliating posture; since to argue that something is obscure—or, no one will get it if they don't, and they don't—implies a prior suspension of judgment.]

9. Peter Brooks, "Must We Apologize?" in *Comparative Literature in the Age of Multiculturalism*, ed. Charles Bernheimer (Baltimore, Md.: Johns Hopkins University Press, 1995), 105.

10. The Bernheimer Report, 1993; reprinted in Bernheimer, *Comparative Literature*, 42.

11. The Levin Report, 1965; reprinted in Bernheimer, *Comparative Literature*, 25.

12. *Hegel's Encyclopedia of Philosophy*, trans. and annot. by Gustav Emil Mueller (New York: Philosophical Library, 1959), 1.

13. One letter to the editor read as follows: "SIR,—I will not, like your 'Constant Subscriber' of last week, protest against all foreign languages. I can read some of them myself, and have relations who can read others. But I shall take it very kindly if the next time M. Stéphane Mallarmé occupies your columns, you kindly append a French translation of his article, or what in Decadish might be called 'une française traduction.' I am, yours resignedly, ONE WHO USED TO THINK HE COULD READ FRENCH" (*National Observer*, April 9, 1892, 540).

14. Mallarmé, "Crise de vers," in *Oeuvres complètes*, 368 (my emphasis).

15. Walter Benjamin, *Selected Writings*, ed. Marcus Bullock and Michael W. Jennings, vol. 1 (Cambridge, Mass.: Belknap Press, 1996), 257.

16. "Letter to a Japanese Friend," in *A Derrida Reader: Between the Blinds*, ed. Peggy Kamuf (New York: Columbia University Press, 1991), 270.

17. Benjamin, *Selected Writings*, 253.

18. William Blake, *The Poetry and Prose of William Blake*, ed. David V. Erdman (New York: Doubleday, 1965), 151.

19. Writ. and dir. by Amy Heckerling, prod. and dist. by Paramount Pictures, starring Alicia Silverstone as Cher Horowitz.

20. Hans Vaihinger, *The Philosophy of "As If,"* trans. C. K. Cohen (London: Routledge and Kegan Paul, 1924), viii.

21. Andrew Boyd, *Life's Little Deconstruction Book* (New York: Norton, 1999).

22. W. E. B. Du Bois, *The Souls of Black Folk* (New York: Penguin, 1989), 5.

23. Joan Copjec, *Read My Desire* (Cambridge, Mass.: MIT Press, 1994), 174–75.

PART 4

Address to the Other: Ethics and Acknowledgment

The Morality of Form; or, What's "Bad"
About "Bad Writing"?

SEVERAL YEARS AGO Edward Said delivered a series of lectures at my institution. He was introduced by the late Ian Watt. I remember Watt's introduction well but even more Said's response. Watt told the audience that of all the critics writing at the time he most appreciated Said because of the clarity and lucidity of his writing, which Watt attributed to an English education. I must not have been the only one in the audience who held their breath in anticipation of what Said, having grown up under British occupation, could possibly say. What he did say was both gracious and to the point. He thanked Watt for the introduction and then added, "But you know, Ian, some of us learned English in different ways—some of us were caned if we didn't speak English correctly."

I use this anecdote because it addresses not only the issue of writing and the value attached to clarity (however ascertained) but also the intensely social aspect of the current discussion of academic writing. It is to that notion of sociability that I will turn for my emphasis. As Ian Watt had been instrumental in establishing a regard for the humanities at Stanford, and was the founder of its humanities center, there was something very significant about his welcoming Said. What Watt chose to emphasize as a point of commonality, of sociability, was a discourse that allowed him to imagine Said as part of a particular fraternity. Watt's pronouncement indicated that he and Said were brothers, not only in the English language but also in a particular usage of it within specific intellectual protocols. For Watt this bond transcended the particularities of how they each came to write English. But for Said such an affinity could not so easily erase historical specificity, a specificity that challenged the notion of a seamless social bond produced by a common language and a shared sensitivity about its proper use.

Debates over language ("national language," bilingual education, ebonics, and so forth) are never about language alone or even primarily. Rather, such arguments point to the social functions of linguistic communication and the assumptions of sociality that are to be at once vouchsafed and reproduced by communication. These issues have everything to do with the social positioning of the practitioners of language—the actual speakers and writers themselves and the extralinguistic situations that englobe acts of communication, that is, the arenas in which words circulate and are recognized, responded to, or rebuffed. The most significant issue behind the flurry of activity that has surrounded the controversy over "bad writing" is the issue of sociability and the attendant matter of social responsibility.

The issue of responsibility is located in two related areas: first is the concern that what is deemed "bad writing" is bad because its authors allegedly set themselves up as progressive political thinkers, whereas in actuality they write in such an obscure and difficult manner as to make access to such political thinking impossible for more than a handful of initiates.[1] Alongside the issue of how "bad writing" might be, despite its assumptions and claims, unpolitical, there is the issue of its application in a certain domain—that of the academy, specifically, the classroom. The issue of bad writing is deeply linked to a pedagogical program constructed around a particular vision of an academic community. In both cases "bad writers" are chastised for their moral dereliction.

To make this charge stick, however, requires the establishment of norms and propriety. An intellectual community is construed that is populated by a specific group of individuals whose norms and capacities guide the production of discourse. If norms supposedly have been broken, contracts voided, responsibilities dodged, then we need to first assume the existence of a "common person" whose level of intelligence or discernment would be used to adjudicate the proper form of language, the degree to which language should conform to its social contract. From a conglomerate of such individuals one posits an ideal community in order to arrive at some sense of what the most acceptable degree of transparency would be or how much complexity, nuance, indirection could be tolerated in social discourse.[2]

Here one discovers an affinity between the notion of "bad" writing and what one might call "deviant" writing, that is, writing that departs from presumed norms and threatens by its example to lead others to reproduce not only that sort of writing but a bad sort of behavior as well. Such language and behavior challenge the norms, the grounds for sense making, truth asserting, and rational discussion in the community. From early rhetorical debates between the Atticists and Asiaticists there has been a specific concern over the manners in which "unplain" language might persuade (indeed, seduce) listeners better than "plain" language and convince them to do bad things. Unplain language is assumed by its critics to be not only less than transparent but also untrue by virtue of its opacity.[3] The assumption on the part of those arguing against "bad writing" is that it irresponsibly and immorally beguiles its readers into taking on its own behavior and norms, into becoming complicit with its own reproduction. Furthermore, these norms are at a significant remove from anything that might be construed as not only true but honestly arrived at as well. Critics of "bad writing" remark on a double loss—the loss of a social world in which "truth," to which they held the keys, no longer takes the same linguistic form, no longer is configured in the terms most familiar to them, and the loss of the power to enforce those norms and by consequence to discipline those who dare to write deviantly.

Thus, "bad writing" presents more than simply a spiritual loss, a loss of kindred community. The present attack on "bad writing" is a multifaceted attack that goes beyond its disappointingly ad hominem facet to an assertion regarding the types of scholarship central to today's academy and the ways in which such scholarship and its conventions seem to have deprived its critics not only of voice but of a place to be. It has taken away an entire topos, a situation of speech and sociality in which their kind of behavior is not only sanctioned but required. If, in the fifth century B.C., Corax, the person to whom the "invention" of rhetoric is attributed, elaborated rhetorical skills in order to help people regain their property after the expulsion of the tyrants and to maintain social order, here we find a battle over language that differently enlists a particular set of rhetorical devices centered on a particular notion of "clarity" and its absolute value to secure intellectual property and rights.[4] The similarity between these two otherwise quite different cases is that in each a particular kind of language/writing is seen as proper to the task of normalizing social relations and the power to claim property. In the academy it is a matter of making sure that the correct modes of expression and argumentation are in use, and in use to secure and convey a particularly configured notion of not only truth but ways of knowing the truth.

For "good writing" now to become urgently necessary requires three interrelated elements: first, the instantiation of a normative community whose reproduction is essential; second, a viable threat to that community and its values; and third, a particular realization of this threat. Here, the threat is manifested in a figure at once inside and outside of the community. This figure occupies this double status because although it has certain claims to membership within the community, it is not a full or equal member. This figure is, precisely, that of a student. "Good" academics are needed to deliver knowledge properly to the bereft figure of the average student in need of proper guidance. Without this particularly imagined, abject object of instruction, we would not need academic writers. To argue a disease and a patient is to legitimize the presence of the physician. To substantiate the existence of this abject figure, critics of bad writing go to some lengths to construct a scenario of powerlessness and fear, of subjection and contempt.

Most important, along with this contempt for readers/students comes a contempt for academic responsibility. D. G. Meyers, one of the editors of the journal that awards the prize in "Bad Writing," asserts that "bad writing" expresses a "contempt for readers" and "not so much a lack of concern for clarity" as a "lack of concern for *clarification*." This distinction is important, for it focuses our attention not on a value but on a pedagogical process. Bad writers should even "take pains" to make themselves clear.[5] According to this critique bad writers are bad because they refuse to honor the contractual obligation all academic writers have with their readers and all teachers have with their students.[6]

The rhetoric of Meyers's sentence snowballs from an abrogation of "responsibility," a dereliction of "duty," and, indeed, the evasion of the "pain" necessary for writers and teachers to fulfill their contract: this community is invented not only by the pleasure of learning but also by a constitutive pain. The assumption is that writers and teachers are to absorb the pain of difficulty in order to spare the reader and student. The proposition is that the scene of reading and learning should have a precisely delimited ratio of difficulty (if it need be difficult at all). But such a notion of obligatory self-sacrifice is again premised on a particular notion of the character and identity of the members of the community—the very individuals whose pain and pleasure, capacity and willingness to understand and to clarify, is presumed to be uniform and discernible. It is also premised on the proposition that learning should not hurt. Meaningfulness must thus be delivered in a particular fashion that clearly delineates a product to be consumed in ways that are similar to the consumption of all such products, that is, in ways that do not unwarrantedly challenge the consumer beyond a certain point.

Hence, Martha Nussbaum argues that academic writers "assume the responsibility of advancing a definite interpretation."[7] Using Judith Butler as her example, Nussbaum states: "[Butler's writing] bullies the reader into granting that, since one cannot figure out what is going on, there must be something significant going on." This argument is weak in two regards: first, it again constructs a "straw-student," a gullible, weak, and unintelligent individual, to represent the victim of bad writing. Second, it assumes the absence of any redeeming pedagogical value. But one could easily argue against the assertion that "bad writing" is "bad" because it lacks determinacy. Rather than deliver a predigested commodity for absorption by an innocent student body, one could imagine that "bad writing" is a provocation to think outside received categories and that "indeterminateness" is exactly what prompts critical inquiry and further speculation. Yet I doubt that the critics of bad writing would argue with this point. Rather what would likely result again would be an argument about the proper degree of difficulty. And, again, that is an abysmal argument, which calls for a stable and clear calibration of the ratio between requisite clarity and acceptable difficulty.

But although one might respond to such criticism by arguing that a new set of concerns and problems now calls for different discursive strategies, and that new forms of linguistic expression have to at least be entertained (if not accepted outright) in order to make possible the representation of new problems, this is not really the point of the controversy. Although there is the need to debate the issue of whether the production of new knowledge calls for a commensurate change in the way we write, as I read and reread the various position papers in this debate, what seems most irksome to critics of "bad writing" is not its existence but rather its supposed predominance. My own suspicion is that on this count those who worry about the dominance of "bad writing" have little to worry about, especially if the issue is the "common person," whose intelligence has to be protected from the tortuous meanderings of bad academic writers. The vast portion of news venues around the world that covered "the story" sided with the critics of bad writing, and hardly any of its defenders were cited at all. The basis for this attack on "bad writing" therefore seems faulty and its moral charge less than persuasive simply because it is not an absolute critique (bad writing is bad) but rather relative and qualified (there is *too much* of it). The issue thus becomes a purely political one. The criticism of bad writing has less to do with lofty moral issues than with social practice and power. Students are to be cured of their ignorance, but equally important for the critics of "bad writing" is the reproduction of healthy bodies, not only to legitimate their own endeavors but to add to their numbers. By casting themselves as the parents and guardians of the next generation, the critics of bad writing attempt to achieve the moral high ground and at once assure that the right kind of reproduction, of the right social world, will be continued.

The critics of "bad writing" are concerned that it persuades a particularly constructed audience to become themselves bad writers. Says Deborah Knight, one of the judges for the "Bad Writing" award: "The *real* risk is that students will be exposed and start writing like this, thinking they ought to [emphasis added]."[8] What is needed, then, is the reinstantiation of the proper community created by "common" language and behavior—what would be more horrible than the production of another sort of community? The issue ultimately is not the degree of difficulty and pain imposed on the reader/student, or even the need for Truth, but another quantitative issue— the *number* of practitioners of bad writing and their likely proliferation and domination over those who envision another sort of community. That is, if all this fuss were about a couple of isolated writers, why would it matter? What indeed emerges from this diagnosis of a few instances is an entire so-

ciology of domineering types and personalities that are necessary to substantiate and give weight and durability to this phenomenon.

For example, we have Nussbaum's imputation of an "air of in-group
knowingness" in Butler's prose, and Robert E. Clark's "Letter to the Editor"
in the *New York Times* (March 27, 1999), which accuses bad writers of play-
ing "a self-perpetuating and insular game . . . speaking only to and for their
colleagues." Meyers elaborates on this to name an entire renegade "community" at odds with all the usual standards of academic communalism: "Academic writing wasn't supposed to be this way. Even at its most stylistically
awkward it was supposed to seek truth. Instead, what we have in academic
writing nowadays is the circulation of authority—the replacement of the
ideals of scholarship and academic community with the principle of a political party."

And it is here that we can disentangle the accusation of "bad writing" as
irresponsible socially and professionally from the much more relevant charge
of its being "bad" because it is partisan. But even partisanship in itself is not
necessarily bad. The issue is not power (academics has of course always been
involved with power: its acquisition, loss, trade-offs, various sites, and inter-
relations) nor the mechanisms that perpetuate it (for example, who cites
whom, who sits on which nominations or awards committees) but rather
that the *wrong kind of people* have it—*bad* people. Meyers writes, "Although
Butler wishes to disrupt 'the workings of capitalism,' the effect of her writing is exactly the opposite. Its effect is to safeguard the power and privilege
of academic capitalists—among whom she is one of the great robber
barons." As titillating as this sounds, this "discovery" of a conspiracy, this
Manichean schematization, is hardly new; in fact, it is as old as the academy
itself.

In *The Sociological Imagination* C. Wright Mills argues the need to understand better the phenomenon of academic "cliques":

> If we are to understand what is going on in any area of cultural and intellectual
> work, we must understand its immediate social context. . . . The whole business of
> "cliques" and "personalities" and "schools" is . . . complicated . . . ; their importance
> in shaping the development of social sciences deserves more awareness on our part.
> . . . The function of the academic clique is not only to regulate the competition, but
> to set the terms of competition and to assign rewards for work done in accordance
> with these terms at any given time.[9]

Most germane for my discussion here is Mills's comment on the reproduction of cliques:

> [I]f there is competition among several cliques in a field of study, the relative posi-
> tions of the several competitors tend to determine clique strategies. Cliques that are
> small and considered unimportant can in due course be expected by leading cliques

to go out of business. Their members will be ignored or won over or rejected, and in the end die off without having trained the next generation. It must always be kept in mind that one important function of cliques is the shaping of the next academic generation.[10]

Meyers herself finally drops the whole issue of writing and discloses the real agenda behind the granting of the "award":

The problem, finally, is not that academic writing is "ugly" and "stylistically awful." It's rather that bad academic writing conceals the political reality of the contemporary university. No longer defined by the common attachment to ordinary rational principles, our universities have become institutions of one-party rule. . . . Young scholars must toe the party line in their writing—and pay a protection fee to the party bosses in the form of quoting them.

The very vagueness of the notion of "ordinary rational principles" and the openness of such a notion to precisely partisan debate forces us to focus instead on the issue of dominance. The issue is not bad writing itself, or even the badness of the people who write badly, but rather the assumed monopoly of authority in place in academia and its effect on "young scholars," that is, the production of new generations along the wrong axis of power. But, again, if this is the real issue, it falls seriously short of being anything worth spending much ink on. This is true for two reasons. First, there is, again, no proof that this is actually the case. Apart from some anecdotal evidence, we have no other data with which to support the assertion that "our" (!) universities have become "institutions of one-party rule." But even if this were so, it would behoove Meyers to prove which party, exactly, is in power. The second reason why this argument falls short is that, as mentioned previously, universities have long been exposed for not being exempt from deeply personal battles over authority and the loyalty of students—such battles belie any claim of "ordinary rational principles" holding sway over individual or group egos. For instance, the judges of the Bad Writing Contest claim that it "exposes the workings of entrenched power" and in so doing seeks to liberate all those docile and intimidated students held under the gun by bad writers. Yet what would happen if "they" succeeded in doing so? They simply would have rooted out the enemy and established themselves as the new party. The debates over "bad writing" may thus be seen within a tradition of internecine academic institutional battles over influence—here the critics of bad writing have taken up the gauntlet supposedly laid down by bad writers. Whether the gauntlet was ever thrown is hardly the issue—it provided a pretext on which to launch a more general attack against a largely invented opposition.

When examined on its basic claims, the critique of "bad writing" discloses a vacuous argument and tremendous bad faith. But, beyond that, there are important issues attached. Returning to my beginning anecdote: although there is something quite poignant and real about the sense of value placed on the intellectual community evoked by Ian Watt, one wonders what has been relegated outside the margins. Is it a community vouchsafed by its common pursuit of "the truth"? Not exactly, because critics of bad writing appropriately make the qualification that the real issue is the method that is to be deployed to not only pursue the truth but to deliver it. Is it indeed a community with common standards that might appear positively and independently from an opposing party? So far, no positive evidence has been proffered. We have no way to identify good writing and, in fact, no real way to determine what, exactly, "bad writing" is, outside of appeals to a still unspecified normative reader. The threat posed to this community by "bad writing" is that truth and the proper pedagogical methods of conveying it are under attack. This is a serious charge, but there is no evidence that this is actually taking place outside the imagined topoi invented by Nussbaum and others, at least not as pervasively and deeply as they assert.

Having now questioned the "clarity" and substance of such a schematization, can we entertain instead a much more nuanced, and perhaps more real, picture? Can we imagine that "good writers" can be bad teachers or that their wonderfully clear ideas are intellectually weak? Can we imagine that "bad writers" may be good teachers, that their style of presentation is not incomprehensible to a differently imagined "implied audience"? Can we imagine that "bad writers" (or any writers, for that matter) write, teach, and speak in different registers for different occasions and to suit different purposes and audiences? And can one imagine students who are not simply cowardly, docile, narrow-minded careerists? In this case we would have to imagine a much more complex and, again, real, world in which we live, that is, a series of topoi that break up the simplistic formula invented by critics of bad writing and open the windows of their rather claustrophobic scene.

In doing so, we might imagine a different sort of implied reader, one who would be looking to a text for a serious challenge to pre-existing ways of thinking, a challenge that might require different and indeed difficult modes of articulation and reading. This reader might be part of an open-ended community-in-the-making that arises not to reproduce a pre-existing community, but rather evolves around an unpredictable set of common interests and concerns stimulated by the reading of the text. In such a case sociability is not reduced to a program of academic reproduction and power grabbing but widened to accommodate a broader spectrum of endeavors that are more in keeping with a difficult, nonconclusive critical inquiry into the possibilities of knowledge. In such a case, would it not be possible to argue that it is precisely "bad writing" that is ethical? For in refusing to bind itself immediately to "determinacy," does it not allow the reader a real freedom of association and the power to think differently?

Notes

Many thanks to Jonathan Culler for his helpful suggestions regarding this essay.

1. Interestingly, in an article published in the May 25, 1918, issue of Il Grido del Popolo, Gramsci cautions against assuming that political language has in all cases to be "easy":

> Let us admit that the article in Il Grido was the ultimate in difficulty and proletarian obscurity. Could we have written it otherwise? It was a reply to an article in *La Stampa*, and the *Stampa* piece had used a precise philosophical language which was neither a superfluity nor an affectation, since every current of thought has its particular language and vocabulary. Our reply needed to stay on the same ground as our opponent's thought, we needed to show that even with, indeed because of that current of thought . . . the collaborationist line was wrong. In order to be *easy* we would have had to falsify and impoverish a debate which hinged on concepts of the utmost importance, on the most fundamental and precious substance of our spirit. Doing that is not being easy; it amounts to fraud, like the wine merchant who passes off coloured water as Barolo or Lambrusco. A concept which is difficult in itself cannot be made easy when it is expressed without becoming vulgarized. And pretending that this vulgarization is still the same concept is to act like trivial demagogues, tricksters in logic and propaganda. (Cited in *Gramsci: Cultural Writings*, ed. David Forgacs and Geoffrey Nowell-Smith, trans. William Boelhower [Cambridge, Mass.: Harvard University Press, 1991], 32)

2. For some useful essays on the subject of communities, speech, and deliberation see Seyla Benhabib, ed., *Democracy and Difference: Contesting the Boundaries of the Political* (Princeton, N.J.: Princeton University Press, 1996), esp. the contributions of Habermas, Mansbridge, Benhabib, Young, Mouffe, and Gutman.

3. One should not forget, however, that the most apparently transparent discourse may be precisely the most devious, as it exploits certain notions of common parlance to obscure its actual content—which president of the United States was called "The Great Communicator," after all?

In book 5 of the *Confessions* Augustine makes a similar point: "In your wonderful, secret way, my God, you had already taught me that a statement is not necessarily true because it is wrapped in fine language or false because it is awkwardly expressed. . . . You had already taught me this lesson and the converse truth, that an assertion is not necessarily true because it is badly expressed or false because it is finely spoken" (Saint Augustine, *Confessions* [London: Penguin, 1961], 97).

Consider also Judith Butler's statement: "No doubt, scholars in the humanities should be able to clarify how their work informs and illuminates everyday life. Equally, however, such scholars are obliged to question common sense, interrogate its tacit presumptions and provoke new ways of looking at a familiar world. Many quite nefarious ideologies pass for common sense" (*New York Times*, March 20, 1999, op-ed).

4. This assertion is found in Aristotle, *Rhetorica*, trans. John Henry Freese, Loeb Classical Library, vol. 193 (Cambridge, Mass.: Harvard University Press, 1975), xii–xiii.

5. D. G. Meyers, "Bad Writing: Judith Butler Did It," *Weekly Standard*, May 10, 1999 (Lexis-Nexis). All references to Meyers are to this article.

6. Interestingly, the reader's obligation to read carefully and consideredly is omitted from these accounts.

7. Martha Nussbaum, "The Professor of Parody," *New Republic*, Feb. 2, 1999 (Electronic Library).

8. Quoted in Tom Spears, "A Contest No One Wants to Win: 'Loopy' Academic Prose Vies for Top Honors," *Ottawa Citizen*, Feb. 9, 1999 (Lexis-Nexis).

9. C. Wright Mills, *The Sociological Imagination* (New York: Oxford University Press, 1959), 107.

10. Ibid., 109.

The Politics of the Production
of Knowledge

An Interview with Gayatri Chakravorty Spivak

STUART J. MURRAY: Let us begin with the general question of communicability and critical writing.[1]

GAYATRI CHAKRAVORTY SPIVAK: In a recent interview I was trying to talk to the general American book buyer.[2] This is what I said about communicability and critical writing, answering a question about my book, *A Critique of Postcolonial Reason*: I think I have learned something from this big book, and that it is perhaps not fair to the reader to go from one end of the spectrum to another.

There will be a question later about my work in Asia, so that is one end of the spectrum, and Columbia University in New York is the other end of the spectrum. But I also go very much from high theory to activist discourse in my book.

If the general reader wants to approach the book, Chapter Three, which is on history, might be the place to begin. The point is not to be turned off too quickly. If it seems wordy at times, move right along. We skim when we read long books, don't we? Even in Chapter One, which is a little daunting for people because it is about philosophy, if one moves on deciding not to be turned off by the fact that I include German words because the translations are not always satisfactory, there is an argument which is not just for philosophers, but for the general reader who hasn't decided that where his or her understanding stops, elitism begins.

I would really like to challenge and invite the general reader to move through this as if it were not a difficult book, even though I say that I do go here perhaps too violently from one end to the other. But I think the experiment is worth making. I don't think a little self-doubt is bad. That's how

I myself read when I read a complicated text or even popularized science, or when I read philosophy, even when I read Aristotle with my negligible Classical Greek. It's not easy and I feel daunted. I do feel self-doubt. It's like going to the gym for me. Have you seen the people who are really trying at those machines—groaning, but pushing? No pain, no gain? We know that in terms of the body. Why have we forgotten that in terms of the mind? A little bit of pain is not bad. Of course, one will never really understand everything of anything. It's a challenge and an invitation to the general reader not to be turned off. The argument is not hard. It requires a little imaginative charity, but I believe there *is* something when you've finished all those pages.

There is some degree of shared assumptions in a so-called public language, but nonetheless, we all know that the *exact* thing is not getting communicated to each and every one. The general law of communication is that it's never a straight line—it's always a curved one. Given this, what am I going to do? Am I going to engage an ever more general reader, lower my sights, so that I can speak to this person? No, I'm going to be as precise as I can be; I'm going to assume a reader who is going to take the trouble to find out what it is I'm speaking about.

The critical must reemphasize the counterintuitive. In the essay that I've written for *What's Left of Theory?* I try to show how Marx is actually pushing the counterintuitive—because that's what you teach, after all, that which is not exactly already understood by everyone.[3] When we're trying to make it accessible, we are constantly running interference.

We are not *obliged* to question common sense, we are not *obliged* to question grammar, we are not *obliged* to question language, but if we are obliged to do so in order to make a point, we ought to have the freedom to do so and to count on a reader who is interested enough to see why. There is a perfect example in someone having ridiculed me for putting a hyphen inside the word *geo-graphy*. Of course, that person was absolutely unsympathetic to the fact that by doing such a thing—such an "uncommonsensical" thing, even though it is a common word—I was asking the reader (who happened to be a man) to understand that I was talking about the fact that when we look at a map, we are looking at stuff that has been—literally!—written, written on, an imagined surface of the earth. My argument was about the disappearance of the aboriginal. It was a pretty serious gesture, putting that hyphen there, but this guy was so fixated on the fact that I had done such an outlandish thing that he couldn't see that there was a reason why.

So, to repeat, it is not *necessary* that we question grammar, or question common sense, or question language, but if we do so, I think that the question of writing, the question of the politics of writing, the politics of the production of knowledge, must be kept separate from the question of difficulty. It's not the same question. I quite often find that people criticize me for writing in this confused way and then take *that* as a dismissal of everything I want to say. That's my objection. My objection is not that one has to be difficult. My objection is that *if* one has to be difficult or if one *is* difficult—and has a style that is perhaps not always easy to handle for the reader—that should be kept separate from the question of the validity of the production of knowledge. It's not identical.

There is a further point I wish to make—and again I'm speaking personally here—I have tried over the years to make my language clearer. I believe my language *is* clearer now, but I assure you, it is not easier to understand. In fact, it may be more difficult to understand, because the simple words seem to be easy, and they're not. The question of difficulty is much more complicated and much more layered and nuanced than one would imagine. I don't think that it's necessary to meddle with "ordinary language," but *if* it is necessary to do so, one must have the confidence in the readership to see what the point of it is and that the question of the politics of the production of knowledge should be kept separate from—only related to—the question of the difficulty of language.

SJM: So, by having such a confidence in your readership, and by refusing to level-down your language—"lower your sights"—are you ensuring the curvature of language, throwing your reader a "curve ball" now and then?

GCS: No, I'm just saying that the law of curvature is the general law of communication. Whatever you say, to whomever, alone, or in crowds, it's common sense that the words are not going to convey some unified meaning from me to you the way in which we copy a file from one diskette to another. There is no question that one is subject to that law; and in fact we try and try to turn that law into a straight line; that is the effort. But one has to remember that at the end of the day one is subject to that law of curvature, which is an iron-clad law; we cannot break it up.

But that was not my main point. My main point was about the fact that one must be allowed to be counterintuitive, that in critical writing or when we're teaching anything, it *is* counter*intuitive; otherwise we're just repeating what the other person already knows. And I'm suggesting that the question of the politics of the production of knowledge must be kept separate from— although it's related to, it's not identical with—the clarity of the speech or prose. Finally, I'm saying that a seemingly clear prose is not, by that token, easier to understand.

There's another problem that people have, and, generally, South Asians have come forth with this one; and that's that I don't seem to be writing about Kant writing about colonialism and that I seem to focus instead on the place where Kant is *not* writing about that. Well, if they took a moment to read—and the reader's role with difficult writing is *transactional*—they would see that that is exactly the point I am making. If one were to look at expressed sentiments, and there are many noble sentiments about *cosmopolitheia* and perpetual peace and so on in Kant, there has been a lot of criticism but also a lot of much deserved applause for such arguments; but in fact for me what is more interesting is the rhetoric of the moment where, in his central philosophical writings, he comes to a central philosophical moment, and therefore I focus there. This is the signature of a literary critic, not an intellectual historian. In fact, a literary critic, by training, focuses on those kinds of moments where a truth is betrayed.

And so by the same token I'm taken to task for not being an Indianist. But I'm not interested in being an Indianist. I'm not even interested in being a kind of refurbished Orientalist who believes that the essence of knowledge is knowledge about knowledge. That's not my problem. In fact, I am a Europeanist who believes that the study of European materials is done best when the wider picture is taken into account. So, indeed, if one goes into the genealogy of this particular objection, one will see that it began the moment I was invited to theorize the work of the subaltern studies group.

At that time I described the preoccupation with subaltern consciousness as a strategic use of essentialism. I think, in hindsight, that it was not such a strategic use of essentialism but simply an assumption that there was such a consciousness. It was at that moment that this particular piece of criticism, that I am not an Indianist, had its origin. To go back to that initial occasion, one of the things that the leader of the collective asked me, in a rather intransigent way, was, could I make a revolution with what I was saying—as Mahasweta Devi could make a revolution with what she was writing. That was in 1986, I believe. I was at that time new to the Indian intellectual scene because I had gone away and had not come back to teach in India until 1987. Today I think I have been enough involved in the subcontinental scene to say that in the current context—in today's globalized world, without the East-West divide—it is much more likely that the kind of educational involvement with a part of the largest sector of the electorate that I have will bring about a revolution of another model than any kind of nationalist strategy.

In fact I had a conversation with Mahasweta Devi, maybe just a month ago. Having secured a good deal of money from the United Nations development fund (which of course, since 1989, is completely uncritical of the transnationalist scene), she said to me: "I want to give to these tribals what will last, like schools and roads." And I looked at her, and I said, look, I want to give them something that will last also, which is to say, in the very long run, changed minds, so that they will not need to be patronized by aid. And I must say that she is such a sympathetic and intelligent woman, that when I was working in the villages, there came a letter from her acknowledging that, indeed, people do not understand what it is that I am doing with my time and skill. So, to that particular criticism, originally from that disingenuous question—can you make a revolution with your work?—I would now answer differently. At that time I had given an honest answer—I am a literary critic; that is my trade—and that has been misunderstood in order to produce a lot of contempt for what I do; but I believe, sixteen years later, I can say that I now answer that question differently.

That comes at a bit of an angle to the question of difficulty, but it certainly is relevant to the question of a wider audience. I am interested not in oral history, but I am interested in providing the kind of education one gives here to extremely opulent students—in terms of quality—I'm interested in providing *that* sort of education for the vastly disenfranchised. I've been teaching for thirty-eight years. My effort in a corner of rural India is now thirteen years old. I hope I remain alive to have one of the students from these aboriginal schools, after a university education, tell me: Gayatri, your writing is too difficult. I am waiting for that day; I am waiting to have such criticism honestly directed at me from one of them. That criticism—I'll wear it like a crown! I cannot take it seriously when people talk to me about "wider audiences," when this comes from the lazy or reactionary parts of the academy or from the person who would like to use words like *activist*, etc., when all they mean is me, my group.

One's wider audience is a choice. If I wrote a book in Bengali about Marx, that would be a wider audience choice. The wider audience choice is not just simply to banalize or make less precise one's argument for lazier or more reactionary academics. As I've said before, difficulty starts where one's own understanding stops, where there's no attempt at wanting to exercise one's own critical capacity.

SJM: I wonder about writing politics back into difficulty in some sense, because if the "choice" to be lazy or reactionary is not a political choice per se, does it not have political implications?

GCS: Yes, but difficulty as such is not a goal, and by that very token the avoidance of difficulty at all costs is nonsense—avoiding difficulty *at all costs*, that is, to have it as a goal above all else, for an academic audience. That's what I'm talking about; I'm being extremely simpleminded here. Now, there is a question about the commitment to democracy. Don't forget that there is, in democratic action, a coercive edge, whereas education is a noncoercive theory in terms of desire. Obedience in the classroom is scary. In democratic forms of government the fact that democracy has, to quote Lefort, an "empty space" at the end is what distinguishes it from other systems. You never know what the decision will be in democracy.

That undecidability is what we want to close up *at all costs*; that's what all the campaign rhetoric, all the polls, all the conventions, all the talks, all the kissing your wife elaborately in public are trying to do—that *is* part of democracy; that's not a failure of democracy. Like most rational abstractions, democracy operates by denying its nature, so the undecidable edge of democracy is always won back to decision, always won back to voting results, etc., so that once again it can be opened up to an undecidability, after a period. In the functioning of democracy there is for sure a good deal of coercion—it's not physical or violent; then it wouldn't be called democracy. But as one well knows, coercion is not confined to manipulating ballot boxes and exercising recognizable and visible violence at polling stations. So that's what this whole business of having campaigns is related to.

Now, in both teaching and this kind of democratic procedure, the point is not to have the word *democracy* mean generally that everyone must understand what you're saying. If that were so, then there would not be contending parties. Reasoning people would all reason at once, so everybody would believe the same thing, wouldn't they, if we were to take that to its logical consequence? That's not the point in democracy. Democratic minorities are not just something we should forget; they're not just racial minorities or cultural minorities—the democratic minority is a body count. So, therefore, when one looks at democracy in a thick way, rather than as just a nice buzzword, then it's simpleminded to think that democracy does not have a coercive moment worked into the structure of its functioning. Whereas, at best education is an uncoercive theory in terms of desire, in the humanities, the social sciences.

And then there is the book. One has to accept the fact that the book is an archaic form now, and we want to keep it residual, rich in wonderful vocabulary. Given the way modes of communication are operating now, the book has to have a different contract with its reader, one that acknowledges that reading, as I said, is transactional. A book is not the functioning of democracy, nor is it the textuality of classroom teaching; the book is a different kind of negotiable instrument. If one wants something that comes more easily, then it is not to the book that one will turn, and so we must give the book its due.

A book is an impacted thing. Either you have that contract with the reader, or the reader has that contract with you—or it won't work. And the humanities are trivialized; the idea of taking time to learn—which is different even from knowing—is being trivialized into just information-command, until even that is no longer pertinent. So, therefore, let us at least, if we are going to engage in that archaic activity, let us insist it be what it can be— that instrument that goes at a slower speed in a world where speed seems to be of the essence. That's what a book is. It is archaic, must remain residual, can become alternative and oppositional because it is a defective form—a virtual enclave in which people can think. There is no such thing as speed reading—that is why people don't like it.

There is the question of people "not schooled in the same idiom." Now here again I will talk about the other end of the spectrum, those aboriginal schools. I do that stuff—the teacher training—for my own education, because there what I have to do is to learn to learn from below, and it's difficult. For thirteen years I've been doing this, and I'm just beginning to break the ice, so that the very poor, the very badly educated—and some of these teachers are extremely badly educated—are beginning to have some faith in my way of devising an education, which does not resemble anything like the education available on a rural level. It's scandalous how different the education is below the middle class. Nothing I say, nothing, can stand up against the common sense of that dreadful system of rote learning and getting through exams by memorizing answers to antiquated questions and so on, unless I learn how to teach the counterintuitive.

How long do I stay there? Not long at all, because if I supervise, once I am gone, it will break. These people have been kept millennially uneducated—this is not like going down to Brooklyn! I've been trying very hard not to have them "obey" me. It has taken a very long time to have bits of trust come from the other side. That's been my education, and it's hard to do—hard to read the other's text to the extent that I will be able to think of a way of changing minds uncoercively that would seem plausible to them.

Just today I was looking at *"The Wall Street Journal" Report*[4] on television, which was about "the hottest new demographic in town": ten percent of eight-to-ten year olds own bonds. To quote the television program: an eleven-year-old sister and nine-year-old brother have learnt at school and have inspired their father to become an investor. And they're using the thing that Marx knew more than one hundred years ago: the bourgeois ruse—your money keeps growing on your money. Merrill Lynch, Salomon Smith Barney—they're sending people into preschools. . . . Morgan Stanley, American Express, kids' parents and money programs—instead of buying the car, buy the car company! They're called "Generation Y." There are seventy mutual funds especially designed for kids, and they have managed to spend $105 billion on their own. I'm just quoting the television program! This is given very positively, right?! We have here how we enter into pliable minds, how children become a part of globalizing financial networks, how exploiters are being trained.

The same day I also saw on NBC: "The MTV generation is driving the economy"; teenagers are the "heads of households" because most parents are working. So we're going from preschoolers, through eight to ten, eleven, and twelve—teaching them investment—into the MTV generation. This is the real core of children's education. And then, the same morning, a bit later on ABC—you see, all the networks, first CBS, then NBC, now ABC: Elizabeth Cady Stanton's granddaughter comes on; she says her grandmother said that women's votes are instruments for social change (we see the regulation documentary footage), and then she praises the female executive of Merrill Lynch—we've just seen Merrill Lynch sending people into schools, right?— saying Merrill Lynch is "working for her."

So, you see, this is a textile, this is a cultural fabric, this is children's education. As far as I'm concerned, for your own education you want to do the thing counter to this kind of effort. Remember, this is just one morning, I was doing my own work, but as I was moving around, I turned on the TV a bit, and I got these three wonderful nuggets—it's not research.

This is the idiom being placed within children's minds; this is the cultural fabric being woven; this is what says, "We won't read anything difficult." When we are training children in this way, these things are against turning globalization around constantly for better social redistribution. I believe that you cannot turn capitalism around to anything that is not within capitalism, in other words, corporate philanthropy, development-sustaining cost efficiency, impatient human-rights intervention with no time to respect local assumptions. We need strong virtues that one must not call "precapitalist" because then you're some kind of a social Darwinist, and we all know that that's a crock! We need other virtues defective for capitalism. But that doesn't mean that that's what should cover the world because globalization cannot, and in fact, should not, be stopped. In order for globalization to globalize all over the world, to be strategy driven, rather than each time crisis driven (the crisis of the North upon the South), we need those other kinds of virtues.

Now, if you like, my effort is at this other end of the spectrum—with the aboriginal children, because they're part of the larger system in countries of the South, the rural poor. When you work here, at this end you can only hope that one person's mind will change, one person who will perhaps become interested in this unglamorous work that is interesting in other ways.

SJM: One at a time. Sort of a "strategic particularism," if you will?

GCS: Of course! Of course! Now, I should also say that problem-solving activists reject what I'm talking about as well because they're impatient with problems to be solved; they don't have the time to construct extremely fragile collectivities that aren't just already there. By their supervision and their constant insistence to present a real collectivity they must remain focused on the moment of *freedom from* oppression. They assume that once the problem is solved and the time for the *freedom to* be responsible comes, that the oppressed somehow will do good. That just isn't true; the facts don't bear that out. My kind of work suffers from the rejection not only from these wonderfully investment-trained preschoolers but rejection also from the problem-solving activists who are just interested in going from problem to problem and solving them. They're absolutely crisis driven.

I think the hope is really for an open future so that one teaches in such a way that there will be some kind of other-directed thinking when things will have changed. But somehow, without any infrastructural support, and therefore not particularly effective within a global context, that sort of hope is all that one can have.

Now, as for the relationship between the academy and journalism. The vast field of journalism should certainly not be ignored—entertainment, infomercials, MTV, and what is the Internet? Is it virtual journalism masquerading as something like books? Is it some kind of simulacrum of that archaic mode? What is the nexus of telecommunication and finance capital, where any kind of information picture moving is okay? Where does journalism end these days? Where does it begin? Should we accept little magazines as also a defunct residual form? I am not talking about fanzines and stuff, because there is within journalism now this move toward the other medium that, even if it is between covers, does not resemble a book because it does not have that transactionality. It's not a question of high and low. It's a question of different kinds of production in language.

SJM: Could we call this "criticality"?

GCS: I don't know if you could call it criticality; but if you like, you could. I think that the concept of criticality itself is more toward one end. They're all using some form of verbality, but I don't know what journalism is anymore. The newspaper, little magazines, journals—these are beginning to shade off into the instant. And not only an instant, but an alternative instant. And sometimes a kind of noninstantiable virtuality. So, if you bring me to the question of journalism and critical writing, I will repeat: we are in a residual mode, which I don't think of on an evolutionary scheme because I'm not a social Darwinist. But nonetheless I welcome Raymond Williams's model that we keep the residual, not just as alternative, but oppositional, by insisting on the fact that the book is transactional; in order to survive as it is, it has to negotiate a different kind of contract with the reader. Finally, that hope is not a very strong one because of the trivialization of the humanities and the quality of the social sciences—and at the same time the weaving of the textile of the cultural fabric gets lower and lower as training turns into this kind of virtualized investment.

SJM: Let's return to the question of your writing with a more specific question. You mention in several places that you write with great difficulty,

190   STUART J. MURRAY

both in English and in your mother tongue, Bengali. You say: "I would like to be able to write more sober prose."[5] Can "sober" prose readily be distinguished from its "inebriated" counterpart? What would it mean to understand your prose as "inebriated"?

GCS: Sober prose—a lovely question. When I did that interview, I was really talking about the rhetoric of expressed desire and not of a goal. Expressed desire, half thinking, half projecting—that's the medium. It's not really an expressed thing. I believe I was using *sober* somewhat more figuratively than you imagine—like *clearly*—and I think what I was contrasting it to was the fact that my passions show.

We need not just a weapon, but a recognizable weapon, an up-to-the-mark, effective weapon. If the "subaltern"—which is a word for those who do not have infrastructural support—resist on their own, it will be useless: it will not be recognized by other women, even by other women in their own families. Therefore, I have said—in a very enraged and passionate way: "The subaltern cannot speak." This was picked up by a kind of narcissism in the academy, where anybody who feels she has not had a good deal immediately decides that she herself is a subaltern. And so we hear Spivak takes away the voice of resistance. "The subaltern cannot speak" was something like saying there is no justice in the world—you know, that sort of passionate rhetoric. But I decided that rather than confront the kind of nonsense I was hearing, it was better to take the rage out and rewrite it in simpler language. That is, if you like, "sober" language, serious language.

And I think, you know, I cannot say that I regret that passion makes me confusing sometimes. So that desire is just an expression of desire that is perhaps not being fulfilled. It's like I wish I could be something that, clearly, I don't quite want to be—that was the mode of my statement, because when you cannot do something, you say, "Oh, I wish I could." And it's often the frivolous and not just the passionate; but if you really want to get the weight of that frivolous, maybe we should talk about the archaeology of the frivolous—but that would take us too far afield. . . .

SJM: I understand you are passionately involved in grassroots literacy projects in Asia. Would you talk a bit more about your activism in this sphere and how it informs the language of your theoretical commitments? What act of "translation" takes place for you, Gayatri Spivak, as you shuttle between Asia and America, trying to effect a communication?

GCS: I'm really not involved in "grassroots literacy projects." It would be difficult for me to really run literacy projects. My real schools, these decade-long schools, are in Western West Bengal. They are not "literacy projects"—they are schools that I run. I feed the children, I pay the teachers, I have small schoolrooms built, I hang out—going again and again, never staying too long—to find ways of being responsible, so that I can tell them how to do things, and teaching teachers to teach by learning from the children. You know, it's that kind of labor-intensive work; there is no project there—it's all my moving around with my teachers in these one-room schools.

What act of translation takes place? I almost don't know what act of translation takes place, but I do know that something happens. I don't try to effect a communication between the two. Over the last few years there are many ways in which my experience there is teaching me how to teach here. After all, it is useful to be far from the triumphant culture with its sense of manifest destiny. As I revise I am on a bus returning from a UNIFEM luncheon, wonderful women, but talk about a sense of "manifest destiny"! The idea of being in an indispensable country, you know, cultural rights everywhere—as if all of this took place so that one could be sitting in a classroom.

So, I try more and more to teach. I teach in my classroom that at the speed of slow reading of difficult books there are no stock options. The idea is to see that reading literature in its literariness is to practice accessing the other as other so that the reader is adrift—determined by the text—in unpredictable alterity. This is what I see *here*, and basically it is something that I have learned from my experience *there*. In the beginning I thought of teaching here as just instrumental, as earning my living so that I could work there. But truly my work there has begun to show that a similar kind of work can be done here as well. Is that a translation? I don't know. But I feel the two ends of the question coming together more and more.

There is another thing. I teach Longinus to my undergraduate students in the history of critical thought. At a certain point Longinus says one of the ways one can produce sublime writing is by thinking one is addressing "the illustrious dead." Now, I don't think they necessarily have to be the illustrious dead. The men and women of these areas with whom I've been involved for the last thirteen years, when I try to learn to learn from below, *they* are my silent judges, they, like Longinus's illustrious dead, these persons so far removed from the dominant idiom; they're always there. They have no power over me, but they have all the power over me. It is in their ghostly presence that I read, write, and teach. Nothing that I read, write, or teach wouldn't be endorsed by the fact that they are. And that does indeed give a certain kind of responsibility, which should not be confused with the obligation to be clear for the lazy or reactionary.

SJM: If I may quote you here: "You have to hypercathect what you translate. That is the politics of translation."[6] Would you mind elaborating on the crossing of the libidinal, the political, and the ethical within translation? How ought we to make sense of "culture as translation"?

GCS: I think translation is something one cannot avoid. When I said hypercathexis, I was really thinking of "attending." What is interesting about hypercathexis is what one would call not attention but attending. Cathecting has a more libidinal application, and I meant something less given over to the libido. How do you understand hypercathexis?

SJM: I was thinking of hypercathexis along the lines of what Freud discussed in his paper on psychoanalysis and the so-called war neuroses. There he found that a neurosis might be prevented by a hypercathexis of the injured body part—effectively binding the libidinal energy. If I recall, the hypercathexis was seen by Freud almost as a prophylactic against psychic trauma.

GCS: Yes, so the hypercathexis is the enigma of survival, as it were. That's very interesting and would relate to the idea of translation. What one "translates" is the untranslatability of language, the untranslatability of idiom. One is translating for content, so it's the language that's falling out; there is no language there. I'm thinking of the lost limb: it is language that is the lost limb there.

SJM: Well, what survives then?

GCS: What survives? Nothing survives. Just as the arm is not there, the language is not there. And yet, it is the enigma of survival: we survive without the arm.

SJM: You have said that the infant "invents his or her mother tongue. That is how the infant begins, by creating a language which then the parent learns, as it were. Through that it develops into a language with a history."[7] Would you elaborate on this notion of "invention," and might there be implications here for the project of cultural translation?

GCS: Cultural translation, the idea that the infant invents his or her mother tongue—these notions come to me from Melanie Klein. But I always insist when I talk about Melanie Klein that this is not the Melanie Klein that you will find in Kleinian psychoanalysis or even in most readings of her. Thankfully, I have read Melanie Klein with the kind of passion I was describing to you, so what I offer is a kind of digest of Spivak using Klein with this sort of focus. Did you read "Translation as Culture"?[8] I'll quote from there:

"Melanie Klein . . . suggested that the work of translation is an incessant shuttle, that is, a 'life.' The human infant grabs on to some one thing, and then things. This grabbing (*begreifen*) of an outside, indistinguishable from an inside, constitutes an inside, going back and forth and coding everything into a sign-system by the thing(s) grasped. One can call this crude coding a 'translation.'" The point is that we, "the reader . . . translating the incessant translating shuttle into that which is read, must have the most intimate knowledge of the ruse of representation and 'permissible narratives'—Klein's words—which make up the substance of a culture, and must also become responsible and accountable with the writing-translating presupposed original."

Now this idea of the subject and the shuttling described by Klein is something that *will have* happened, not something that definitely happens. In this understanding of translation in Melanie Klein, therefore, the word *translation* itself loses its literal sense. That is Melanie Klein's narrative. Although she does talk about Oedipus, etc., because she was devoted to Freud, I think this is secondary in Klein; it's part of the permissible narrative. In fact, if you really look at Klein carefully, you'll see that the subject's an economy; it's a constant shuttling, and Oedipus is only a resource rather than an object-choice narrative that one adopts. Klein doesn't go from Imaginary to Symbolic, etc. She's very, very interesting from this point of view. I believe Deleuze and Guattari misunderstood her, and Lacan did not acknowledge her.

SJM: Perhaps I could ask another question in this vein. Psychoanalytic theories posit an unconscious of various sorts that gets taken up critically as a model of radical alterity. Here at the heart of the "I" resides something irreducibly Other, and yet it is also, after a fashion, "mine." But how much of this, to follow Lacan, is "structured like a language"? You have said, "When you say it's structured like a language, when it's structured like metaphor and metonymy, everything begins to go astray."[9] What is this going astray? Is it a productive crisis? And, conversely, might there be a better model, outside the vagaries of language, to theorize unconscious alterity?

GCS: Now, my idea of "radical alterity" is not psychoanalytic. I cannot think of this resident other—which, indeed, psychologically I cannot access but nonetheless is metapsychologically imbricated in whatever can be called a "me," if not an "I"—I can't think of it as "radically" other. It is only psychologically other; I cannot access it psychologically. My notion of radical alterity is—if it can be a notion—that to be human is to be angled, that is to say, leaning toward another. It's more philosophical than psychoanalytic. This entails an assumption of a radical alterity, so therefore it is in fact not an antonym of the self; an antonym of the self would not be a radical alterity—it would be alterity but not "radical." A radical alterity *is* not, as it were. And so for me the psychoanalytic theoretical fiction of the unconscious is not a radical alterity insofar as it is the "it" of the "I."

I would like to point you to this essay, which you no doubt have read, which is part of Lacan's twentieth seminar, called *Encore* (Again)—where he's talking to Jakobson, "À Jakobson." He says, "[I]f one considers everything that, given the definition of language, follows regarding the foundation of the subject—so thoroughly renewed and subverted by Freud that it is on that basis that everything he claimed to be unconscious can be grounded— then one must, in order to leave Jakobson his own turf (*domaine réservé*), forge another word. I will call it linguistricks (*linguisterie*)."[10] He is trying to say he was not doing linguistics when he took that line from Jakobson: he was "linguistricking." Now, this is the important part. Lacan continues: "The fact that I say (*Mon dire*) that the unconscious is structured like a language is not part and parcel of the field of linguistics." So, the fact that it was taken to mean, literally, the transposition of the linguistic model of metonymy and metaphor working on the chain of the production of signifiers—desire and the symptom—that is what here, quietly, in the 1970s Lacan is dissolving as he is moving into his postsemiotic phase.

I'm but an aficionado of psychoanalysis. I have the same kind of feeling about psychoanalysis as I have about any sort of ritualized behavior: it works because it works. And so I would say that the effort to tap the production of the subject in order to restore social agency—I think that is incredible, because one must work with this distinction between subject and agent, although at the limit they are shifting. But nonetheless, I would not want to theorize unconscious alterity because my idea of unconscious alterity is precisely that which resists theorizing. So it may be that language is the best model. But that is a problem, rather than a solution. By doing this I'm simply repeating a lesson learned from Derrida early on, which he hasn't turned his back on. In the very first thing of Derrida's—his introduction to Husserl's "Origin of Geometry"—the point was that Husserl solved the problem too quickly and too easily by falling on the model of language. Of course that's the model that will always solve the problem—but what's the use? That solution *is* the very problem.

SJM: Would you comment on South Africa's "Truth and Reconciliation Commission," presided over by Archbishop Desmond Tutu? The idea is, basically, that perpetrators of crimes under Apartheid publicly confess their crimes—a ritual intended to bring peace and a sense of justice to post-Apartheid South Africa, even if this does little to change the material conditions of its citizens. What faith do you have in such ventures; are you hopeful? Can past horrors be represented adequately in/by language, without Nuremberg-style trials, and to what end?

GCS: First of all, I will say that in the idea of stating something ritually we're not thinking about psychotherapy. We're thinking about the fact that ritual works because it works. That's the power of ritual. In fact, what we're looking at here is a tremendous exercise in the literalization of a kind of de-hegemonized Christianity. De Man used to say that in order to be political, you have to literalize the metaphor. To an extent that's what this is. And therefore what is happening here is not an adequate representation of horrors. In other words, it's not an adequate *Darstellung* of horrors in speech but that other meaning of representation, that is to say, a metonym. Speech becomes an accepted agential, rather than subjective, metonym for the unrepresentable. And therefore it does not remain unrepresentable. The very unrepresentability, the unrepresentability of a horror that approaches the absolute, is represented by its metonymic substitution in speech. That's how ritual works.

When penance is given—from within a generalized discourse—in exchange for confession in the more classic structure of confession, one would have to think that all Catholics are fools or naive to imagine this is taken by a subtle Catholic mind as some kind of actual substitution. It is the act of faith in the substitution that works because it works. Like an exchange, it's not reasonable. That functioning of the value form—that's what it is in the classic structure of confession—that functioning is as symbolic as all exchange.

SJM: You have recently said: "Triumphant global finance capital/world trade can only be resisted with irony."[11] Would you talk a little about irony and the possibility of a resistance in language?

GCS: De Man's definition is that irony is permanent parabasis, which is the move in Attic comedy when the Chorus steps forth and there is a kind of collective voice that interrupts the main action of the play. Even there, however, one voice wants to take over in the Chorus, etc. These counterglobalizing movements, if you globalize globalization rather than see it as just metropolitan migration, these movements are constantly disrupting, not at meetings but by small initiatives, one after the other, one after the other . . . turning capital around and trying but not succeeding because of the absence of infrastructural recognition and what I call relative restricted permeabilities—so that stuff from the top (for example, the WTO demonstrations in Seattle [December 1999]) permeates down, but not much percolates up. This is what I call the irony of global finance capital—permanent parabasis: constant interruption of the operating of the main story (finance capital and world trade) by a collective voice. That's what I meant; I did not mean ironic language.

There are people who know about this: there is a Third World network; there is an Asian Women's Human Rights Council; it's not like no one knows. But in the sector that calls itself the international civil society, or the

196 STUART J. MURRAY

general northern-based radical sector that goes on demonstrations—the people who go to the Beijing plus Five meetings at the UN headquarters in New York—with them there isn't enough of an infrastructure that percolates up. If you look at the big email circuits produced by the Beijing plus Five meetings, etc., you will see that what is often being reported is people making NGOs and asking for help. But we're not talking about how nicely they work as NGOs, and so on! It is amazing if you actually read the reams of stuff that's produced. But for the actual non-English-speaking, local-language-speaking workers in the field, there is no infrastructure that will allow the news of this resistance to reach up as such. It *is* taking place—the permanent parabasis is taking place—but it remains inaccessible to northern-based, somewhat impatient organizational do-gooders. The northern-based stuff or the NGO-level southern stuff *is* not, strictly speaking, interruptions. Those ruptures are critically continuous with the system.

SJM: Back in 1988 you said, "There is a practical political left in the United States, but it has no connection with the academic left."[12] Very recently, however, you have lamented the *absence* of a "'practical' left in the United States," suggesting the left is now consigned entirely to "a dwindling enclave in the academic and journalistic world."[13] Have your views changed in the last decade? And is the academic left "impractical"? These academic and often esoteric debates take place, as you say, "with a vigor matched only by [their] lack of consequence outside the academy."[14] How do you reconcile the need to be critical of "ordinary language" politics and the need to be accessible, to "go public as often as we can"?[15]

GCS: I won't give you a direct answer because I've talked at length about this in the first part of our conversation. But I would like to end with an anecdote. I cotaught a course in fall 2000 with the head of the Political Science Department—an enlightened, rational choice kind of colleague. I did this because we don't often enough talk to such colleagues to recognize that our account of the most radical in left thinking is incomplete. Here, for example, I hold in my hand a book written by another colleague of mine—Professor Elster—with whom I have had only one casual conversation in all these years! The academic subdivision of labor is so strong, and the dismissal of the kind of work we do—which is the occasion for our conversation—is so Olympian in the other part of the academy, that he would be completely dismissive of my work.

I've just started to read his book *Alchemies of the Mind*, which has for a subtitle: *Rationality and the Emotions*. Rationality and the emotions—very promising, and indeed, I find his earlier work, *Ulysses and the Sirens*, for example, extremely suggestive. But look at this. He is talking about psychic causality as "a recurring and intelligible causal pattern," a "mechanism." This is so far from our understanding of a lot of the psychic as being metapsychological! The difference between the psychic as apparatus (although he's using the word *mechanism*, his understanding of mechanism is "an intelligible causal pattern") and the fact that there is a metapsychological that is not accessible to psychology, that is not continuous with psychology and a kind of taxonomy of phenomenal emotions and affects, etc.—that difference is so commonsensical to us. Consider the question: "Who dreams?" or that to dream is normal. I'm not even going into any kind of theoretical thicket here. This immediately gives the lie to this notion of psychic causalities. So in the interest of a coherent theoretical system, which presumably enriches the rational choice idea of political theory by an account of the emotions, one must impoverish the psychic field even by ignoring what I'm calling common sense.

When the best in the discipline is like this, and the discipline is broken by the question that brought us into this conversation—this distrust of a language that sinks or swims in order to come to grips with something that may not be an intelligible "mechanism"—then, I think, the binary opposition between the criticism of ordinary language and the need to go public, claimed by our neck of the woods, becomes a bit risible.

I notice in rereading that I have bypassed the question of the left. Why have we identified "the left" with simplemindedness? The teaching rôle of the left intellectual is an economy of the uncanny, making the familiar unfamiliar enough so that critical practice can happen. But that is simply to prepare the field. Is that enough? That leads to another conversation.

Notes

1. This interview took place at Columbia University, New York, August 20, 2000.

2. "Moving at Both Ends of the Spectrum: A Conversation with Gayatri Chakravorty Spivak," interview by Lopamudra Basu. The interview took place four months prior to this one, and is posted at the Barnes and Noble Web site: http://www.bn.com/. It is accessible via the link "Interviews and Essays, Read More From the Author" from Barnes and Noble's web page for Spivak's book, *A Critique of Postcolonial Reason.*

3. Gayatri Chakravorty Spivak, "From Haverstock Hill Flat to U.S. Classroom: What's Left of Theory?" in *What's Left of Theory? New Work on the Politics of Literary Theory*, ed. Judith Butler, John Guillory, and Kendall Thomas (New York: Routledge, 2000), 1–39.

4. CBS, August 20, 2000.

5. Gayatri Chakravorty Spivak, *The Post-Colonial Critic: Interviews, Strategies, Dialogues*, ed. Sarah Harasym (New York: Routledge, 1990), 160.

6. Gayatri Chakravorty Spivak, "Lost Our Language—Underneath the Linguistic

Map," interview by Rainer Ganahl, in *Imported: A Reading Seminar*, Semiotext(e) 18, volume 6, issue 3 (New York: Semiotext(e), 1998), 192.

7. Gayatri Chakravorty Spivak, interview by Geert Lovink, ed. Linda Wallace, *Pax Electronica*, July 23, 1997.

8. Gayatri Chakravorty Spivak, "Translation as Culture," in *Parallax: A Journal of Metadiscourse Theory and Cultural Practices* 14 (Jan.–March 2000): 13–34.

9. Spivak, *Post-Colonial Critic*, 150.

10. Jacques Lacan, *The Seminar of Jacques Lacan, Book XX: On Feminine Sexuality, The Limits of Love and Knowledge, Encore 1972–1973*, ed. Jacques-Alain Miller, trans. Bruce Fink (New York: Norton, 1998), 15. Originally published as *Le Séminaire, Livre XX, Encore, 1972–1973* (Paris: Éditions du Seuil, 1975), 20.

11. Spivak, "From Haverstock," 33.

12. Spivak, *Post-Colonial Critic*, 134.

13. Spivak, "From Haverstock," 1.

14. Ibid.

15. Spivak, *Post-Colonial Critic*, 103.

Values of Difficulty

I AM WONDERING how to write this essay. Will I be intelligible or not? And if I am intelligible, does that mean that I have succeeded? And if I am not quite intelligible, or if I am unintelligible, then will that be a failure of communication? Or will it be making a different point? This is a rhetorical predicament I am in, writing here, and it is one not only I am in, but which many of us are in as we try to explain why certain kinds of scholarship in the humanities assume the voice that they sometimes do. In many venues, these days, there is an obligation, a need, to make clear what we do. And this is not always easy because what we do is not always easy. It is sometimes necessary to take up the challenge of making clear what we do, of making clear what we do without precisely denying what we do. That the presentation cannot and will not always conform to modes of communication that are familiar and consoling may seem to some as if the project of communication has failed. But is it not part of a critical practice, a critical approach to language and, indeed, to rhetoric, to ask what constitutes the norms of communicability, and what challenges them, and how it is that a critical consideration of the norm and its challenges forms part of the project of a comparative approach to literature? Indeed, the norms that govern communicability are not singular, and if they were, there would be no place for translation, no need to ask, how might I make this text communicable here and there? Or how can it travel? And what are the limits to its traveling? Part of my point will be that to pass through what is difficult and unfamiliar is an essential part of critical thinking within the academy today, an academy whose dedication to "comparative" work is not a field or subfield of its operation but a fundamental and irreversible condition of communication itself. I hope to make clear along the way that this passage, which is not smooth, through the unfamiliar and the difficult is especially crucial for a version of the humanities that seeks to maintain a connection to social theory and to the project of social and political transformation. Whereas some critics, such as Rorty, have suggested that literature is deprived of its inspirational possibility once it becomes sullied by the work of social theory and social science, I would like to suggest that it is virtually impossible to think the practice of criticism, much less critique, without this important implication of literary theory in its relation to social life. I will be making a counterpoint, however, as well, about the specificity of literary language and the limits of its translatability into social theory.

A certain paradox has emerged within debates on the politics of language. The questions of how we speak and to whom we speak are traditionally rhetorical problems. They become acute when we seek not only to speak but to persuade, and to persuade others of our political views. Now, one view on this problem, a view from the left, is that it is therefore crucial that we speak in ways that most people can understand, that we reach them where they live so that the "we" who speaks and the "them" to whom we speak are not separated, so that we are a member of the very community that is our audience. That same position holds that it is important that we reach the largest audience possible with our views and that politics relies fundamentally on a rhetoric with popular appeal. What this means for academics on the left is not only that it will be important to speak in a way that does not become lost to the internal workings of academic language but that it will be important to take popular culture as an object and venue for academic work itself. I take it that this position is one that insists that any progressive use of politics must be popular, and it must be popular in several senses: it must reach a wide audience, it must address topics that concern most people, and it must speak in the language of the broader community.

This strikes me as a sound view. But I do want to outline a paradox, and the other side of the paradox looks like this: Adorno and others working in the context of critical theory made the argument that one of the most important ways to call into question the status quo is by engaging language in nonconventional ways. He worried, and surely many others worried as well, that language gives us a world, a sense of its meaning and its intelligibility, and that many assumptions about how the world should be are built into language use. I take it that he did not mean that whatever we say the world is, is the way the world appears but rather that certain kinds of assumptions about, for instance, the natural status of money, the inevitable existence of class structure, of what the human is, of "who" constitutes the human, of what the limits of community are, of "who" is included in prevailing notions of community, what communicable speech might be, "who" is intelligible and who is not are embedded in the everyday use of language. Now, this use may appear to be "common," but here again we have to ask: whose language assumes the status of "common" language, who polices the "common," and what uses of language are thereby ruled out as uncommon or, indeed, unintelligible? Adorno thus claimed that a critical theory must use language in ways that call into question its everyday assumptions, precisely because some of the most problematic views about reality have become sedimented in everyday parlance. His worry was that to speak in ways that are already accepted as intelligible is precisely to speak in ways that do not make people think critically, ways that accept the status quo and do not make use of the resource of language to rethink the world radically.

So this strikes me as an interesting and sound view, even though it appears to be in conflict with the first view that I laid out above. Whereas the first view claims that any left position must speak the language of the popular, the second worries that the language of the popular is that of an uncritical consumerism. Whereas the first might accuse the second of elitism, and with some justification, and might also claim that forms of critical consumerism exist, that popular culture, including popular language, is a scene for critical subversion of the status quo, the second might accuse the first of selling out thought or, indeed, of premising politics on a dogmatic anti-intellectualism.

Surely there are a number of viewpoints that fall between the two I have just outlined. There are those, for instance, who might claim that critical theory does not need to be popular or have an effect on what is popular, that its value is intellectual and that it does not need to change the world or always be referred to the project of changing the world. And there are others who might claim that changing the world is the paramount thing and that it will always be a pragmatic consideration which language to use in the process or who might feel that language is one instrument among many for effecting that transformation. It is also unclear that what Adorno means by "common sense" is the same as what defenders of popular culture mean by the "popular." Surely, popular culture can function to challenge common sense; the popular is not one, and it is often the venue for minority cultures to weigh in against high culture, often the vehicle through which the new comes into confrontation with what has been commonly accepted.

So what do I mean by *critical?* I will turn to Adorno to see what might be made of this term, but here are a few remarks to keep in mind: Adorno was an elitist, and his views on popular culture are for the most part radically lamentable. He thought that film stupefied the senses and dulled the critical mind, that jazz lacked the proper characteristics of culture: even the most generous reader of his work would be hard-pressed not to call those reflections of his racist. So my point will not be to embrace Adorno but to let him represent one extreme within a reflection that I hope to conduct, a reflection that seeks to embrace a paradox without precisely resolving it.

So, with such caveats in mind, let me cite a passage from Adorno, one that illustrates his deep distrust of communicability, a distrust that would be nearly impossible to hear replicated within our current cultural climate. Adorno put his view most acutely in his *Minima Moralia*,[1] a text he wrote while in exile in New York and published in 1951 in Germany:

A writer will find that the more precisely, conscientiously, appropriately he expresses himself, the more obscure the literary result is thought, whereas a loose and irresponsible formulation is at once rewarded with certain understanding. It avails nothing ascetically to avoid all technical expressions, all allusions to spheres of culture that no longer exist. Rigour and purity in assembling words, however simple the result, create a vacuum. Shoddiness that drifts with the flow of familiar speech is taken as a sign of relevance and contact: people know what they want because they know what other people want. Regard for the object, rather than for communication, is suspect in any expression: anything specific, not taken from pre-existent patterns, appears inconsiderate, a symptom of eccentricity, almost of confusion. The logic of the day, which makes so much of its clarity, has naively adopted this perverted notion of everyday speech. Vague expression permits the hearer to imagine whatever suits him and what he already thinks in any case. Rigorous formulation demands unequivocal comprehension, conceptual effort, to which people are deliberately discouraged, and imposes on them in advance of any content a suspension of all received opinions, and thus an isolation, that they violently resist. Only what they do not need first to understand, they consider understandable, only the word coined by commerce, and really alienated, touches them as familiar. Few things contribute so much to the demoralization of intellectuals. Those who would escape it must recognize the advocates of communicability as traitors to what they communicate. (101)

Adorno, of course, belonged to that earlier formulation of critical theory that believed that social criticism ought not to be separated from aesthetics and that, in particular, a critical perspective must actively trouble the received conventions of language, risking a certain "isolation" from common-held standards of linguistic satisfaction. Of course, this has always been the conceit of high literary modernism, namely, that the world can only be given anew when redescribed by heightened and unconventional language that reworks the settled meanings of words into those that are explicitly unconventional. Within literary modernism the point of undoing conventional forms of communication was to produce the new, and the new had a value, since it seemed to signify cultural progress and the possibility of renewing a sense of experience out from under the shackles of technology. Part of what critical theory did in its pre-Habermasian phase was to transpose this insight of literary modernism into social theory. Thus, the question of language became central to the rethinking of social reality. Language not only communicates to us about a ready-made world but gives us a world, and gives it to us or, indeed, withholds it from us by virtue of the terms it uses. Then the critical question emerges: what world is given to us through language, and how might the alteration of our language give us a different sense of world? Is one way that social reality, capital, class difference, relations of subordination and exclusion come to seem natural and familiar precisely through the language that impounds these notions in a subtle and daily way into our sense of reality? And if this sense of reality is built up, solidified, rendered immutable, imprisoned through repeated kinds of language use, then where do we intervene on that repetitive use to transform the world into a site of possible action and of possible transformation?

It may seem that I am asking for a certain kind of emancipation through language, but I do not mean to be so happy. Adorno makes clear in the above that the risk of difficult thinking is a certain isolation and estrangement, so it is not a bounteously collective moment in which critical thinking emerges. Indeed, it can come from the depths of isolation. One might object and say that Adorno moves too quickly to identify the familiarity of the common with consumerist notions of satisfaction and that the reason writing must risk obscurity and isolation is therefore to establish a perspective that is not immediately co-opted by consumer culture. Although Adorno may have all sorts of misbegotten ideas about consumer culture, he does have an idea of what makes a perspective critical. The demand that language deliver what is already understandable appears to be a demand to be left alone with what one already knows. But Adorno gives this notion of self-satisfied ignorance a twist when he writes, "Only what they do not need first to understand, they consider understandable." The "they" here do not need to understand, and that very need not to understand conditions their judgment about what is understandable. The paradox that emerges is that what is not understood becomes what is best understood, and for Adorno this is no understanding at all; it is, in fact, a defense against understanding, one performed and maintained in the name of understanding itself.

Of course, one political response to such a view is to claim that to reach people and to have effects one must write in an accessible and popular way. And perhaps it is that Adorno fails to understand the critical or subversive potential within consumer culture itself. But is he also making another point about criticality that might be separated from his claim about consumer culture? Is he telling us that the moment in which understanding is challenged and risked is the one in which a critical perspective emerges? Is this not the moment, the occasion, when I come to recognize that it is my ignorance, and my tenacious hold on ignorance, that dictates what I will come to call communicable knowledge? What does it say about me when I insist that the only knowledge I will validate is one that appears in a form that is familiar to me, that answers my need for familiarity, that does not make me pass through what is isolating, estranging, difficult, and demanding?

Adorno is not referring to certain kinds of truths that are hard to take but rather to the way in which those truths are presented, a presentation that is essential to the truth that is articulated. If communication does not take place through familiar conventions that house and protect my ignorance, then does it take place at all? If I call "communicability" that moment in which I already know the convention by which communication takes place, what risk of difference do I foreclose, and what form of cultural parochialism do I protect?

To say that the communication of truth depends on its presentation is to say that such communication is rhetorical. This means that the presentation of truth that is made may well produce meanings that call into question the truth that is communicated or add something more, something different, to what is explicitly intended. The language in which one offers one's views does not always carry the meanings that one intends, and our words often return to us as hauntings from another order. For words are not first spoken and then received, they are received and spoken, received and imparted at once in the act of speaking. That I am born into a language does not mean that it speaks me as if I am its ventriloquization, but it does speak as I speak, and my voice is never fully or exclusively my own. Indeed, I speak and listen, and then later ask, "Who was speaking there?" And the answer may not be conclusively given. That the speech act is not governed by the intention by which it is animated does not mean that there is no intention, only that the intention does not govern. That the intention does not govern does not mean that it does not sometimes orchestrate and effect its intention, only that if it does, it is lucky. Similarly, this does not mean that we cannot fully intend to get across a certain point, but we should probably be aware that even the same words resonate differently, depending on the semantic dimensions of their circulation, and that our intentions will become derailed to some extent in the course of the trajectory of our words. I think that this situation is not simply reducible to a formal character of language, to a relation between intention and force, or to fields of intention and fields of reception but takes its own specific form within the context of a multicultural linguistic condition. The use of a term or a locution in one context may or may not travel appropriately into the next.

This happens surely with contemporary human rights discourse, where rights are attached to kinds of persons or practices that make no sense in one cultural venue and are, as it were, the foundation of sense in another. And it happens when we consider the term *universality*, which, by definition, should include all people, and it is regularly misunderstood by those it describes, or refused by those it includes, or used in syntactical ways that are incompatible with other such uses. And speaking locally, for the moment, this problem of translation, and its limits, takes place in gay politics as well, a lesson learned from AIDS activism in the 1980s, when activists sought to enter Spanish-speaking communities, for instance, to do AIDS outreach by asking who was "homosexual" only to find that very few people would answer to the term. When they returned to ask who practiced anal sex with other men, many more people came forth, and a lesson was thereby learned by Anglo activists. To engage in activism is not to start with the concept of a shared language but to be prepared to find that communication can sometimes take place only when the terms that initiate a discussion undergo an expropriation that bears no resemblance to the original, where the term abandons the animating conditions of its own efficacy in order to live elsewhere as another term or as a term subjected to a radically unanticipated use.

Such examples make at least two points about political rhetoric that I would like to underscore today. The first is that we may think that effective activism requires that we use language that is direct, straightforward, and commonsensical. Indeed, we may even think that a popular democratic movement must use the language of the people, and we may even conjecture that we know what that language is and how best to use it. But if one of the tasks of activism is to cross cultural barriers in a nonimperialist fashion, that is, to learn how to speak across various languages in ways that do not assimilate this variety of languages to a dominant notion of speech, then it seems to me that we must do without a notion of common language. And although some may think that doing away with common sense and a common language is the sure road toward divisiveness, it seems to me that accepting the heterogeneity of language is a necessary point of departure for any left politics that does not seek to reestablish the terms of cultural dominance through recourse to what is publicly accepted as the doxa of the common.

The second point is that there is no effective politics without accepting translation as the common predicament. To claim that translation is a common predicament is not to claim that there is a common language among us but only that speech will require translation to be received, that activism that seeks to extend information in particular (and we can think of many instances in which that is the paramount goal of activism) will founder if it does not take up the task of translation. What I mean here is that even the core terms, the ones we cannot do without, such as *universality* and *justice* and *equality*, the ones we believe are essential to politics, do not have a simple or already established meaning. And although we often think that we must secure the meaning of such terms before we can proceed, that otherwise we will have no anchor and no ground, we will find that as soon as these terms enter into a political field, they are contested and that no recourse to an ideal or precultural semantics will settle the question of what they mean or, indeed, within institutions, how they will mean. The question, for instance, of how *universality* means, and how *universality might mean*, is an example of one key question that must remain open for politics to maintain its status as a critical enterprise, for it to resist the lure of foundational certainties that reduce it to the doldrums of dogmatism. And it may be that there are different ways, within different languages, within different political syntaxes, of understanding *universality*, but it also might be that that term has no translation in certain contexts and that a certain failure of translation is presented there for us to undergo. For when we assume that translation is possible, we assume that every language, every political syntax has a place for what we call *universality*, but that place may not be a place: it may be an inflexion, it may be a sign for colonialism, it may be no sign at all. And then we will be up against the limits of universality, for if it cannot translate everywhere, then the only way it can translate is through ignoring what it finds, through an imperialist move that claims to find itself in the Other, or through a developmental perspective that assumes that the colonized has not yet assumed the insights of the colonizer and that it is the white man's burden to prod them along. And this challenge to translatability—its interruption, its arrested moment—is the one that compels the violence of a certain colonial expansionism, but it is also the possibility of meeting up with the limits of our own epistemological horizon, a limit that challenges what we know to be knowable, a limit that can always and only function as the radically unfamiliar within the domain of ordinary language, plain speaking, common sense.

And although this is a philosophical point, and in some ways a political point, I want to make it again briefly and to make it through a brief reference to Henry James, not because he is a political hero or because he represents brilliant class politics but because the kind of difficulty he presents for us is one with a clear ethical implication. And then finally, briefly, I'd like to return to it by asking what happens to Adorno when he reads Benjamin on Baudelaire, why it is that Benjamin seems to Adorno too obscure, too difficult, too untheoretical. But first, what is the relation between linguistic opacity in James and the question of an ethical relation? Consider what James has to say about judgment, our ability to make it, and the necessary limits of our capacity. We may think that without the capacity to judge we are surely at sea in the realm of ethics, that judgment must anchor us, that judgment is what we must secure.

At the end of *Washington Square* the main character, Catherine, refuses to marry Morris Townsend, the man to whom she was earlier engaged and who left her quite unceremoniously and without good explanation some twenty years before.[2] Catherine's father never believes anyone would want to marry her and believes in particular that Morris wanted to marry her only for her wealth. But she very much wanted to marry dear Morris and wanted as well to believe in the transparency of his words. She believed, as it were, in the transparency of his authorship, that his words manifested his intentions, and that the words and the intentions were nothing but good. Catherine was not only believing but also obedient, and she refused to marry Morris until and unless she could secure her father's approval. But that approval never comes; it is ferociously withheld, and daughter and father become locked in a battle of wills. In the meantime she keeps Morris waiting, Morris, who turns out not to have a job, not to have a cent, very much in need of her money, to be very much a cad, a smooth cad, one with a wonderful and engaging way with language. Before the father dies, he asks that Catherine promise that she will not marry Morris, even though it has been twenty years, and no one has heard from him. She refuses to promise. More suitors arrive in the interim, and she refuses them all. And then the father does die, and Morris arrives, and he banters, and he appears to mean what he says, and he asks about a future, and she shows him the door, which is her act. And she takes up her embroidery and assumes her solitude for the time that is left to her. Morris can't understand and asks, well, why didn't she get married all this time, assuming she was waiting for him. And we ask, well, if she wasn't going to marry old Morris, why didn't she make the promise to her father? But she didn't, no, she didn't. And everyone thinks they know her; everyone thinks they can predict her. The father dies thinking that she was unwilling to make the promise because she intends to marry Morris. Morris arrives thinking she has been rejecting suitors with the hope of marrying him. But she won't. She won't make that promise, and she will not take that vow. And these refusals, we might say, make her virtually incomprehensible to everyone.

> Morris stood stroking his beard, with a clouded eye. "Why have you never married?" he asked abruptly. "You have had opportunities."
> "I didn't wish to marry."
> "Yes, you are rich, you are free; you had nothing to gain."
> "I had nothing to gain," said Catherine.
> Morris looked vaguely round him, and gave a deep sigh. (218)

She offers him some words in this instance, but he cannot seem to understand them, and he doesn't seem to know what questions to ask of these words in order to gain elucidation. Indeed, she seems to understand that the answer she has to give is one that he will not be able to understand as an answer: "I meant to tell you," she adds, "by my aunt, in answer to your message—if you had waited for an answer—that it was unnecessary for you to come in that hope" (219). She offers him no hope for an answer, and in this moment it is the reader, too, mindful that this is the last page, who is cautioned against hope in this sense. When Morris then says good-bye, he adds, "Excuse my indiscretion," suggesting that he has broken from accepted form or that her refusal is in some way an indication that he arrived with inappropriate expectations. Her response does not take the form of words but rather an extended silence, as if whatever meaning this refusal has for her will not and cannot appear in speech. The final act between them is one of movements, not words: "He bowed, and she turned away—standing there, averted, with her eyes on the ground, for some moments after she had heard him close the door of the room" (219). As he leaves, he expresses his exasperation to Mrs. Penniman: "She doesn't care a button for me—with her confounded little dry manner." And then he comes up against the enigma of her decision: "But why the deuce, then, would she never marry?" (219). Mrs. Penniman, whose own desire, deflected and sustained through the triangularity of their relations, fears the impending end. Catherine has taken herself out of the circuit, and there is no future if this enigma stays intact, if no fresh explanation can incite more plot. Morris then leaves them both, and the "inadequacy of the explanation" finally stills their conspiracy. "Catherine, meanwhile, in the parlour, picking up her morsel of fancy-work, had seated herself with it again—for life, as it were" (219).

And she does not give her reasons in language. Indeed, this is a moment when language recedes, when handiwork is taken up, when the idioms of the novel cannot approach the final enigma that she is, when what we might be tempted to call her autonomy has no language but takes place, as it were, through marking the limits of all speaking that seeks to bind her, that offers itself to her as a way of binding herself. She performs, we might say, the limits of language and the "inadequacy of explanation" at this instance. The work she takes up "for life, as it were," makes clear that this is a life constituted only metaphorically: the "as it were" closes the story, but the figure retrospectively extends back to the whole story, as if, all along, a figure of speech that does not quite capture the referent has been the story's way of proceeding, only stated explicitly at the end, as a defining and definitive aside. The reader is also left, in a sense, exasperated, cursing, staring. As readers we are effectively asked whether we will judge her, supply her with a motivation, find the language by which to know and capture her, or whether we will affirm what is enigmatic here, what cannot be easily or ever said, what marks the limits of the sayable. And if we cannot join with Morris and the other chatterers to judge her, then perhaps we are asked to understand the limits of judgment and to cease judging, paradoxically, in the name of ethics, to cease judging in a way that assumes we already know in advance what there is to be known.

And this suspension of judgment brings us closer to a different conception of ethics, one that honors what cannot be fully known or captured about the Other. Her action, her nonaction, cannot be easily translated, and this means that she marks the limits of the familiar, the clear, and the common. To honor this moment in which the familiar must become strange or, rather, where it admits the strangeness at its core, this may well be the moment when we come up against the limits of translation, when we undergo what is previously unknown, when we learn something about the limits of our ways of knowing; and in this way we experience as well the anxiety and the promise of what is different, what is possible, what is waiting for us if we do not foreclose it in advance.

So one might think that this brings me back to Adorno's point and that in a way all I have been saying is a support for Adorno's claim about passing through the unfamiliar.[3] Adorno at once helps to articulate this conception of passing through difficulty as part of what is necessary for critical thinking, but he also exemplifies the limits of the very capacity he recommends. When Walter Benjamin sends Adorno in October of 1938 his Baudelaire manuscript, per agreement, to be considered for publication in the journal edited by the Institute for Social Research, Adorno takes some time in responding; and when he does respond, he lets Benjamin know he is "disappointed" (281). Benjamin is living in Paris at the time, in exile from Germany, under a collaborationist government, with little money. He has no other livelihood than the meager payments he receives for his articles; Adorno and others are responsible for keeping Benjamin on the payroll of the institute. Fearful of the Germans entering France, Benjamin is voicing his desperation to Adorno, and indeed writes to Adorno only one year before he is interned in a camp in Nevers. So we might say, and with reason, that there is a certain ethical urgency to Benjamin's situation at the time. He earlier corresponded with Gerschom Scholem to see whether he might emigrate to Palestine, and Scholem suggested to him that it might be difficult, since Benjamin might need to embrace Zionism.[4] And now Benjamin is waiting to see whether the Institute for Social Research will help him, and they do eventually help him, but it is Max Horkheimer who makes sure that the visa is at Marseilles in September of 1940, Horkheimer who could never really read Benjamin, who wanted the journal to go in a different direction: more social theory, more social science. So Benjamin sends his Baudelaire essay to Adorno, and Adorno responds by vacating the position of the "I" and writing as the "we," the editorial board: he writes about "the attitude of all of us to your manuscript" (280):

motifs are assembled but they are not elaborated (*durchgeführt*). In your cover letter to Max you presented this as your express intention, and I am aware of the ascetic discipline you have imposed on yourself by omitting everywhere the conclusive theoretical answers to the questions involved. . . . Panorama and "traces," the *flâneur* and the arcades, modernity and the ever-same, all this *without* theoretical interpretation—can such "material" as this patiently await interpretation (*geduldig auf Deutung warten kann*) without being consumed (*verzehrt*) in its own aura? (281)

So Adorno's complaint seems to be that Benjamin fails to give an elaboration and that an elaboration, a true elaboration, will be one that qualifies the work as theoretical. Benjamin's writing is allusive, inconclusive, too ascetic, withheld, guilty of ellipsis. It needs to give itself, and to give itself in the form of a theory that renders explicit the meaning of the disparate elements of analysis at hand. What would qualify for Adorno as such a theory? And is this theory as it must be, or is this theory as Adorno wished it to be? We get a better sense of what is required as we continue to read this fateful letter of November 10, 1938. There he writes, for instance, that Benjamin's work belongs to a "realm where history and magic oscillate" (282); that the work is "lacking in one thing: mediation" (282); that Benjamin relates "the pragmatic contents of Baudelaire's work directly and immediately to adjacent features in the social history, and wherever possible, the economic features, of the time" (282). For Adorno, Benjamin fails to relate these aspects of the text and its conditions of production in a way that can be conceptually elaborated; Benjamin offers metaphors for this relation and, Adorno writes: "I am struck by a feeling of artificiality (*Künstlichkeit*) whenever you substitute metaphorical expressions for [obligatory expressions (*verpflichtenden Aussage*)]" (282, my correction). And then he makes clear, without doubt, that for the connection to be authentic, and not artificial, for the relation to be conceptual and elaborated, and not metaphorical and elliptical, it would have to fulfill the requirements of a true materialism: "I regard it as methodologically inappropriate to give conspicuous individual features (*sinnfällige Züge*) from the realm of the superstructure a 'materialist' turn by relating them immediately, and perhaps even causally, to certain corresponding features of the substructure. The materialist determination of cultural traits is only possible if it is mediated through the *total social process* (*gesamtprozess*)" (283).

So we see that what theory is or, rather, must be is precisely the kind of practice that relates every particular cultural trait to the total social process.[5] But we also understand that Adorno is writing to Benjamin at a time of need, rejecting his piece on Baudelaire, and calling into question his relation to the institute, which supplies his wage at this time and which holds out his last hope for gaining a visa out of collaborationist France. This somehow remains in the background here, even as Adorno apologizes for Horkheimer's failure to respond directly to the essay originally addressed to him, citing "the enormous commitments connected with [Max's] move to Scarsdale" (285).

The impression which your entire study conveys—and not only to me . . . —is that you have here done violence upon yourself. Your solidarity with the Institute, which pleases no one more than myself, has led you to pay the kind of tributes to Marxism which are appropriate neither to Marxism nor to yourself. Not appropriate to Marxism because the mediation through the entire social process is missing, and because of a superstitious (*abergläublisch*) tendency to attribute to mere material enumeration a power of illumination (*Macht der Erhellung*) which really belongs to theoretical construction alone rather than to purely pragmatic allusions. (284)

And then Adorno truly assumes the mantel for both Marxism and theory, not to mention patron, father, and judge, when he writes:

I speak not only for myself, unqualified as I am, but also for Horkheimer and the others when I say that we are all convinced that it would not only benefit "your" production if you could elaborate your ideas without recourse to such considerations . . . , but that it would also prove most beneficial to the cause (*am förderlichsten ist*) of dialectical materialism and the theoretical interests represented by the Institute, if you surrendered to your own insights and conclusions without combining them with other ingredients, which you obviously find so distasteful to swallow that I cannot expect anything good to come of it. (284)

The letter concludes by explaining to Benjamin why the work cannot appear in the journal pages as is, and Adorno justifies this decision by claiming that this is "for your own sake and for the sake of Baudelaire" (285).

So maybe it is for Benjamin's sake, or the sake of Baudelaire, but we don't really find Adorno weeping over the cause of Baudelaire in this writing or elsewhere. We do see him clearly laying out the stakes of a dialectical materialism, however, that takes the process of mediation to be central, that thinks the truly theoretical operation is the one that relates the particular to the social totality through this mediation, fully conceptualized, according to norms of conceptualization to which Adorno subscribes. Indeed, Benjamin's refusal to supply the satisfying link between the particular cultural trait, the duty on wine, the stroll of the flaneur, and the total social process seems to be costing him his livelihood at the moment. And perhaps it could be said as well that the subsequent delays on the part of the institute in supplying that visa in time might be due to the lapse in correspondence that followed this rather stunning rejection of Benjamin's work by Adorno. For months follow after this: Benjamin replies in December with an even and laconic response, and Adorno waits until February 1 to reply, offers a lengthy engagement with Benjamin's essay again, and mentions the impending threat of a German invasion, but does not mention the visa. Benjamin writes back on February 23, 1939, and Adorno waits until July to write again. By September Benjamin is interned at Nevers.

If Scholem earlier asked Benjamin to sign on the dotted line to commit himself to Zionism, and linked that to the plausibility of Benjamin emigrating to Palestine, now Adorno invokes not only dialectical materialism but the collective voice of the institute, inducing Benjamin either to join his view or to disavow Marxism altogether. And although Adorno does not deliver an ultimatum to Benjamin, he withholds work and payment and even delays their correspondence precisely at the moment in which Benjamin's livelihood and life are imperiled. Significantly, Scholem had written Benjamin earlier about the prospects of Benjamin getting a visa to New York, but in the context of that deliberation Scholem lets Benjamin know that he thinks the writing is too obscure, too unintelligible, and that the possibility of getting the necessary support from influential intellectuals in New York is in some way made more difficult because of Benjamin's difficult prose.[6]

You might think that Benjamin would cave in, would simply write what they want, if it would make them all more satisfied, if it would induce them to go to the consulate, get the visa papers in order, make sure he had a way out. But that was not Benjamin's route, and, as you know, he ended up, visa in hand, committing suicide at the Spanish border on the one day when the border was closed in early September of 1940.

In defending his work, Benjamin suggests that theory must risk a certain incoherence, that it must fail to be fully explicit, that it must founder on relations that might be figured, through metaphor, but not captured through conceptual elaboration. "I, too," he rejoins to Adorno,

regard this as a theory in the strictest sense of the word (*eine Theorie im strengsten Sinne des Wortes*) and my discussion of the *flâneur* culminates in this. This is the place, and the only place in this part [of the text], where the theory comes into its own in undistorted (*unverstellt*) fashion. It breaks like a single ray of light into an artificially darkened chamber. But this ray, broken down (*zerlegt*) prismatically, suffices to give an ideal of the nature of the light whose focus lies in the third part of the book. (290)

Although I cannot take the time here to trace the treatment of the flaneur, it seems important, for our purposes, to see how Benjamin insists on the invocation of metaphor when he makes the claim for "theory in the strictest sense," theory that "comes into its own in undistorted fashion." And the metaphor at work, the metaphor of light, is precisely the central metaphor of truth in Kabbalistic writings.[7] Suffice it to say that Scholem will be no more pleased with Benjamin's appropriation of Kabbalah (see Scholem, *Walter Benjamin and Gerschom Scholem*, 106) than Adorno will be pleased with Benjamin's appropriation of Marxism and that despite the clear relation of need and friendship Benjamin has for both Adorno and Scholem, he will refuse, refuse until death, to satisfy either one of them. Benjamin does a certain violence to Kabbalah, a certain violence to Marxism, yet he insists on both. To Adorno he writes, "If I refuse (*wenn ich mich dort weigerte*) . . . to pass on to other matters beyond the interest of dialectical materialism and the Institute, there was more at stake than solidarity with the Institute or simple fidelity (*blosse Treue*) to dialectical materialism, namely, a solidarity with the experiences (*Erfahrungen*) we have all shared during the last fifteen years" (291). And to the charge that he has done violence to himself, Benjamin continues:

[I]t is therefore a question of my own [most productive interests (*eigenste produktive Interessen*)] as a writer. I will not deny that these may occasionally do violence to my original interests. There is an antagonism here of which I would not wish to be relieved (*enthoben*) [not even once (*nicht einmal*)] in my dreams. And overcoming (*Bewältigung*) this antagonism constitutes the problem of my study, and that is a problem of construction. I believe that speculation can only begin its inevitably audacious flight with some prospect of success if, instead of donning the waxen wings of esotericism, it seeks its source of strength in construction alone (*statt die wächsernen Schwingen der Esoterik anzulegen ihre Kraftquelle allein in der Konstruktion sucht*). (291, my translation)

Whereas Adorno understands the construction of social reality to be a theoretical elaboration of the mediating structures that relate specific cultural traits to the total social process, Benjamin understands that social reality is riven precisely by the absence of such mediation, an absence that produces an inevitable tension and antagonism, one he would not want to be without and one that has a specific value for him. Esotericism, yes, precisely because the uncanny way in which the pipe, the stroll, the wine tax, the windows relate to each other and to some social totality is not to be grasped, and that ineffability must be figured, relentlessly, through metaphors in which the relation of substitution between terms does not culminate in a mediation between them, in which, rather, a disjunction and irretraversibility is restaged again and again. When Benjamin writes in February of 1939 to Adorno, he makes clear that conceptual elaboration, if there is to be one, if there is to be one of the flaneur in particular, will have to assume a metaphorical form that instates an antagonism that will find no resolution. Satisfaction will not be achieved, not even in one's dreams. He makes clear his version of Marxism when he claims: "the commodity economy arms [the] phantasmagoria of sameness (*des Gleichens*) which simultaneously reveals itself, as an attribute of intoxication, to [become believable as (*begläubigt*)] the central image of illusion" (310, my correction). In making his point clear to Adorno, he writes, "the *flâneur* makes himself thoroughly at home in the world of [saleability (*Käuflichkeit*)]. In this, he even outdoes (*überbietet*) the whore; he takes the abstract concept of the whore for a stroll" (310). Here, quite literally, Benjamin subjects the conceptual to a metaphorical mode of transport. But whereas the translator adds "so to speak" at the end of this line, there is no *"sozusagen"* or any similar marking of the figural status of this claim in the German. There is no "as it were" that marks off the figural dimension from something more objective, more grounded, more conceptual. For Benjamin, as he argues against Adorno's equation of metaphor with artificiality (*Künstlichkeit*), the figural is the means by which the conceptual is fulfilled, and the figure of the strolling whore is a concept that fulfills itself only in another figure (310). If the concept is fulfilled by such figures, the concept appears to become articulated only through its disarticulation as a figure. Indeed, if for James, Catherine takes up life "as it were," we are asked to understand the life she takes up as a figural one, a life that is as proper to fiction as, say, the life of a fictional character must be. And we are asked at that moment to consider the slide between fiction and life, since there are lives that are lived in the mode of "as it were," resembling something we might call life that carries no quotation marks around it. Benjamin's translator tries this Jamesian move when he supplies the "so to speak" to Benjamin's claim that Baudelaire "takes the abstract concept of the whore for a stroll." Benjamin is insisting here that reality has been transfigured by the commodity, that new forms of animation are possible as a consequence, and that the figure has become literalized in this instant. James's explicit affirmation of the figural status of Catherine's life fails to restore us to a sure distinction between figural and literal. Since we might say that her life is only "as it were" a life because it is a fiction, taking place within one, the uncanniness of the story resides precisely in the positing of a life that can be lived in the mode of the "as it were," one that fiction lets us see but that does not, for that reason, exempt the possibility from life. If Baudelaire is said to "take the abstract concept of the whore for a stroll," then the concept is animated in and by its figural dimensions, and there is no way to separate the two without losing the animation that is, as it were, its very life.

Oh Benjamin, he makes our heads hurt. Why does he torture us so? Must we follow him here, or can we stop following him, tell him, simply, clearly, that he is no longer a Marxist, no longer a Kabbalist, no longer knowable according to the terms by which we have, conventionally, established knowability? Or is he telling us something about what truth has become for us, historically, that it has become a certain difficulty, and that if we are unwilling to be disarmed and to become, suddenly, unknowing, we assume instead a posture of dogmatism that may well sidetrack us from the evanescence, if not the ineffability, of a life?

Notes

1. Theodor Adorno, *Minima Moralia: Reflections from Damaged Life*, trans. E. F. N. Jephcott (London: Verso, 1978).

2. Henry James, *Washington Square* (New York: Penguin, 1979).

3. See Theodor Adorno and Walter Benjamin, *The Complete Correspondence, 1928–1940,* ed. Henri Lonitz, trans. Nicholas Walker (Cambridge, Mass.: Harvard University Press, 1999). The German text consulted and cited here is *Theodor W. Adorno, Walter Benjamin, Briefwechsel, 1928–1940*, ed. Henri Lonitz (Frankfurt: Surhkamp, 1994).

4. See Scholem's letter to Benjamin, dated July 26, 1933, in which he remarks, "In our experience, in the long run only those people are able to live here who, despite

all the problems and depressions, feel completely at one with this land and the cause of Judaism" and then counsels Benjamin to "assess the degree of your commitment to Judaism," in *The Correspondence of Walter Benjamin and Gerschom Scholem, 1932–1940*, ed. Gershom Scholem, introduction by Anson Rabinbach (New York: Schocken, 1989), 66.

5. Of course, Adorno makes clear elsewhere that this totality is not given at once but only negatively and in parts that indicate the always vanishing whole.

6. See Scholem's letter to Benjamin, March 25, 1938, regarding how Benjamin is regarded as a "mystic" in New York (Scholem, *Walter Benjamin and Gerschom Scholem*, 215).

7. Benjamin was reading Scholem on Kabbalistic writings (in manuscript form) throughout the 1930s and doubtless had exposure to them before. Kabbalistic writing has centered on the *Sefer ha-Zohar*, a multiauthored text that centers on the theory of divine emanation. This emanation both informs and transcends figures of speech so that words contain and indicate a divine light that precedes them and passes through them. The account of emanation has undergone several forms in the course of Kabbalistic writings. The Safed Mystics, exiled in the early sixteenth century from Spain, included Isaac Luria, who, in Palestine, offered a theology in which "the first divine act was not emanation, but withdrawal." God, deemed Ein Sof, withdrew from this space both to eliminate "harsh judgement" (15) and to subsequently endow the space of withdrawal with the power of light. The light entered this space only to shatter and to produce sparks that became contained as bits of material existence. The Hasidic phrase "raise the sparks" refers to the act of finding the holiness within material reality and, indeed, within letters of the alphabet. See Daniel C. Matt, *The Essential Kabbalah, The Heart of Jewish Mysticism* (New York: HarperCollins, 1994), 1–19.

Contributors

JOHN BENDER is Professor of English and Comparative Literature, Jean G. and Morris M. Doyle Professor of Interdisciplinary Studies, and Anthony P. Meier Family Professor in Humanities at Stanford University. He is also director of the Stanford Humanities Center, author of *Imagining the Penitentiary: Fiction and the Architecture of Mind in Eighteenth-Century England*, and coeditor of *The Ends of Rhetoric: History, Theory, Practice; Chronotypes: The Construction of Time*; and *The Columbia History of the British Novel*.

PETER BROOKS is Sterling Professor of Comparative Literature and French at Yale University. His most recent books include *Troubling Confessions: Speaking Guilt in Law and Literature*; and a volume edited with Alex Woloch, *Whose Freud? The Place of Psychoanalysis in Contemporary Culture*.

JUDITH BUTLER is Maxine Elliot Professor of Rhetoric and Comparative Literature at the University of California at Berkeley. She is the author of numerous works in feminist theory and continental philosophy, including *Antigone's Claim: Kinship Between Life and Death*; and, with Ernesto Laclau and Slavoj Žižek, *Contingency, Hegemony, Universality: Contemporary Dialogues on the Left*.

REY CHOW is Andrew W. Mellon Professor of the Humanities at Brown University and the author of several books, including, most recently, *The Protestant Ethnic and the Spirit of Capitalism*. Her publications in English have been translated into a number of Asian and European languages, including Chinese, Japanese, Korean, French, Spanish, and German.

JONATHAN CULLER is Class of 1916 Professor of English and Comparative Literature and senior associate dean of the College of Arts and Sciences at Cornell University. He has published widely in the field of literary theory and criticism and continental philosophy. His books include *The Pursuit of Signs: Semiotics, Literature, Deconstruction; On Deconstruction: Theory and Criticism After Structuralism*; and *Literary Theory: A Very Short Introduction*.

MARGARET FERGUSON is Professor of English at the University of California at Davis. She has also taught at Yale, Columbia, and the University of Colorado. The author of *Trials of Desire: Renaissance Defenses of Poetry*, she has also coedited numerous volumes, including *Rewriting the Renaissance: Discourses of Sexual Difference in Early Modern Europe*; and *Postmodernism and Feminism*. Her most recent book, *Dido's Daughters: Literacy, Gender, and Empire in Early Modern England and France*, is forthcoming from the University of Chicago Press.

BARBARA JOHNSON is Professor of English and Comparative Literature and Frederic Wertham Professor of Law and Psychiatry in Society at Harvard University. She has published widely in literary criticism and theory and is the author of, among other works, *The Critical Difference: Essays in the Contemporary Rhetoric of Reading*; and *Mother Tongues: Sexuality, Trials, Motherhood, Translation*, forthcoming from Harvard University Press. She is also the translator of Jacques Derrida's *Dissemination* and coeditor of *The Norton Anthology of Theory and Criticism*.

ROBERT KAUFMAN is Assistant Professor of English at Stanford University. He is currently completing two related books, *Negative Romanticism, Almost Modernity: Keats, Shelley, and Adornian Critical Aesthetics*; and *Experiments in Construction: Frankfurt School Aesthetics and Contemporary Poetry*. He is also at work on a third project, *HAMLET's Form of the Modern*. His articles have appeared in various journals and edited collections, including *Critical Inquiry*, *October*, *American Poetry Review*, *The Cambridge Companion to Adorno*, *Modern Language Quarterly*, and *Studies in Romanticism*.

KEVIN LAMB is a Ph.D. candidate in the English department at Cornell University. A former high school mathematics teacher, he also spent time working in Russia in the field of HIV/AIDS activism and queer politics prior to pursuing his interest in contemporary theory and modernist literature.

JOHN MCCUMBER is Professor of Germanic Languages at the University of California at Los Angeles. He has taught at the New School for Social Research and Northwestern University and is the author of *Time in the Ditch: American Philosophy and the McCarthy Era*; *Philosophy and Freedom: Derrida, Rorty, Habermas, Foucault*; *Metaphysics and Oppression: Heidegger's Challenge to Western Philosophy*; and other books and articles.

STUART J. MURRAY is a Ph.D. candidate in the Department of Rhetoric at the University of California at Berkeley. He is writing a dissertation on spectral subjectivity and the sacred.

DAVID PALUMBO-LIU is Professor of Comparative Literature and director of the program in Modern Thought and Literature at Stanford University. His most recent work includes an essay on Jean-Luc Nancy, "The Operative Heart," forthcoming in *The New Centennial Review*; and "Multiculturalism Now: Civilization, National Identity, and Difference Before and After September 11th," published in *boundary 2*.

GAYATRI CHAKRAVORTY SPIVAK is Avalon Foundation Professor in the Humanities at Columbia University. Her numerous books include *The Post-Colonial Critic*; *Outside in the Teaching Machine*; *A Critique of Postcolonial Reason*; and, most recently, *Red Thread*; and *Death of a Discipline*, both in press. She has also translated Jacques Derrida's *Of Grammatology* and Mahasweta Devi's *Imaginary Maps*; *Breast Stories*; *Old Women*; and *Chotti Munda and His Arrow*.

ROBIN VALENZA is Assistant Professor of English at the University of Chicago. She wrote a dissertation at Stanford on the emergence of the modern academic disciplines in the eighteenth and nineteenth centuries in Britain.

MICHAEL WARNER is Professor of English at Rutgers University. He is the editor of *Fear of a Queer Planet* and coeditor, with Gerald Graff, of *The Origins of Literary Studies in America*. His most recent books are *The Trouble with Normal: Sex, Politics, and the Ethics of Queer Life*; and *Publics and Counterpublics*. His essays and journalism have appeared in *The Village Voice*, *VLS*, *The Nation*, *The Advocate*, *POZ*, *In These Times*, and other magazines.

ROBYN WIEGMAN is the Margaret Taylor Smith Director of Women's Studies and Associate Professor of Women's Studies and Literature at Duke University. She has published *American Anatomies: Theorizing Race and Gender* and five edited collections: *Who Can Speak? Authority and Critical Identity*; *Feminism Beside Itself*; *AIDS and the National Body: Writings by Thomas Yingling*; *Women's Studies On Its Own*; and *The Futures of American Studies*. She is codirector of the Dartmouth Institute on American Studies.

Index

Addison, Joseph, 40
Adorno, Theodor, 11–12, 19, 26n4, 68–69, 111–14, 124n8, 144–50, 200–203, 206, 209–14
aesthetic education, 135
aesthetic experience, 143–50
aesthetic judgments, 54–55, 58–59, 144
alienation effect, 19
Apollinaire, Guillaume, 130
argument, formal, 50–51, 52
Aristotle, 10, 20, 60–69
audience, 17, 106–8
Augustine, Saint, 179n3
Austin, J. L., 47, 51, 54
avant-garde, 130–32, 138

Bacon, Roger, 20
Bad Writing Award, 1, 6, 12n1, 43, 45, 47, 53, 115, 175–77, 179
Bakhtin, Mikhail, 137
Balibar, Renée, 27n6
Barthes, Roland, 9, 100–102, 137
Baudelaire, Charles, 145–48, 150, 151, 152, 158–60, 209–14
Bender, John, 9–10
Benjamin, Walter, 19, 144–50, 152, 162, 206, 209–14
Berkeley, George, 36
Berlant, Lauren, 94
Blake, William, 163
Bonitz, Herman, 62
Bourdieu, Pierre, 20
Boyd, Andrew, 163, 164
Brecht, Bertolt, 19
Brooks, Peter, 11, 150
Brown, Wendy, 93n15

Burckhardt, Sigurd, 22
Burke, Kenneth, 135
Butler, Judith, 6, 11–12, 15, 17–19, 43, 45–47, 68–69, 109, 111, 113, 116–17, 136, 175, 176
Canguilhem, Georges, 124n8
Cavell, Stanley, 10, 47–56
Charnes, Linda, 129–30
Cheney, Lynne, 134
Chow, Rey, 10, 89
Christian aesceticism, 99
clarity: history of, 62; ideology of, 15, 60–69, 95–97, 111–17; metaphysics of, 58–69
Clark, Robert E., 176
Claudel, Paul, 137
Clueless, 163–64
Cocteau, Jean, 143–44
common sense, 9, 36, 39, 97, 111–12, 130
Comolli, Jean-Louis, 136
comparative literature, 160–63
confession, impersonal, 52
"conversable" language, ideal of, 29–41
Copjec, Joan, 166
Corax, 173
critical thinking, 199–206
criticism, literary, 8, 131–38, 166, 184
Culler, Jonathan, 10
cultural studies, 123, 134–35, 160
curvature, law of, 182–83

Dante Alighieri, 9, 16, 21–25
De Man, Paul, 5–6, 97–98, 99, 104n6, 136, 195
deconstruction, 8, 162
defamiliarization, 9, 19, 111–2, 117–18
Derrida, Jacques, 8, 46, 194

Devi, Mahasweta, 184–85
difficulty, 130–37, 139–54, 181–83, 185–87, 199–206, 209–14
domination of matter by form, 64, 66–67
double consciousness, 165
DuBois, W.E.B., 165
Ducker, Dan, 48
Duncan, Robert, 152,
Dutton, Denis, 137

Eliasoph, Nina, 120–21
Elio de Nebrija, Antonio, 25–26
Eliot, T.S., 132
Elster, Jon, 196–97
Emerson, Ralph W., 49
epistemology, sciences contrasted with humanities, 8–9, 30–32, 34, 38–40
exegesis, 131, 135–36

Fanon, Frantz, 164
feminism, 10, 75–94
Ferguson, Margaret, 9
Fischer, Ernst, 143–44
Fleming, Richard, 48, 49
Foucault, Michel, 82, 109, 124n8
Frankfurt School, 111, 145, 155n7
Fry, Paul, 6, 9
Frye, Northrop, 131, 135

Gautier, Théophile, 158
gender, performance of, 7, 46–47, 82–84
globalization, 10, 103, 188–89, 195–96
Glouberman, Mark, 48
Gorky, Maxim, 130
Graff, Gerald, 37
grammar school, 24–25
Gramsci, Antonio, 45, 179
Grewal, Inderpal, 92n14
Gubar, Susan, 78
Guest, Barbara, 150–54
Guillory, John, 119

Habermas, Jürgen, 118
Hartman, Geoffrey, 134–35
Hawking, Stephen, 39
Hegel, G.W.F, 49, 67- 8, 161–62
hegemony, 45–47
hermetic language, 130
Hirsch, E.D., 15
Hobbes, Thomas, 67
Horkheimer, Max, 209

Hull, David, 63
Hume, David, 9–10, 17–19, 29–41

ignorance, power of, 3
Italian vernacular, 22–25
Jakobson, Roman, 194

James, Henry, 206–9
Jameson, Fredric, 26
Johnson, Barbara, 7–8, 11
Johnson, Samuel, 29

kabbalah, 212
Kant, Immanuel, 54–55, 58–59, 144, 183–84
Kaplan, Caren, 92n14
Kaufman, Robert, 11
Kenny, Anthony, 48
Knight, Deborah, 175

Lacan, Jacques, 161, 166, 194
Laclau, Ernesto, 45–47
language: as normative community, 172–73, 175–78; materiality of, 98–99; politics of, 200–208; specialized versus general, 24, 30–40,
Latin, ideal of, 19–21, 24–25
Lefort, Claude, 185
Levin, Harry, 161–63
Locke, John, 29, 33
Longinus, 191
Lusignan, Serge, 20
lyric poetry, 139–54, 157–62

Mallarmé, Stéphane, 130, 158–60, 162
Marxism, 98, 144–45, 210–14
mass culture, 108, 110–11, 121
McCumber, John, 10
Messer-Davidow, Ellen, 78
Meyers, D. G., 174, 176–77
Miller, James, 110, 111, 113, 114, 115
Mills, C. Wright, 176–77
modernism, 99, 102, 131, 139–54, 202
Modleski, Tania, 78
moral superiority, 2–5, 16–19, 96–97, 160
Mulhall, Stephen, 48
multiculturalism, 161
myth, 100–102

Nabokov, Vladimir, 132
New Criticism, 82, 131, 135

Newman, Jane, 92n13
Norma Rae, 140–43, 150
Nozick, Robert, 44–45, 54
Nussbaum, Martha, 6–7, 15–17, 62, 70n9,
    116–17, 174, 176; misreading of Greek
    philosophy, 62–63

Orwell, George, 106–11, 113, 115, 122, 124

pain, 182
Palmer, Michael, 152–54
Palumbo-Liu, David, 5, 11
Parker, Patricia, 25
Pascal, Blaise, 164
penetrate past assessment, 52–53
performative, 3–4, 7
philosophical utility, 52–53
philosophy as writing, 50–51
Plath, Sylvia, 157
Poe, Edgar Allan, 162
Pollitt, Katha, 109, 116, 117, 123, 124
Poovey, Mary, 91n6
postcolonialism, 95
post-structuralism: and myth, 100–104; and
    politics, 75–90, 95–97, 19
preservation of form, law of the, 60–62
Priestley, Joseph, 32
psychoanalysis, 82–83, 191–94
public, creation of, 108, 114–19, 121–24
public intellectual, 109, 118–24
public sphere, 107, 118–21
publishing, 121–23
Puttenham, George, 21

queer theory, 19, 79, 82–83, 87
questions, in writing, 17, 53

radical alterity, 193
reader, kindness to, 17, 25
Reed, Laurie, 150
Reid, Thomas, 36
reviewing of books, 122–28
Rich, Adrienne, 77, 81
Richards, I.A., 135
Rimbaud, Arthur, 153, 158
Ritt, Martin, 140–43
Rodden, John, 110
Rorty, Richard, 66, 69, 200
Rosenbaum, Ron, 129–30, 135
Russell's paradox, 59

Said, Edward, 171
Saussure, Ferdinand de, 164–65
Schiller, Friedrich, 135
Scholem, Gerschom, 209–14
Schor, Naomi, 78
science, epistemology of, 30–35, 38–39, 63–
    64, 96–97
Sedgwick, Eve, 3
Segal, Lynne, 76, 78–80, 83–88
self-indulgence, 50–51
Sexton, Anne, 157–58
simplicity, 17–19
Slaughter, Sheila, 93n17
solecism, 16
Sophists, 9, 15–17
Spivak, Gayatri, 11
Stevens, Wallace, 134
style, masculine and feminine, 23–25
subaltern studies, 184–85, 190
Sutton, Crystal Leem 140–43

Taylor, Charles, 132
teaching, 2, 11, 135–36, 164–66, 174–78,
    183, 186–89, 191
theory, 5–6, 129–30, 133, 160–62, 181–82,
    200–202, 210–14; resistance to, 5–6, 97–
    104
Thomas, Dylan, 140–42
Thoreau, Henry David, 111–12
translation, 10, 37–38, 160–62, 190–92, 205–
    6, 208–9
truth, relation to clarity of, 60–69
Tutu, Desmond, 194

undecidability, 186
universality, 204–6
unknowing, epistemological privilege of, 3
unreadable book, ideal of, 44–45

Vaihinger, Hans, 163–64
Valenza, Robin, 9–10
vernacular, 16, 19–26

Warner, Michael, 10–11
Watt, Ian, 171, 178
Wiegman, Robyn, 5, 10
Williams, Raymond, 27n7, 189
Wittgenstein, Ludwig, 47–49, 51–54
women's studies, 61–62, 86

Cultural Memory | *in the Present*

Jonathan Culler and Kevin Lamb, eds., *Just Being Difficult? Academic Writing in the Public Arena*

Jean-Luc Marion, *The Crossing of the Visible*

Eric Michaud, *An Art for Eternity: The Cult of Art in Nazi Germany*

Anne Freadman, *The Machinery of Talk: Charles Peirce and the Sign Hypothesis*

Alain Badiou, *Saint Paul: The Foundation of Universalism*

Bernard Faure, *Double Exposure: Cutting Across Buddhist and Western Discourses*

Stanley Cavell, *Emerson's Transcendental Etudes*

Stuart McLean, *The Event and Its Terrors: Ireland, Famine, Modernity*

Beate Rössler, ed., *Privacies*

Gil Anidjar, *The Jew, the Arab: A History of the Enemy*

Jean-Luc Nancy, *A Finite Thinking*, edited by Simon Sparks

Theodor W. Adorno, *Can One Live after Auschwitz? A Philosophical Reader*, edited by Rolf Tiedemann

Patricia Pisters, *The Matrix of Visual Culture: Working with Deleuze in Film Theory*

Talal Asad, *Formations of the Secular: Christianity, Islam, Modernity*

Dorothea von Mücke, *The Rise of the Fantastic Tale*

Marc Redfield, *The Politics of Aesthetics: Nationalism, Gender, Romanticism*

Emmanuel Levinas, *On Escape*

Dan Zahavi, *Husserl's Phenomenology*

Rodolphe Gasché, *The Idea of Form: Rethinking Kant's Aesthetics*

Michael Naas, *Taking on the Tradition: Jacques Derrida and the Legacies of Deconstruction*

Herlinde Pauer-Studer, ed., *Constructions of Practical Reason: Interviews on Moral and Political Philosophy*

Jean-Luc Marion, *Being Given That: Toward a Phenomenology of Givenness*

Theodor W. Adorno and Max Horkheimer, *Dialectic of Enlightenment*

Ian Balfour, *The Rhetoric of Romantic Prophecy*

Martin Stokhof, *World and Life as One: Ethics and Ontology in Wittgenstein's Early Thought*

Gianni Vattimo, *Nietzsche: An Introduction*

Jacques Derrida, *Negotiations: Interventions and Interviews, 1971–1998*, edited by Elizabeth Rottenberg

Brett Levinson, *The Ends of Literature: The Latin American "Boom" in the Neoliberal Marketplace*

Timothy J. Reiss, *Against Autonomy: Cultural Instruments, Mutualities, and the Fictive Imagination*

Hent de Vries and Samuel Weber, eds., *Religion and Media*

Niklas Luhmann, *Theories of Distinction: Re-Describing the Descriptions of Modernity*, edited and introduced by William Rasch

Johannes Fabian, *Anthropology with an Attitude: Critical Essays*

Michel Henry, *I Am the Truth: Toward a Philosophy of Christianity*

Gil Anidjar, *"Our Place in al-Andalus": Kabbalah, Philosophy, Literature in Arab-Jewish Letters*

Hélène Cixous and Jacques Derrida, *Veils*

F. R. Ankersmit, *Political Representation*

Elissa Marder, *Dead Time: Temporal Disorders in the Wake of Modernity (Baudelaire and Flaubert)*

Reinhart Koselleck, *The Practice of Conceptual History: Timing History, Spacing Concepts*

Niklas Luhmann, *The Reality of the Mass Media*

Hubert Damisch, *A Childhood Memory by Piero della Francesca*

Hubert Damisch, *A Theory of /Cloud/: Toward a History of Painting*

Jean-Luc Nancy, *The Speculative Remark (One of Hegel's Bons Mots)*

Jean-François Lyotard, *Soundproof Room: Malraux's Anti-Aesthetics*

Jan Patočka, *Plato and Europe*

Hubert Damisch, *Skyline: The Narcissistic City*

Isabel Hoving, *In Praise of New Travelers: Reading Caribbean Migrant Women Writers*

Richard Rand, ed., *Futures: Of Jacques Derrida*

William Rasch, *Niklas Luhmann's Modernity: The Paradoxes of Differentiation*

Jacques Derrida and Anne Dufourmantelle, *Of Hospitality*

Jean-François Lyotard, *The Confession of Augustine*

Kaja Silverman, *World Spectators*

Samuel Weber, *Institution and Interpretation,* expanded edition

Jeffrey S. Librett, *The Rhetoric of Cultural Dialogue: Jews and Germans in the Epoch of Emancipation*

Ulrich Baer, *Remnants of Song: Trauma and the Experience of Modernity in Charles Baudelaire and Paul Celan*

Samuel C. Wheeler III, *Deconstruction as Analytic Philosophy*

David S. Ferris, *Silent Urns: Romanticism, Hellenism, Modernity*

Rodolphe Gasché, *Of Minimal Things: Studies on the Notion of Relation*

Sarah Winter, *Freud and the Institution of Psychoanalytic Knowledge*

Samuel Weber, *The Legend of Freud,* expanded edition

Aris Fioretos, ed., *The Solid Letter: Readings of Friedrich Hölderlin*

J. Hillis Miller, *Black Holes*; and Manuel Asensi, *J. Hillis Miller; or, Boustrophedonic Reading*

Miryam Sas, *Fault Lines: Cultural Memory and Japanese Surrealism*

Peter Schwenger, *Fantasm and Fiction: On Textual Envisioning*

Didier Maleuvre, *Museum Memories: History, Technology, Art*

Jacques Derrida, *Monolingualism of the Other; or, The Prosthesis of Origin*

Andrew Baruch Wachtel, *Making a Nation, Breaking a Nation: Literature and Cultural Politics in Yugoslavia*

Niklas Luhmann, *Love as Passion: The Codification of Intimacy*

Mieke Bal, ed., *The Practice of Cultural Analysis: Exposing Interdisciplinary Interpretation*

Jacques Derrida and Gianni Vattimo, eds., *Religion*